Living the Dream

Previous books by Ken Piesse for Wilkinson Publishing

CRICKET

2023: *David Warner, The Bull, daring to be different*
     Reprinted 2024

2022: *On Ya Warnie* (updated)

2018: *Australian Cricket Scandals*

2009: *On Ya Richie*

2007: *On Ya Warnie*

1999: *T.J. Over The Top* (with Terry Jenner)

AFL FOOTBALL

1995: *The Goal King* (with Jason Dunstall)

1994: *The Gary Ablett Story*

Living the Dream

60 YEARS IN CRICKET & FOOTBALL

KEN PIESSE

Published by:
Wilkinson Publishing Pty Ltd
ACN 006 042 173
PO Box 24135
Melbourne, Vic 3001
Ph: 03 9654 5446

enquiries@wilkinsonpublishing.com.au
www.wilkinsonpublishing.com.au

Copyright © 2024 Ken Piesse

All rights reserved. No part of this publication may be reproduced, stored in a retrieval system or transmitted in any form by any means without the prior permission of the copyright owner. Enquiries should be made to the publisher.

Every effort has been made to ensure that this book is free from error or omissions. However, the Publisher, the Author, the Editor or their respective employees or agents, shall not accept responsibility for injury, loss or damage occasioned to any person acting or refraining from action as a result of material in this book whether or not such injury, loss or damage is in any way due to any negligent act or omission, breach of duty or default on the part of the Publisher, the Author, the Editor, or their respective employees or agents.

Title: Living the Dream
ISBN (softcover): 9781922810601
ISBN (hardcover): 9781922810557

A catalogue record of this book is available from the National Library of Australia.

Design by Spike Creative Pty Ltd
Ph: (03) 9427 9500
spikecreative.com.au
Printed and bound in Australia by Ligare Book Printers.

PHOTOGRAPH CREDITS

Front cover photo of Ken Piesse at Echuca Over 60s state cricket championships, 2023, courtesy of Peter Glenton, Australian Cricket Society. Back cover picture of Ken with Ron Barassi, in 1979 by Terry Phelan, the Sporting Globe. Ken's cricket caps (from left to right) are Beaumaris CC, Australian Cricket Society, Kingston Saints, Port Melbourne, Frankston, Crusaders and Mt Eliza.

Inside pictures are from the Ken Piesse collection. Ken's Elsternwick hat-trick pictures courtesy of Ian Gibson from Jeeralang Junction.

Ken Piesse's website: www.cricketbooks.com.au
Ken's email: kenpiesse@ozemail.com.au

To Susan

Thanks for not doing a runner.

CONTENTS

Foreword: Ian Crawford AM ix
Author's introduction xi

1   Meeting with a hermit 1
2   Baby Bradman 5
3   Dead man walking 18
4   Living the dream 34
5   Sobie & the Stones 43
6   Scarred for life 52
7   Demolition man 63
8   'What's this shit, Tolstoy?' 72
9   Lessons from the legends 91
10 Competing like there's no tomorrow 107
11 Back to kindergarten 122
12 Enter AB 128
13 A secret comeback 136
14 Tracking old Bert 148
15 In Sigley's shoes 158
16 Scoop of a lifetime 163
17 Ghosting the stars 171
18 Nugget 184
19 Dermie 191
20 Learning to listen 194
21 Organised chaos 203
22 Smokin' Joe 212
23 A leg-break from heaven 219
24 Tubby's time 226

25	Ambushed	236
26	Discovering Steve Smith	247
27	High society	252
28	Crossing Don Bradman	262
29	Thrill of the hunt	272
30	Tim Tams at Monbulk	285

Last word	292
Acknowledgements	299
Glossary	300
Bibliography	303
Clippings	308
Toasts & roasts	314
Stats	322
Premiership Pics	328
Index	331

FOREWORD

By Ian Crawford AM

Kendrick and I go back 50 years and more. It's a friendship we have maintained to this day through our mutual love of cricket and football.

He played his first game as a 16-year-old under my captaincy for the Prahran Cricket Club's fourth XI in round 1 of the 1971-72 season at Como Park. He'd come the same year as Dav Whatmore, our greatest modern-day player. They'd catch the train up each training night, Ken from Cheltenham and Davvy from Highett.

Being the youngest member of the side, he was a natural for short leg, despite being 188cm (6ft 2in)! What an induction. No helmet, mouthguard, shin pad or box back in those days; very courageous. One of our icons John Malligan was coming back through the lower grades after injury and having made a nice save at gully, young Ken called: 'Not bad for an old man!' Jack was 35 at the time! Even then Ken made sure his voice was heard.

After games I'd often give some of the boys a lift home. We'd talk about the game and what was ahead. His knowledge, even then, was amazing.

I saw him make a 100 against our thirds late one year at Como. It was a wet wicket and he led from the front. Only a few years previously I'd telephoned and asked if he fancied making a comeback with us – with the ones. At 35, his leggies were that good. He thanked me and recommended a younger teammate who also bowled wrist spin. 'He's the future,' he said.

I have watched with great pride Ken's progress with his family and, of course, his love of sport. He has become a magnificent contributor to cricket and AFL football. Few share his reputation as a writer of class and credibility. Most of us have at least one 'Ken Piesse' book in their bookcases. I have almost two whole rows in mine. And now this one, the best of all.

It was fortuitous that we were honoured on the same day at the mighty MCG with Sport Australia Medals, recognising our 50-year contributions to cricket.

As Prahran Cricket Club's historian, he pushed determinedly and was successful in having our historic oval at Toorak Park named after the great Sam Loxton, one of Victorian cricket's mightiest. Sam had first played as a 12-year-old and Ken interviewed Sam and many of his older teammates who said Sam was better than all of them, even then. Ken's flair for interviewing is unsurpassed. But I am biased...

His 16-year leadership stint as chair of the Australian Cricket Society was of dedication, determination and commitment. He rejuvenated and revived the Society's fortunes, injecting a rare expertise and passion.

His commentaries are still heard most weekends on RSN radio in Melbourne and beyond. He is fair and fearless, trusted and respected.

I've been privy to some of the early chapters of *Living The Dream*. What a 'read' this is.

I'm so honoured, Ken, to write these words for a great mate, a true master of his craft.

August 2024

AUTHOR'S INTRODUCTION

I was a child of the '60s, one of the luckier ones. We didn't have to endure a Depression or a World War and National Service was ending. We had the Beatles, Clark Kent, sliced bread, decimal currency and takeaway Chinese in saucepans. The clip-clop of the horse-drawn milk cart was as familiar as the dawn wake-up calls from our resident kookaburra from our old eucalypt dominating our corner block in bayside Beaumaris.

Our Dad, Ken snr, worked hard and so did we, earning pocket money by assisting outside, mowing the lawns, raking leaves and stoking the briquette hot water booster. On Thursday nights Dad would leave pocket money outside our rooms. My dawn paper round ensured early starts until year 12 when sleeping into 7am became preferable to getting up shortly after 5.

On cold, crisp, often-foggy Saturday mornings, the siren from the nearby footy oval was irresistible. I'd be there from nine to five, watching all three Bowie games, including the seniors which went unbeaten through the entire 1965 South-East Suburban season, its star a full forward named Geoff Skinner from nearby Martin Street who marked tall and roosted drop punts as far as another of my heroes, Collingwood's famed goalkicker Peter McKenna. Nineteen-year-old Skinner booted 112 goals that year, 18 in one match. The team's unbeaten run was in peril one day and at three quarter-time, the coach, Frank Reade, who'd been to the War, was red-faced and ropable, accused the players of half efforts and playing like show ponies.

Tearing a jumper off the back of one of the younger ones, he roared, 'This... THISSSS... is what you're playing for.'

Born in 1955, I was 10 at the time and can still remember that fire and brimstone speech at Oak Street. From that day, team was everything for me and I was proud to be first ruck in several Bowie premierships, one with Frank as selection chairman.

But cricket was the game I *really* loved. Dad would take me to our local library in Parkdale and I'd withdraw all 18 of its cricket books and lovingly arrange them in order of size in a bookcase I'd made at school, imagining they were mine. Dad would ask if I wanted to borrow anything else. 'No,' I'd say, 'but thanks Dad.'

We'd attend Sheffield Shield matches at the mighty Melbourne Cricket Ground, always 20 rows back at fine leg. I'd have my NSW Junior Cricket Union scorebook, several sharp grey leads, a rubber, a Herbert Adams pie and a can of fizzy drink. He'd sit with me for a time before catching up with his mates in the Cigar Stand.

In the winter of '65, Dad allowed me to move my bed into the lounge room next to our new Healing radiogram so I could listen to the night-time descriptions of the Tests from the faraway Caribbean. The Barbados Test from Bridgetown was my favourite. Famed opening pair Bobby Simpson and Bill Lawry started with 382. And against the might of Wes Hall and Charlie Griffith, the two fastest bowlers in the world.

When Dad and Mum gifted me the 1965 *Wisden Cricketers' Almanack* that Christmas, I was truly hooked and read and re-read all of its 1042 pages, thrilling particularly to the feats of Simpson who had an insatiable appetite for mountainous scores. On three consecutive early-season weekends in 1963-64, he amassed scores of 359, 4 and 246 and 247 not out. Later, we became friends and we'd talk often. With Lawry, he said, calling became unnecessary, especially when they had defended the ball to their feet. Just a half look in each other's direction and they'd take off, their daredevil tip-and-run singles triggering near-hysterical screams from many of the women in the member's. 'We always reckoned the safest place to be was at the non-striker's end and we'd do everything possible to get there,' Simmo said.

I was fortunate, in time, to be friends and interview so many of the game's most illustrious.

Dad worked for the Americans in Queen Street in the heart of Melbourne, directly across the road where the Great Bookie Robbery was to occur, in 1976. Armed with my paper-round funds, he'd queue at lunchtimes at the grand gothic ANZ bank on the corner of Queen and Collins to purchase International Bank Drafts to send with my cricket book orders to England. Dad also brought home most of the morning newspapers, from the Adelaide *Advertiser* to Brisbane's *Courier-Mail*, triggering my 40-year habit of keeping newspaper clippings in scrapbooks, both footy and cricket. Mum, ever resourceful and always budgeting, found a recipe for home-made Clag (glue) which we'd store in large jars in the fridge alongside the Schweppes bitter lemon.

With four kids under eight, Dad had originally sold encyclopaedias door-to-door after work to help keep us afloat. Like the celebrated Keith Miller, he could remember names and relate to all from the most notable Arbitration Commission judges to Tony our Italian greengrocer at Cheltenham Railway Station. 'Ciao Tony,' he'd say each Saturday morning. 'Come Stai' (how are you?). 'Bene, bene (very good),' Tony would reply, grinning. Tony would give us kids sixpence a roll for parcelled up newspapers which he used to wrap up customer's veggies. The Saturday *Age*, then a broadsheet, was always the best. It had three or four huge advertising sections. Shopping done, there would be an 'arrivederci' (goodbye), between Dad and Tony. It was the happiest of vibes.

My inspirational Dad, Kenneth Charles Piesse. He loved that I shared his passion for sport. We were the closest of mates.

Dad was the 'talkiest rascal' – as one of his more dangerous mates Mr P. Harris, a tennis coach from Hobart used to say – and in hours could placate tempers and avert wildcat strikes among the oil rig workers off Lakes Entrance. A luxurious Ford Fairlane 351 T-bar automatic had been included in his package and I'd often wait outside the back gates for him to round the corner into St Aubin Street. On summer nights I'd ask him to park in the street so he could bowl an over or two at me under the carport. Never once did he say no. He loved that I shared his passion for sport. Mum would keep dinner warm until we'd finished. Depending on the time of year, conversation at our table automatically centred around our beloved Hawthorn Hawks or the fortunes of the Test XI. On wintertime Friday nights, Harry Beitzel's Football Show was unmissable with Thorold, Chick, Bigs and the smooth-talking Doug Heywood.

A Saturday lunchtime staple was yellow cod. Have never had it since. Another was Mum's cabbage and we'd all have to sit at the dining room table until our plates were clean. My brother Jim never seemed to have any trouble with his greens. One weekend Dad opened the trap door to his small, mysterious cellar where he stored his hock and best reds only to discover all this rotting cabbage which had surreptitiously been pushed down into the cellar when no-one was looking.

Mum, Patricia, was a golfer and good at it, breaking into single figures during her years in Southern GC's top pennant teams. She played No.6 behind the likes of team stars Jean Thomas and Gina Roughead, a beautiful, sweet swinger from Leongatha. The Hawthorn legend Jarryd Roughead hails from the same big family. During school holidays I'd practise with Mum at Southern and help pick up the balls. She had a Sam Snead-autographed Little Slammer and was virtually impossible to beat at match play. She stitched her own clothes, insisted we all attend Sunday school and championed our achievements.

Having been captain of cricket, football and the school at Beaumaris state, I was set to repeat the treble in my final year at Beaumaris high, only for the head prefect's role to be given to an older kid repeating Year XII. I'll share his initials: Noel Peters. One of my Geelong mates, Ken Davis, still calls me 'AA' – almost a head prefect.

As the youngest and the one offered the most leniency, it's a family joke that if ever Kendrick (me) got into financial trouble and had to rob a bank, Mum would say: 'Oh well, Ken must have needed the money…'

DAD WAS BARELY shaving when he went to War, serving on the islands of Timor and Tarakan and, alongside his commando buddies, hindering the advances of the Japanese, who'd already taken Singapore and were bombing Darwin incessantly. My grandmother Christina's hair turned white when for weeks there was no news of Dad's unit, the 2nd/4th Independent Company. So successful were their hit and run jungle missions that the Japanese reckoned there must be 2000 Aussies on Timor, when in fact there were 200. The Australians befriended and protected the locals, each soldier having a criado, a second pair of expert eyes, who were like family and integral to everyone's safety.

One morning, before first light, Dad's unit was jumped and it was hours before the enemy was repelled. Afterwards Dad looked down at his feet, which were unusually sore. He'd put his right boot on his left foot and left on his right.

Dad had badly banged a knee parachuting out of a plane, but refused to have it stiffened, despite being in pain most days. He liked to bowl to me, his cricket-mad son, under our tin-roofed carport. We were the closest of mates. He'd take me to cricket on Saturday mornings and organised specialist coaching which fast-tracked my game. Happily, I'd told him how much I loved and appreciated him in a card not so long before his early death, at 61. As Mum says, he'd be thrilled with my achievements. But I'm the proud one.

The war knocked Dad around. Tuberculosis was to take one of his eyes, but not his sense of fun and frivolity. Often during the six o'clock swill, Dad would deliberately dislodge his artificial eye and drop it into his glass to catch the uninitiated. 'It's your shout,' he'd say. Mum sometimes exploded, but only occasionally. She knew what he'd been through.

One of five impish brothers from Merridale – still one of Kew's most gracious Federation mansions – Dad attended Scotch College, on the

Glenferrie Road hill and represented Victoria juniors at hockey. He and his brothers loved jazz and having a good time. They would co-host dances at The Barn, on a corner of the family's large acreage. Up to 70 would attend. For a time Jim Piesse sat in, playing piano for Graeme Bell and his All-Stars. Having raged most Saturday nights, all the boys liked their Sunday sleep-ins and the bell at nearby St. Hilary's was far too loud and would sound far too early and often for their liking. Late one very dark Saturday night, Fred, the eldest, wrapped the bell in cotton wool, much to the consternation next day of the local minister. The boys thought it hilarious. Everyone knew who was responsible. When the local policeman arrived for a 'please explain', a few of the boys happened to be up an old fig tee directly above the wooden back gate. Told of the accusations, my grandmother, CP, smiled at the officer and said emphatically: 'Sir, my boys would NEVER do that.' Bless her.

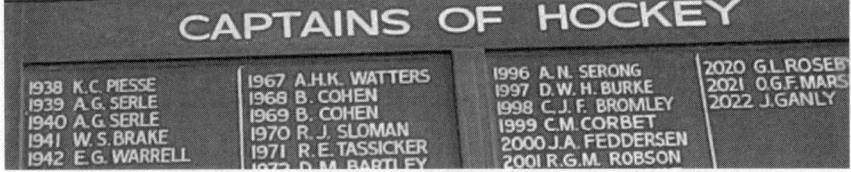

GRAND FINAL NIGHT 1961 was eventful. Our team Hawthorn won its first flag and Dad was picked up by the police zigzagging along Brighton Road and driven home by an officer. Mum answered a knock at the door to find Dad, the hell-raiser, alongside a uniformed policeman. 'Is this your husband Madam?' he asked. 'Yes.' 'Here are his keys.' Even on her 100th birthday, memories of that night were still vivid. 'Dad could be very good,' Mum said. 'But he could also be very bad.'

Born in Scone and raised in Charlton in the west of NSW, Mum's upbringing was austere. She was shy and closeted. When Dad first brought Mum home to dinner at Merridale, one of his brothers mischievously tapped her on the ankle. 'That's a hot one you've got there, Kenny,' he said.

Dad was building an extra room onto the family house and asked Mum for the latest cricket score. 'I'm not sure,' she said, 'but someone has just been caught in Bedser's leg trap.' 'And Patty,' said Dad, smiling mischievously. 'What is Bedser's leg trap?' 'I've got no idea.'

One day, rising comedian Rod Quantock arrived on our front doorstep, ready to take my sister Annie out. He was barefooted and Mum immediately ushered him away.

Mum's mother, Amanda, liked to be addressed very formally as 'Mrs Wilfred Thomas' – her married name. Buoyed by multiple beers with his wartime buddies on Anzac Day, Dad would waltz through the door, put on his favourite dance records, like Ella Fitzgerald's *The Dipsy Doodle*, grab Nan and say: 'C'mon Mandy, let's dance.'

When Nan and Pa's 1950 Holden FX ute went to God, Dad bought them a new Ford Falcon to tow their caravan. One incredibly hot summer amid severe water restrictions, Dad and I would drive to Ricketts Point and collect bags of seaweed to help nourish Mum's prize roses.

For years Hawthorn's Glenferrie Oval and the MCG were second homes for both of us and, in time, as my hobbies became my livelihood, I was to meet so many of the most important. I shook hands with Hollywood icon Jimmy Stewart, played golf with Richie Benaud and Bob Shaw, cricket with Ian Chappell, Colin Cowdrey and Ian Botham, caught a Prime Minister, sacked another, interviewed Slim Dusty, chatted with Ronnie Corbett, Michael Parkinson and the Welsh songstress Katherine Jenkins and met Jack Nicklaus and Gary Player, among a host of sport's biggest and most high-profiled. To borrow a line from Mark Twain: 'Find a job you enjoy doing and you'll never have to work a day in your life.' I'm truly living my dream.

1
MEETING WITH A HERMIT

'You're the first person to come here for years. If I keel over tomorrow, no-one will find me for weeks...'

BANG. BANG. BANG. I was hammering on the Frog's wooden front door with all my strength, but so loud was the classical music inside that he couldn't hear me. Finally, he emerged, unshaven and dishevelled. 'Sorry about that Ken,' he said. 'Didn't I tell you to bang the door like this?' And with his sledgehammer of a hand, Alan Lloyd 'Froggie' Thomson all but knocked it off its hinges.

His recollections were integral to my Golden Jubilee reunion booklet for Bob Cowper and his 1969-70 Victorians which won the Sheffield Shield; a delightful nostalgia trip revolving around some of the most magical cricketing names of my youth. The Frog had been pivotal in the triumph, his high-pace in-swing delivered with a unique front-on windmilling action resulting in a swag of wickets and triggering his first

Australian selections. He was the heart and soul of the XI, exuberant, willing and comical – no other Victorian or Australian No.11 was so appreciated for his hilarious attempts in connecting bat with ball. The Frog's theatrical 'leaves' would often trigger standing ovations from his appreciative hometown mates in Bay 13.

But, into his 70s, he was in a bad way. Life after cricket had soured. Once a strapping 188cm (6ft 2in), the Frog was barely 177cm (5ft 10in), had severe breathing and respiratory issues and his balance was dodgy. His wife had left him, his son was living off-shore and he had little or no contact with his grandkids. 'It was tempestuous,' he said describing his marriage to Diane, a fellow schoolteacher. 'I was probably not the easiest to live with.'

Memories had all but faded of his finest cricketing moments on the third morning of his one-and-only hometown Ashes Test match in Melbourne in January 1971 when he dismissed grand masters Geoff Boycott and John Edrich before lunch and led the Australians from the field to all round acclaim. Almost 50 years on, the Frog was a hermit, living alone and emerging only on Fridays for his weekend shop. 'Doing anything physical knocks me around,' he told me. 'No one visits. You're the first person to come here for years. If I keel over tomorrow, no-one will find me for weeks.' We sat at his simple kitchen table looking at a scrapbook his wife had kept during happier times. His best had been electric. Opposed to Garry Sobers' 1968-69 West Indians, he took five wickets in the first innings and six in the second and swept to 100 wickets in his first 16 Victorian matches – matching the feats of the wayward genius Chuck Fleetwood-Smith years earlier. Unlike Fleetwood, who lived life on the edge, smoking, drinking and cavorting before finishing a penniless derelict sleeping under the Princes Bridge, Thomson was a solid citizen and a teetotaller, rarely indulging in anything stronger than Fanta or Schweppes pelato.

He still loved cricket, but rarely attended games as he couldn't get a disabled park close to the gate. He listened to podcasts and tuned into matches all over the world via Fox and Kayo. In-between Tests, he'd watch cricket videos long into the night when he couldn't sleep. His nickname had been bestowed at school. 'I was always loud,' he said. 'So loud that one teacher reckoned I could be heard four blocks away, like Foghorn Leghorn. And I've been the Frog ever since.'

Of his fleeting frontline new ball role with Australia – lasting just 10 weeks – Thomson said he was constantly encouraged to intimidate the English, in particular John Snow. 'I didn't want to bounce Snowy. I'm not brave. I'm not suicidal.' He showed me a draw overflowing with his music CDs and another of his precious cricket videos. He posed for a photo outside in his Australian jumper and a baggy green cap, crumpled and out of shape.

Afterwards I rang the Australian Cricketers' Association and said the Frog desperately needed help – at the very least some funding for a Medi-alert buzzer to hang around his neck, in case he collapsed. The lass said he'd always rejected any outside assistance. 'He's very proud, Ken,' she said.

We duly produced *Bob's Boys*, featuring the Frog's heartfelt foreword, in which he told his story: an ugly duckling who had dared to be different. The celebrated Frank Tyson had once told him to ditch his windmill action. 'But I didn't know any other way,' he said. 'It never felt strange to me. I've only seen a small amount of footage of me bowling. But when I do I still get a giggle out of it.' The Frog delayed his annual time-share holiday booking on the Mornington Peninsula to attend the reunion and launch of the booklet, limited to 307 copies, mirroring Cowper's epic mid-'60s Test triple-century. Everyone signed, Thomson's flowing autograph among the most readable.

I shared news of the fallen old star's ill health with the readers of sportshounds.com.au, the resting room for old sports journos waiting to go to God. Dean Jones saw my piece and broke into tears. The Frog had also been one of his childhood heroes. Just weeks before Froggie's death, aged 76, late in 2022, he rang and asked about the availability of my annual *Universal's Cricket Summer Guide* – 'the one with all the stats'. His voice was raspy and initially I didn't recognise it. 'It's Alan Thomson,' he said. Finally, it dawned. 'Oh, it's you Frog,' I said. 'Why didn't you say so mate?' He'd been moved into a nursing home, had a fall and broken his hip. 'But it doesn't stop me from reading,' he said. He duly sent me a cheque, probably the last one he ever wrote.

His celebration of life was held in a small beer garden of a Richmond pub during the 2022 Melbourne Test, the only match he'd bother to see each year as he was given a ticket in and lunch as an ex-Test player.

Among those to attend were many of his old cricket buddies including fellow internationals Cowper, Keith Stackpole and Ken Eastwood and his old Shield 'keeper, Normie Carlyon who had shared in almost a third of the Frog's 55 victims during that title-winning summer of '69. Carlyon reckoned no one could make the new Kookaburra bounce and veer as drunkenly as the Frog. Stacky had brought along some old photographs, including one of Froggie at Australian catching practice. 'That wasn't his go much,' he said. 'But he could bowl.' Cowper loved Thomson for his big heart and stamina. 'He always ran in with purpose and, on his day, could be menacing with his bounce and slant,' he said. In the lead-up to the Frog's send-off, Cowper sent me a message. 'Please keep me informed,' he said. He didn't want to miss farewelling one of his boys. Friendships in sport are for life.

2

BABY BRADMAN

'Instead of congratulating Potter on his brilliant pick-up and return, the Don said: "You've just ruined the match. He's their best player."'

Back in the swinging '60s there was no internet. No Kayo. No Fox Sports. ABC Radio was our cricketing lifeline. Its capital city stations, like 3LO (774) in Melbourne or 2BL (702) in Sydney, had three five-minute summaries each and every Sheffield Shield day, the last always right on 6.30pm. Sometimes they'd also do ball-by-ball descriptions. I hung on every word. The exact times were published in the Green Guide in the Melbourne *Age* each Thursday. ABC television broadcast the final two hours of the Tests. Dinner at 26 Deauville St. would invariably be delayed on cricket nights.

There was great hilarity during a cross to Perth one springtime evening in 1967. Earlier in the week, on Channel 7's *World of Sport*, Melbourne's 30-year Sunday institution, twinkle-eyed old international Doug Ring had playfully suggested that Victoria would create a new world record and make at least 1107 runs in its opening match of the new season against lesser lights Western Australia in Perth. Jim Fitzmaurice, ABC Perth's sporting anchor, started the formalities at Sunday tea-time:

> 'Welcome to the WACA Ground here in Perth where Victoria has fallen almost 1000 runs short of its anticipated first innings total...'

Unable to contain his glee, Fitzmaurice then introduced hero-of-the-hour Ian Brayshaw, who in the game of his life, had taken all 10 wickets, for just 44 from five or six different spells, both with and against the Fremantle Doctor – the afternoon breeze which so famously assists the swing bowlers in Perth. With two for 2 overnight, Brayshaw was delighted by his start against such an illustrious top-order. Coach Wally Langdon said: 'Take five for 5 and I'll get Todge (Campbell, the *West Australian's* cricket photographer) to take a photo of the scoreboard.'

Sure enough, late in the first session, Brayshaw had his five for 5, Keith Stackpole edging an in-swinger onto his boot and watching in horror as it ballooned all the way to Jock Irvine at mid-off. Brayshaw's five dismissals were all Australian XI players, past, present and future:

Ian Redpath	21
Ken Eastwood	6
Bob Cowper	7
Jack Potter	0
Keith Stackpole	0

He was to add five more, too, as the Shield champion tumbled to 152 all out in under 50 overs. With 47, Bill Lawry top scored, but even years later was still debating the so-called tickle down the legside to

WA's wicketkeeper Gordon Becker. 'Tell Braysh I never hit it,' he relayed through a friend. Only two other Australians at Shield level had also taken 10 wickets, South Australia's Tim Wall between-the-wars and Queensland's Peter 'Piccolo' Allan, also against the Victorians just a season or two earlier. Allan sent Brayshaw a congratulatory telegram: 'Welcome to the club. Thank God for the Vics.'

I'D BEGUN TO keep newspaper clippings and record all the major stats, state-by-state, player-by-player, match-by-match, in a VANA exercise book. South Africa was visiting for the first time in a decade and Dad had promised we would attend the Melbourne Test. No eight-year-old had as keenly counted down the days approaching a game.

Only one of the 1963-64 Springboks had toured before. Captain Trevor Goddard was also a rookie, never having led at even Currie Cup level, South Africa's equivalent of the Sheffield Shield.

Six debuted in Brisbane, including the much-vaunted teenage left-hander Graeme Pollock from Port Elizabeth. His big brother Peter Pollock was the team's strike bowler. Peter was known as 'Pooch'. Graeme was 'Little Dog'. Peter rarely watched his younger brother bat in case he jinxed him.

Even at 19, RG Pollock was a virtuoso, with a cover drive as imposing as any of the future champions – even India's Virat Kohli. Tall, blond and athletic, Pollock had played for the elite South African Schools XI at 15 and been the youngest ever to notch a Currie Cup century. Just months earlier, at St George's Park, Eastern Province's home ground, he'd made an unbeaten 209 against Richie Benaud's International Cavaliers – including thirty-four 4s and three 6s against the formidable attack of Garth McKenzie, Des Hoare, Benaud, David Sincock and Johnnie Martin. Soon he was to be dubbed 'The Baby Bradman'.

In Eddie Barlow, the Springboks had a highly skilled, world-class opener. Aggressive, competitive and cantankerous, he became one of the players of the season – my first of 60 joyous summers. Barlow often deliberately steered bouncers over the head of second slip and bowled bumpers at the batting specialists, just like England's Ben Stokes years later. With his gold-rimmed spectacles and ample mid-section, he answered to 'Bunter' – after Billy Bunter of comic book fame.

He'd made a six-hour century in the opening Test in Brisbane, a match marred by the callous and unpalatable public execution of Victoria's fast bowling hero Ian Meckiff. Recalled unexpectedly after almost three years in the wilderness, Meckiff, 28, was no-balled four times for throwing in his only over. Mid-match rains made a result impossible, but there was much to like about the Springboks, especially in the field, where two would race for the boundary balls and the first expertly scoop it back to his partner for the return throw. Colin Bland and Peter Carlstein were electrifying square of the wicket, Bland's power arm rivalling Norman O'Neill. So pinpoint were the tall Rhodesian's returns that if one happened to fly just a little wide of the stumps, the Aussie crowds would boo, Bland sometimes waving an apology. It was all so vivid for me. I was fascinated by the game, its nuances and lead players. After a tropical storm consigned the match to a draw, a distraught Meckiff announced he was quitting cricket at all levels. In later years he conceded he'd been victim of a set-up – a Bradman-led purge on those with suspect actions. He conceded his action had changed because of injury and he'd been opening up at release like a javelin thrower.[1] Clem Jones, chairman of the Umpires' Selection Committee and a delegate to the Board of Control said years later that 'something was on'. 'They'd decided to do it a week before the game,' he said. 'The poor bloke had no hope.'[2]

---

1   *Australian Cricket Scandals*, Ken Piesse (Wilkinson Books, Melbourne, 2018)
2   *Inside Story, Unlocking Australian Cricket's Archives*, Gideon Haigh and David Frith (News Custom Publishing, Melbourne, 2007)

Australia's topscorer in the game was the silky New South Welshman Brian Booth, who loved the clear light in Brisbane and its pitch which played similarly to his home ground, St George's Hurstville Oval, in Sydney.

Barlow made another century, in quicker time, on the opening afternoon in Melbourne, but again lacked support, the Springboks trailing badly in mid match after local hero, pencil-thin debutant Ian Redpath from Geelong College, made 97 and shared an opening stand of 219 with his Victorian opening partner Lawry. Having caressed swing specialist Joe Partridge to the cover pickets, he looked to repeat the shot, only to be bowled. Goddard had just taken the second new ball and ringed Redpath with close-in fielders. 'I laid my ears back, but missed it,' Redders said years later. 'At the time I didn't think too much about it but have most days since. It would have been nice to have made a 100 first up.'[3]

The Test had started on New Year's Day. It was to be another five years before the first of the MCG's regular Boxing Day internationals. Victoria had three in the starting XI, plus 12th man Jack Potter. He was preparing for a New Year's fishing holiday with his father-in-law when told of his call-up. Earlier in Christmas week, Australia's No.3 O'Neill had been struck on the gloves by Alan Connolly during the Shield match, x-rays revealing a hairline fracture of his finger. Come the morning of the match, with Australia fielding first, the names of the players were installed hand-by-hand in the massive slots. The name POTTER went up. 'Great,' he thought. 'I'm in.' Walking back to the rooms, barely touching the ground in his elation, he was sorting through some gear when selection chairman Sir Donald Bradman approached and shook his hand. 'That's nice,' thought Jack. 'Recognition from the great man himself.' Looking Potter directly in the eye, the Don said: 'I always say it's

---

[3] It took Redpath five-and-a-half-years and 27 more Tests before finally making his maiden 100

better to be 12th man, than 13th.' O'Neill's batting spot was to be filled by Bobby Simpson, captaining for the first time. Lawry and Redpath were to open. Instead of making a hometown Test debut, Potter spent his New Year's watching from the upstairs viewing area – alongside the Don. He received a baggy green cap and the 25-pound match fee, but never was to make an actual Test XI.

In Melbourne, the young Springboks again under-achieved and were sliding to defeat, having conceded a 173-run lead. Goddard succumbed early before Barlow and No.3 Tony Pithey tamed the new ball pair of McKenzie, known as 'Garth' after the imposing comic book hero and Connolly, then a tearaway operating off a run-up more suitable to a Jumbo jet.

They'd added 48 reasonably comfortably when, for the first time, Potter was called into the match as a temporary substitute. He'd played Claxton Shield representative baseball and was fast, alert and athletic. Simpson immediately enlisted him in the inner ring. Within minutes, Pithey hit one to Potter's right at mid-wicket and called 'yes'. Barlow (on 54) responded, only to be beaten by a fabulous 25-yard throw, low and direct to the striker's end. Potter had just run out the in-form player in the world, denying him the opportunity at twin centuries. 'It bounced up nicely straight into my hands,' said a modest Potter.[4]

Jogging back into the rooms to a standing ovation, Potter walked past Bradman who was seated alone upstairs. Instead of congratulating Potter on his brilliant solo, he had his head in his hands. 'You've just ruined the match,' said the Don. 'He's their best player.'[5] Weeks earlier in Melbourne, representing an Australian XI, Potter had thrown out Carlstein for a duck from side-on – and Carlstein was lightning between wickets.

---

4   *Born Lucky, the story of Jack Potter, Australia's finest 12th man*, Jack and Sarah Potter (cricketbooks.com.au, Mt Eliza, Melbourne, 2019)
5   *Born Lucky*

In Adelaide, Barlow and Pollock shared a pulsating 341-run partnership for the third wicket in a massive series-squaring victory. It was the Australia Day long weekend. Dad was painting our lounge room at home and we listened to the description all afternoon. The famed South African commentator Charles Fortune was working alongside the doyen Alan McGilvray and Vic Richardson, then almost 70. Fortune spoke in slow-rounded vowels and pronounced seagulls as 'seagles'. 'Do you think we will ever get them out Dad?' I asked. 'Not sure Bill (his pet name for me). They seem well set.' Barlow scored 201 and Pollock 175 and in Saturday's final session scored at a rare rapidity: 80 runs an hour. Richie Benaud's first four overs cost 36 and Bobby Simpson's first two 31. Barlow and Pollock were unseparated for five exhilarating hours. Three of Pollock's 6s disappeared high over mid-wicket, now the site of the Victor Richardson gates, one speeding down a bitumen path and finishing 150 yards beyond the ground.

It was a coming-of-age afternoon for South African cricket. The Springboks were soon to be the unofficial champions of the world. That night a few of the players joined Sir Donald next door in the South Australian Cricket Association's committee room. At the tour start, in Perth, when Pollock made an electrifying century, Sir Donald shook his hand. 'If you're going to bat like that again,' he said, 'let me know and I'll come and watch.'[6] This time the Don just smiled and said: 'I'm glad I was here.' Even McKenzie, the fastest white bowler in the world, was collared, Pollock clubbing anything wide to the shorter extra cover boundary and Barlow delighting with his deliberate lifts over the slips to the third man fence. 'That little ramp shot of Eddie's was unusual and he got a lot of runs from it,' said McKenzie. 'In South Africa a few years later, my tactic to him was to bowl straighter and allow him no width outside the off stump. It curtailed his run flow.'

6   *The Trevor Goddard Story*, Graham Short (Purfleet Productions, Durban, 1965)

McKenzie regarded Pollock alongside Barry Richards and Sir Garfield Sobers as the best of his time. 'They had the most ability,' he said. 'If it was your day you might get them out; their day and it didn't matter how well you bowled.'

No two visiting post-war batsmen had ever combined to so thrash an Australian attack. Among the 20,000 at the ground to stand and applaud Pollock as he left the arena was the legendary Bill O'Reilly, positioned in the open-air press box to the side of the rooms. Tiger Bill reckoned it was simply marvellous.

Had more of the South Africans shared Barlow's incredible self-belief, the tourists could easily have also won the deciding Test, in Sydney – and the series. 'See you at six o'clock boys,' Barlow loved to say as he was walking out. 'Have a beer waiting for me.'[7]

Goddard lost his first four Test tosses. Afterwards Sir Donald said South Africa, massive underdogs pre-tour, had clearly been Australia's superior and was unfortunate not to win the series outright. With 603 runs at an average of 75, Barlow had been the most prolific visiting international since the iconic Englishman Walter Hammond, 35 years earlier.

FOR THE FIRST TIME to Australia, the Springboks had arrived in Perth by jet – a Qantas Lockheed Electra with limited fuel capacity, forcing refuelling stopovers in Mauritius and the out-of-the-way Cocos Islands. Their marathon five-and-a-half month, 28-match program included a dozen 'bush internationals' against Country XIs of various skillsets, on an assortment of wickets, low, slow and not so true. On a green seamer in Ipswich, Don Bichel (Andy Bichel's uncle) grabbed a rare 'seven-for'. In the same game, the tourist's reserve paceman Clive Halse

---

[7] *Peter and Graeme Pollock, Bouncers and Boundaries* (Sportsman Enterprises, Johannesburg, 1968)

took six for 6 and five for 17, including a hat-trick. In Adelaide, against Garry Sobers and South Australia, reserve wicketkeeper Denis Lindsay scored an enterprising two-hour century from No.9. He thrived on the faster pitches.

In Hobart on Boxing Day, play was suspended for almost 20 minutes amid wild, whistling winds, recorded at 106km/h (66mph). Peter Pollock was twice blown off course in his delivery stride and no balled. When a clear catch behind was disallowed, the umpire claiming he'd heard only the wind, an unimpressed Goddard led his team from the field, waiting for the conditions to settle.

The team operated under nightly curfews. Its tour manager Ken Viljeon insisted on high discipline. Players had to be back at their hotel by 10.30pm; earlier during Test weeks. When a movie finished late one night, players asked their taxi driver to turn the engine off and freewheel down a hill to their hotel so as not to wake Viljeon who was often in the lobby anyway, waiting to catch any night owls. As chief selector, he was all-powerful. When Barlow inadvertently wore the wrong travel clothes, Viljeon declared he'd be returning to South Africa immediately – 'on a slow boat'. An incensed Barlow replied: 'You don't have to worry boss (Viljeon). I'll pay my own way.'[8] Barlow reckoned Viljeon treated the squad like naughty schoolboys. He was yesterday's man. Viljeon's relationship with the Australian press was equally fractious. He regarded many as 'sensation seeking mongrels' and warred in particular with one of the most prominent, RS 'Dick' Whitington, Keith Miller's old 'ghost' writer.

Team morale was further affected by a simmering feud between wicketkeeping rivals John Waite and Lindsay, almost 10 years his junior. As a selector, Waite had the advantage, but Lindsay was the superior, sweeter

---

8   *Eddie Barlow, the autobiography* (Tafelberg Publishers, Cape Town, 2006)

striking batsman and his equal as a keeper. His running catch to dismiss Barry Shepherd from a skier in the Adelaide Test was a matchwinner.

Most of the touring party encountered Australian flies for the first time. And television too. They were chilled by the assassination of American president John F Kennedy at faraway Dallas.

In Parkes in the NSW central-west where the New Year temperatures soared above 115 degrees even in the shade, some of Graeme Pollock's sweetly-timed straight hits into the bank of pepper trees, 30 yards over the boundary reminded older locals of the feats of the town's own six-hitting hero Cec Pepper from the mid-'30s. Pollock made 160 retired in under two hours and just days later, scored 122 in the Sydney Test. 'Our own Duncan Macdonald played him into form,'[9] said long-time Parkes' local Greg Morrissey. Pollock thrived on cornering the strike. He cared little for who was at the other end. On the eighth ball, they had to be ready to scamper. He bludgeoned the ball with awesome power through the offside and while his career was shortened by South Africa's isolation from world cricket, he remains a legend of the game and one of the few to average 60 or more in Tests. 'He was a great batsman,' said one of his contemporaries, the mighty Victorian Bob Cowper. 'It was a pity the world couldn't see more of him. Give him any room and he would destroy the bowling. His brother Peter was genuinely quick and part of a great Test team that unfortunately couldn't play more internationally because of South Africa's sad racial system.' Cowper was a quality part-time finger spinner and would come from wide around the wicket and angle the ball into Pollock's middle and leg stump, hoping to negate his offside mastery. 'I tried to bowl into his blind spot,' said Cowper. 'Freddie Titmus would do the same to me. I'd look to do this to Pollock whenever I got the chance to bowl to him.'

---

9   Macdonald conceded 60 runs from six overs.

RICHIE BENAUD'S illustrious career was to finish in 1963-64. Having missed the Melbourne Test with injury he advised Sir Donald Bradman he would be unavailable for the 1964 Ashes tour and was immediately replaced by the run-making colossus Simpson as Australian and NSW captain. That short conversation with the Don remained one of Benaud's few regrets. He would have loved to have finished as Australia's captain. A Sydney bus strike coincided with the final day of his career and just 6000 attended. Ironically, four years later, Simpson was to have a similar heart-to-heart with the Don and declare his unavailability for the 1968 tour. He, too, was immediately benched, despite having made centuries in each of the first two Tests of the 1967-68 Indian summer.

Benaud had been a magnificent allrounder and an astute, inspiring and motivating leader who backed his players unequivocally. 'He seemed to know what you were thinking,' said Booth. 'He always knew the right thing to say.' In the late-'50s Benaud and the left-arm paceman Alan Davidson were the outstanding bowling pair in the world, Benaud's career having revived remarkably after he happened across a NZ pharmacist who suggested an ointment which miraculously repaired his spinning finger, allowing him to once again apply full revs on the ball without breaking the skin.

In the first-class matches in South Africa in 1957-58, he and Davidson were unstoppable, Benaud taking 106 wickets (at 19 runs apiece) and Davidson 72 (at 15). For a time they were as potent a combination as moderns Shane Warne and Glenn McGrath, Davidson with his late in-swing and Benaud with his signature leg-breaks and sliding lbw ball, the flipper.

The Benaud-led Australian teams had a remarkable rapport. Bill Lawry was a great trickster and once nailed Richie's brand-new street shoes to the floor. To the general merriment of the team, Richie went to slip his feet into them and said, 'I must be tired. I can't move.' As a youngster Benaud had once told Keith Miller how he wished he had bowled to Bradman. The great man retired the year Benaud started. 'That was your good luck,' said Miller.

On the last of his three Ashes tours, in 1961, Benaud won a Test match at Manchester almost single-handedly, going around the wicket in the spell of his life, a tactic later perfected by the best of all, Warne. Months earlier on the final afternoon in Brisbane, with Australia needing 120 in even time to win the first Test against the West Indies, Bradman, Australia's selection supremo, approached Benaud in the rooms and asked what he intended to do. 'We're going for the win of course,' he said. 'I'm very pleased to hear it,' said the Don.[10] Benaud's century stand with Davidson was pivotal in the most remembered Test match finish of all. They were the greatest of friends. Davo was always prepared to bowl another over for Benaud – even if he was exhausted.

Aside from the Meckiff fiasco, over which he had little control, the negativity of the 1962-63 Ashes series remains one of the few blemishes on Benaud's arresting leadership file. After the highs of the 1960-61 summer in which Benaud and visiting captain Frank Worrell vowed to play attractive attacking cricket at all times – and did – the 1962-63 internationals were played at such a pedestrian pace that thousands hooted and booed the Australians from the field in the final Test in Sydney. 'People felt they had been let down,' said cricket writer Tom Goodman. 'The jeering drowned out what handclapping there was.'[11] England's touring captain Ted Dexter was a man of many moods. Few batsmen were as electric, but as captain his concentration often drifted and he could often be seen practising his golf swing at cover. He didn't

---

10 *A Tale of Two Tests*, Richie Benaud (Hodder and Stoughton, London, 1962)
11 *With the MCC in Australia 1962-3*, AG 'Johnnie' Moyes and Tom Goodman (Angus and Robertson, Sydney, 1963)

share the same rapport Benaud had enjoyed with Worrell. Set 241 in even time, Australia scored at a snail's pace, just two runs an over – and back then they were eight-ball overs. A stonewalling Lawry finished 45 not out at an average of 11 runs an hour. The Ashes had become a monumental millstone and cricket was back on the doldrums, just two years after the magnificent highs and goodwill generated by Worrell's high-octane, exuberant Calypsos.

Cricketing generals Frank Worrell and Richie Benaud masterminded one of the most celebrated Test series of all, in 1960-61.

3

DEAD MAN WALKING

'The Ashes were cricket's big event, played at an unparalleled intensity. A Test match victory was akin to winning Tatts.'

The past can be intoxicating, compelling, mesmeric. The heroes of our youth are championed, their flaws and foibles forgiven. Like JM Barrie's Peter Pan, they remain ever young, electric, ebullient. In 1965, Jack Potter made a classic double century in the annual Christmas 'test' between traditional rivals Victoria and New South Wales in Melbourne, the quality of his square driving against a high-class attack of Dave Renneberg, Grahame Corling, Doug Walters and 'The Little Fave' Johnnie Martin reminding the selectors of an outstanding player with exquisite timing and flair. Yet, less than two years later, aged 29, Jack walked away from big cricket, having been told he was unlikely to be chosen for the next Ashes tour, in 1968.

The competition for top-order batting places that 1965-66 Ashes summer was ferocious. Nineteen of the 22 who figured in the memorable all-star Sheffield Shield encounter played or toured with Australia. Victoria's top-order was Bill Lawry, Ian Redpath, Bob Cowper, Keith Stackpole, Jack and the Geelong teenager Paul Sheahan. NSW's top six was even more formidable: Bobby Simpson, Barry Rothwell, Grahame Thomas, Norm O'Neill, Brian Booth and the Dungog prodigy Walters. On a steamy, oppressively hot opening day, Thomas motored to 229. No-one in Australia hit the ball harder. He had wrists of steel. It was high holiday season and armed with my MCC Ladies ticket – which juniors could use too – floppy hat, zinc cream and multiple rounds of Mum's home-cut vegemite and walnut sandwiches, I saw three of the four days, scoring the match ball-by-ball. I still have the page of Jack's 221. Some reckoned he lacked self-belief and could be unsettled early by genuine pace. I thought he was a marvellous player. And he was to become an even finer captain and coach. He had the courage to back his instincts and make inspired bowling changes which often triggered a wicket. Years later I published his memoirs *Born Lucky*, which included his mentoring of the precocious Melburnian Shane Warne who, to Jack's amazement, perfected within days a flipper he'd only just been shown. Lawry contributed the foreword and was generous in his praise of Jack's skillset. Many less talented players had represented Australia. Jack had been in the right place, at the wrong time.

Lawry was another early hero. Known to everyone in cricket as 'Phanto' or 'Phanta' for his love of Phantom comics, Lawry had taken a stack of them with him on his first interstate train trip, the overnighter to Adelaide in 1956. While others enjoyed a beer or three, young Bill was quietly engrossed by the daredevil feats of the masked crusader.

Few were tougher on the field or harder to dismiss, Lawry's centuries on his maiden first Ashes Test tour in 1961, remarkably poised and brave. He may not have led with the verve and instinct of his successor,

Ian Chappell, but few were as level-headed, more resilient or prouder to wear his representative caps. There were few more amusing after-dinner speakers and, for four decades, his voice was integral to Channel Nine's summer coverage. So desperate was Nine for him to broadcast one last Test match in Sydney that executives bought him a new $50,000 car.

For years we collaborated in producing his lively column for Melbourne's *Sunday Observer*. Famously, Lawry once wrote how he wouldn't walk his dog on the MCG, so mottled was the outfield. 'It should be a showpiece,' he said. It was an Ashes summer and I dictated the story to a copytaker from a cramped press box chockful with visiting English writers. 'Bill writes differently to the way he batted,' said one. It was our frontpage lead and made all the newsagent banners. Fancy a favourite son being so outspoken about one of the most celebrated cricket grounds in the world – especially his own. Once I asked Lawry if he would play in a one-off media match one Sunday. We'd open the batting. 'No,' he said, 'they'd be bowling against Bill Lawry.' Even years into retirement he didn't want to give up his wicket to anyone. *(In that game, at Fawkner Park, I was run out early attempting the only five of my life.)*

When Sir Donald Bradman and co. sacked him late in the 1970-71 series – a banishment unprecedented in Test history – it cost Australia the Ashes. His replacement Ken Eastwood conceded the Poms would have been far more comfortable seeing him and not Lawry walk out in the deciding Test in Sydney. At 35 and short of match practice, Eastwood made just 5 and 0 in a narrow loss.

Twelve months earlier, Lawry had complained at the length of Australia's seven-month tour of Ceylon (now Sri Lanka), India and South Africa. He was also scathing about the quality of the accommodation, especially on the sub-continent. Once the story broke in the newspapers, Bill knew he was a dead man walking. He learnt of his dismissal via a radio bulletin. No-one crossed the Don.

THE BIGGEST CRICKETING names of my youth were beguiling. Test stars McKenzie, Walters, O'Neill, Simpson and Burge were as big in my eyes as the Animals, Hendrix and Ray Davies. Our house was very musical, my closest brother Jim, a drummer of renown who started at Her Majesty's Theatre at shows like *Charlie Girl* and *No No Nanette* before teaching the technique of the American drum legend Joe Morello, whose touch, flair and people skills were extraordinary. He toured the USA seven times, including a season in Las Vegas as MD and drummer for the Four Kinsmen. Jim had been told by his headmaster on the eve of his Year 12 exams: 'Piesse, you're going to fail.' Having obtained honours, he won a scholarship to Monash University. He and my sister Anne also love cricket. In an orchestra pit one night, Jim was asked to pass the 'Ashleys'. He immediately handed over the mallets. At a cricket dinner in Hobart there were some old-fashioned long necks on the table and I asked Annie for 'the Bill Lawry'. Without hesitation, she immediately passed the opener. Recently Annie sent a Christmas card of Santa with cricket bat in hand, facing the bowling of his reindeer. He was batting left-handed. Thanking her for the card, I said I didn't realise Santa was a mollydooker. 'Oh yes,' she said. 'He loves Usman (Khawaja).'

Another of my youthful heroes was Queensland wicketkeeper Wally Grout, noted for his exuberant stumpings and his sprints to fine leg, pads-and-all, chasing deflections. He was to die young – just two years after his last Test appearance in 1966. Like Warnie years later, he'd had chest pains but ignored them. He was a chain-smoker, two packs a day.

Years later, I published his biography, written by his grandson, which, in addition to his many celebrated achievements, graphically tabled his mania for gambling which twice saw him return from Ashes tours without any gear, all hocked to help fund his addiction. His wife insisted the betting debts be met and negotiated a personal loan from her bank manager. Grout the husband, chain-smoker and gambler was foolhardy, but as a wicketkeeper he possessed sublime skills and was universally popular.

The Australians toured England in 1964, Simpson making 311 at Old Trafford. When one English fan looked up to the balcony and yelled: 'Declare Simpson you bastard', Grout casually leant over the dressing room railings and said: 'What about The Oval 1938?'[12] At the end of the series, Simpson promised a game to all those who hadn't played during the Ashes. Extra Tests had been scheduled in India and Pakistan. Leg spinner Rex Sellers made a one-off appearance at massive Eden Gardens. Reserve wicketkeeper Barry Jarman played two Tests and wrist spinner Johnnie Martin three. Jack Potter was the unfortunate one. He remained in hospital in London for an extra month having had his jaw broken in an exhibition game at The Hague. The left side of his face had fallen and even weeks later he was still slurring his words considerably. He'd missed the birth of his first child and his wife was heavily pregnant with another. Doctors warned against him flying until he could pronounce the words: 'Massachusetts Institution'.[13] Given he'd played only two thirds of the program, Australia's Board of Control for Cricket – not known for its generosity – debated that some of his tour fee (1200 pounds, about twice the average wage) should be withheld. Bradman squashed such talk immediately. Potter was paid, in full.

Earlier, during that '64 tour, Potter had been batting with Simpson on a green county seamer. 'I could hardly put bat on ball,' he said. 'Yet at the other end Simmo was playing so effortlessly, like he was on a different pitch altogether. Years later I related that story to Bill Heller, one of our leading players at Fitzroy. "That's how you made us feel when we played with you Pottsy," he said.' "You were on another level again."'

---

12   When England batted into a third day making 7-903 declared, still the world record Ashes score
13   *Born Lucky, the story of Jack Potter, Australia's finest 12th man*, Jack and Sarah Potter (cricketbooks.com.au, Melbourne, 2021)

HAVING ATTENDED my maiden Test match and witnessed the power and majesty of Graeme Pollock, it was to be 12 months before the next Melbourne Test, a one-off international for the sub-continent's 'Bradman,' Hanif Mohammad and his touring Pakistanis on their way through to New Zealand. The Test had been an after-thought and was allocated only four days. Three other first-class games were also played, but over just three days. The monies offered by the ABC to televise the Test were so meagre it was decided to cover the game only on radio.

Of diminutive build, Hanif had a Sobers-like stature in world cricket and was known as 'The Little Master'. He'd once batted three days to save a Test and had a highest score of 499, which eclipsed even Don Bradman's highest score.

The Test, his only international in Australia, was a great success and included go-slow tactics on the final day which denied Australia any chance of a win.[14]

Hanif all but made twin centuries with timing and elegance. He also kept wickets, taking five catches after the first-choice wicketkeeper Abdul Kadir had his thumb crushed by McKenzie's third ball of the match. With a physique to make girls swoon and teammates envious, McKenzie possessed a beautiful loping, side-on action and bowled the heaviest of balls.

Australia fielded two newcomers, the red-headed left-arm wrist spinner David Sincock, known to all as 'Evil-dick' and another from Adelaide, the emerging 21-year-old batting prodigy Ian Chappell. One of Sincock's early overs to Hanif cost 19. He was a big spinner but erratic and selectors were soon to look elsewhere for a replacement for Richie Benaud, their just-retired champion.

---

14 Pakistan bowled just six overs in the first 37 minutes, fast bowler Farooq Hamid taking two minutes to tie his bootlaces before beginning his fourth over to ironic cheers. Set 166 to win in 127 minutes, Australia faced less than a dozen overs, finishing at 2-88, with rain intervening.

Chappell was to be a long-termer, one of the elite players and captains of his generation. In time, he was to also have access to the most lethal Australian pace attack in history, enhancing his status alongside Benaud and Mark Taylor among the most-famed post-war Australian captains.

Like Ricky Ponting the commentor, Chappell the captain was invariably an over or two ahead of the game. He had flair, panache, timing and a short fuse. His first South Australian selections, at 18, had been triggered by a headlining display at Glenelg Oval against the state's two Shield opening bowlers Alan Hitchcox and Peter Trethewey, both from West Torrens. After dispatching Hitchcox to the square leg boundary, he jogged down the wicket and eyeballed his opponent. 'Fancy *you* opening the bowling for South Australia!'[15] he said disparagingly. Hitchcox fumed, threw his bowling marker back another five or so yards and unleashed a stream of bouncers at the young upstart. He genuinely wanted to scone him. But each were pulled with savage intent to the square boundary, the teenager advancing from 84 to 100 in four balls. Non-striker Des Selby sat back and smiled. 'Here was a young guy who was very special. He was ready to play big cricket,' he said. 'The shorter Hitch bowled, the harder Ian hit 'em.'

Chappell was in at No.3 in his maiden Test and while he missed out, his leg-breaks were handy and he took three catches, having been given immediate responsibility in the slips.

IT WASN'T until the 1970s that itineraries included international tours every summer. While 1964-65 was basically a domestic season, reward for the best performed was a place in Australia's squad for the world Test showdown with the West Indies in the autumn of '65. Peter Burge's withdrawal weakened the batting and rather than include

---

15 *Favourite Cricket Yarns*, Ken Piesse (Echo Publishing, Melbourne, 2014)

a 'project' player like Chappell or the NSW prodigy Walters, the Australians opted for seasoned experience and in one Test, in Barbados, even played seven specialist bats.

Wes Hall and Charlie Griffith were at their most lethal on their bouncy, bone-hard home pitches. Hall was fast and Griffith faster, operated from wide of the return crease, often outside the sightboard eyeline. At Queen's Park, Trinidad, he came from the Pavilion end without any sightboard. He'd been called for throwing previously and Benaud – on tour as a journalist – reckoned he should have been no-balled regularly from the opening Test in Jamaica. Frame-by-frame film taken by a local Trinidadian confirmed a considerable bend in Griffith's arm.

At Sabina Park, famed for its polished grey mud pitch which gleams like a tortoise shell, Hall and Griffith shared 13 wickets as the West Indies recorded its first ever home victory against Australia. All four of Griffith's wickets were bowled. 'Charlie was dangerous,' said Brian Booth. 'I didn't see three of his deliveries in that game. Two were screaming yorkers and knocked my stumps over – never before or after had I been so comprehensively bowled – and a bouncer grazed my chin. I don't recall seeing the ball leave his hand or even whipping past my face. But I felt it.' Grahame Thomas said no one was as menacing or possessed Griffith's sudden burst of withering pace. His angle was particularly confronting for the right-handers. Booth and Bob Cowper shared a double-century stand at Trinidad. As a leftie, Cowper could more easily sway out of the way of the bouncers.

Pre-tour, the West Indian board had refused to agree to Australia's request for legside fielding restrictions, a warning the Australians were to be peppered like in the days of Bodyline. Griffith often started with eight fielders behind the wicket and just one in front. With home crowds roaring, 'Bounce 'im maan, bounce 'im,' he'd meander in before 'delivering' open-chested at express speeds. The shorter the bowling, the more the Caribbean crowds would roar and whistle. 'BOUNCERRR,' they'd chorus. Australia almost lost in Bridgetown despite having started with 6-650 declared. The Windies were just 11 runs short of victory on the sixth and final evening when time was called, a rare McKenzie wide seeing the final over extend to seven balls. Asked years later if he had deliberately bowled it to waste some time and avert the possibility of an extra over, McKenzie said: 'It could have been on purpose. It was really tight in the end. But I'd bowled almost 50 overs in the first innings and there was barely a break before we were bowling again (after a late-match declaration). I was exhausted.' Often McKenzie's role reverted from strike to stock bowler. 'It was frustrating, especially when numbers 5 or 6 came in,' he said. 'If you hadn't bowled so many overs, you'd have had more of a chance against them.'

Despite just two day's rest in-between the fourth and fifth Tests, McKenzie finished the series with five for 33 and three in four balls on the final day of the tour. Having bowled Hall and Griffith, his hat-trick delivery shaved the off-stump of No.11 Lance Gibbs before the next bowled him. It was Australia's only win of a bruising campaign. At the tour end, O'Neill said Griffith was a blatant thrower operating outside the laws of the game. He never wanted to face him again.[16] He'd been forced to retire hurt in consecutive early Tests and had his thumb broken at Bridgetown. Captain Bobby Simpson described Griffith 'as the most deliberate and fearsome chucker of all time'.[17]

I listened to the descriptions of each of the Tests long into the night. Much to my disappointment, the Windies won the first and third Tests and the series 2-1. Garry Sobers was captaining the Windies for the first time. The world's most celebrated cricketer, he soon afterwards released

---

16 *Sydney Daily Mirror*, May 1965
17 *Captain's Story*, Bobby Simpson (Stanley Paul, London, 1966)

his autobiography *Cricket Crusader*. I spied a copy in the side window of our local newsagency, Cutland's in Cheltenham. It was 31 shillings and threepence and it took me a month of Wednesday paper rounds to afford it. I still have the book, which Sir Garfield later signed, along with four or five of his other books. He was a true champion on and off the field.

BY THE TIME Mike Smith's touring MCC arrived in Perth for the much-anticipated 1965-66 summer, I'd turned 10 and was playing on Saturday mornings and scoring in the afternoons for my local club, Beaumaris. One of our neighbours at the top of the street was the formidable Hawthorn-East Melbourne left-hander John Chambers, who had been recruited by Beaumaris. A real estate agent, he had walked away from first-class cricket, aged 25. I was friends with his two boys and John asked if I would score for the firsts. I'd had a season's apprenticeship with the second matting boys, our club's fourth XI. So excited was I by the prospect that on the opening day of the season I sharpened four different pencils and used them all: a 4 was red, 3 was purple, 2 was brown and 1 was black. Our scorebook looked like a giant liquorice allsort. 'Kendrick,' said John, 'this is all very nice, but maybe just stick to one colour from now on...' Later I was to interview John for *Pavilion*, the magazine of the Australian Cricket Society. It was my first byline in the Society's flagship publication.

Our first XI at Beaumaris included my local footy hero Geoff Skinner and John Ward, who later represented Victoria. The wicketkeeper was local Presbyterian Church minister Garry Jacobs. Wardy was 17, broad of shoulder and fast. This particular day, he continued to beat the outside edge. After yet another play-and-miss, Ward yelled out in mid-pitch: 'Geezes $#&%ing Christ... mate, what do I have to do to get you out?' Immediately reproached by Rev. Garry for his bad language, Ward induced another play-and-miss and again started swearing like a sailor. 'John,' called the Rev. 'Never ever use the good Lord's name in vain.' 'Sorry Rev, sorry.' Finally, later in the over – eight balls back then – he feathered one and it flew at comfortable height to Jacobs' right only for him to inexplicably muff it. 'You bastard,' said the Rev, punching his fist and looking skyward. 'Where were you when I needed you?'

THAT SUMMER, I began the first of my lovingly kept scrapbooks, beginning with Percy Beames' 300-word assessments of each of the English visitors, published daily in our staple, the Melbourne *Age*. Mike Smith's profile was the first. He'd been offered the captaincy after Ted Dexter preferred not to tour. His deputy was the seasoned Colin Cowdrey, on his fourth visit. The Ashes were cricket's big event, played at an unparalleled intensity. A Test match victory was like winning Tatts. Smith led with a smile, building a rare unity and team spirit. Everyone was treated as equals, the massive gulf between amateurs and professionals on previous tours forgotten. *(Years earlier they'd enter an arena via separate gates.)*

From the opening over of the tour against Western Australia in Perth the English looked to play attractively, Bob Barber bombing a straight drive back over Garth McKenzie's head, one bounce into the crowd.

Smith's close-in catching, especially in the win in Sydney was inspired. Despite a batting average of under 20, he never allowed his poor form to undermine his spirit or dampen the mood of the dressing room. If he happened to miss out, he'd sit back down, unbuckle his pads and say, 'That wasn't very good, was it,' and keep smiling.[18] Few were as calm, tactful or dignified.

---

18   *The last Corinthian, the cricketing life of MJK Smith*, Mike Thompson (Pitch Publishing, London, 2023)

The English outplayed Australia early, only a fumbled stumping by batsman-keeper Jim Parks robbing them of a Test victory in Melbourne before they won easily in Sydney – the celebrated New Year Test in which his matchwinners Barber and Geoff Boycott opened with 234 at a run-a-minute. Barber was a brilliant shotmaker years ahead of his time. He'd insist on having half the strike and would often refuse Boycott's entreaties for a single from the last ball of an over, sometimes by simply turning his back.

The ABC televised each of the final sessions and I'd sprint home from school to catch the first ball, right on 4pm. On Day 3 of the opening Test, a Monday, so hot was it in Melbourne that we were allowed to remove our school ties at lunchtime. Further north at the 'Gabba – then very much a country ground in the city – the teenage Walters shared a near double-century stand with Lawry in the first Test of the series. They both made big 100s, Walters rifling an impeccable set of drives wide of mid-on against England's two off-spinning specialists Fred Titmus and David Allen. His thrilling advances to anything pitched up were punctuated by powerful pulls through mid-wicket. He was so poised, so unaffected – even if he did spend 50 minutes in the 90s. I watched the last two hours spellbound, marvelling at Walters' nerve and range of flowing strokes. Blissfully, there were no ads, or hiccups. The previous February, in a Shield game, he'd made 253 and taken seven for 63, a sensational solo, the best in a major game in Adelaide since 1891. He'd just turned 19 and was already being labelled a 'batting genius'.[19] According to Lawry, Walters looked as though he had been playing Test cricket all his life. On ABC Radio, ex-Test captain Victor Richardson said he couldn't remember anyone so young hitting a cover drive with such assurance.[20] By stumps Walters was 119 not out and overnight 100 congratulatory telegrams

---

19   *The Cricketer*, April 1965
20   *The Cricketer*, April 1965

arrived toasting Australia's youngest cricket star. It had been almost four decades since Australians had seen a teenager start his Test career with a century.[21] In the next Test, the second in Melbourne, he emulated the feats of a young Bill Ponsford a generation earlier when he scored another ton which helped save the match. The decisive moment in the game came early on the final afternoon when Parks missed stumping Australia's No.4 Burge from a wider-pitched Barber leg-break. It hit him on the shoulder and he was widely condemned, especially as he'd missed a similar stumping on the first morning, reprieving Bobby Simpson. At the time Burge had made just 34 and carried on to a match-high 120.

Writing in the London *Evening Standard*, John Clarke said:

> 'Had Burge been out then, England surely would have won the match, for with half their side out, Australia was only 18 ahead and there was still more than four hours left for play. Instead, Burge and Walters stayed together to save the game and added 198...'[22]

So burly was Burge that in his stance his bat looked like a matchstick. He struck the ball with awesome power and was inventive, occasionally even dispatching bouncers to the long-on fence with a tennis-like smash. Parks' fumbles sparked the push for wicketkeeping specialist John Murray to replace him. But Parks was the superior batsman. 'No stumping is as easy as it looks from the stands,'[23] he said. Had the emerging John Snow, then 24, been included in that Australasian tour – sharing the pace bowling duties with David Brown and Jeff Jones – Smith believed England would have wrested the Ashes, despite the brilliance of Walters.

---

21 Since Archie Jackson in 1928-29.
22 *With England in Australia, the MCC tour 1965-6*, John Clarke (Stanley Paul, London, 1966)
23 *Young Jim, the Jim Parks Story*, Derek Watts (Tempus Publishing, Stroud, Gloucestershire, 2005)

The series ended memorably with Bob Cowper making 307 in Melbourne, the second of the two MCG Tests that summer. The match before, in Adelaide, he'd been relegated to 12th man, selection chairman Bradman telling him he wasn't as fit as the other batting specialists. In Melbourne, he was to run a world record twenty-seven 3s and if the outfield hadn't been so waterlogged, he could well have surpassed Bradman's highest Test score of 334. Ironically, they were pictured afterwards having a celebratory drink. Years later, on the publication of *Bob's Boys*, how Victoria won the 1969-70 Sheffield Shield, I shared a glass of Cowper's favourite chardonnay and he talked of the two 5s he and Bill Lawry had run at the MCG only a few years previously in a Sheffield Shield game. 'And they were from consecutive balls,' he said. 'I was fit enough all right – if not fitter than everyone else.'

No one at Test level has emulated his triple-century feat at the MCG. His Australian-soil Test average of 75 is second only to Don Bradman. He was in Dean Jones' class running between wickets. Long-time state and Test teammate Alan Connolly said Cowper was the best he ever opposed. 'I only ever got him out once,' he said, 'and he was only a 16 or 17-year-old playing for the Combined Schools against the VCA Colts. I bounced him and he hit it down the throat of fine leg. I couldn't get him out at club level. He was near impregnable.'

MELBOURNE'S SUMMER of '66 had a remarkable ending with a four-day Grand Final later recognised as the club match of the century. Star-studded Essendon started with a colossal 9-514 declared – and still lost. 'Someone bat with me and we'll make them,' said the opposing captain, Northcote's Bill Lawry at the innings break. 'Someone has got to stay with me.' [24]

---

24   *Bill Lawry, Chasing A Century* (Hardie Grant Books, Melbourne, 2018)

Lawry made 282 not out[25] and Northcote won an extraordinary play-off by five wickets. The match was at the Albert Ground, a lightning-fast village green, just minutes from Melbourne's CBD. In an earlier match that summer against Essendon, Lawry had been dismissed for a duck. Unimpressed by his send-off, he marched into the Essendon rooms afterwards and said: 'You bastards are going to pay for that.'

The one who stayed with him was Tom Ryan, a 21-year-old university student, in his maiden season of first XI cricket and later theatre critic for *The Age*. In the innings of his life, he scored 82, helping Northcote to its first pennant in 45 years. Even Essendon's two Sheffield Shield strike bowlers John Grant and Keith Kirby couldn't dislodge him. Lawry batted for 509 minutes and hit thirty-two 4s, many from tucks and glides to the Pavilion steps, the fastest boundary on the ground. Dad and I went on the Sunday as Northcote advanced their overnight score from 0-98 to 3-405. It was gripping cricket, Lawry hardly playing a false stroke and mentoring his rookie partner in-between overs. On arrival, Lawry told Ryan: 'Don't watch the scoreboard. Play the game, ball-by-ball and let the score build that way...'

'And,' he continued, remembering a mix-up earlier in the season, 'no risky runs.'[26] Among the 5000 watching the epic finish was the cricket-loving Prime Minister Sir Robert Menzies, whose shiny black Bentley was impossible to miss immediately outside the gates. He was seated in the simple side dining room area and was totally content. Some unable to gain a satisfying view opted to stand on cars parked on St Kilda Road. Fittingly, Lawry hit the winning runs and later rated his innings as satisfying as his famous 'Battle of the Ridge' ton during his first Ashes tour, at Lord's in 1961. Back then Lawry was more of a

---

25   It was the highest score in a Melbourne District final since Bill Ponsford made 295 for St Kilda in 1927.
26   *Bill Lawry, Chasing a Century*

shotmaker, brilliant square of the wicket on the offside and a hooker of renown. By 1964, he'd begun to play more of a risk-free, conservative game triggering the immortal 'Corpse with Pads On' phrase from noted English cricket writer Ian Wooldridge. Once he succeeded Bobby Simpson as Australia's Test captain, he further retreated, playing the percentages and batting time.[27]

As we headed home that night, Dad said: 'Just goes to show you... in cricket, you never stop believing...'

A pivotal moment in the 1965-66 club Match of the Century at the Albert Ground. Having made 205, Bill Lawry could have been out stumped down the legside by Essendon's Tom O'Neill. He didn't give another chance. Footballer Barry Davis was the bowler. Asked later what it was like bowling to an icon, Davis said: 'Tough, very tough.'

---

27   In the summer of his life, Lawry batted for 41 hours in the five 1965-66 Ashes Tests for 592 runs. He also made 153 and 61 for Victoria and 47 and 126 not out for a Combined XI against the tourists.

4

LIVING THE DREAM

'While Mum and Dad relaxed with the Avengers or the FBI featuring Efrem Zimbalist jnr, I would be poring over the District and sub-district first XI scores…'

Every kid has a best mate. Mine was Alan Cowen, a redhead who loved Stevie Marriott and the Small Faces and would play *Itchycoo Park* non-stop on a tiny 45s-only turntable each and every night after school as we snacked on his Mum's dark green cordial and Brockhoff biscuits, taboo at our place. Mrs Cowen had a tiny Chihuahua called Perry and we were both wary of it. Coo bowled nice outswing and could bat and our backyard tests were always full on. We'd try and emulate the actions of our heroes, like Alan Connolly, England's offie Freddie Titmus with his double-fisted start and dragging back foot and later Terry Jenner, the bouncy newcomer from South Australia who flung his leg-breaks and googlies extravagantly into the air. At the peak of the holiday season when the Sheffield Shield matches were on, we'd take bat and multiple tennis balls into the 'G and continue our one-on-ones in the many back corridors in the new Western Stand, named in Bill Ponsford's honour. In football season, tiny Glenferrie Oval was our home-away-from-home. We were among the few kids at school who barracked for unfashionable Hawthorn. Glenferrie was known as the 'Sardine Tin' and was shaped like New Zealand's famed rugby capital Eden Park, only smaller. Melbourne's Hassa Mann snapped an impossible goal from the Linda Crescent pocket in time-on late one game to put us out of the '64 finals. I wept for days.

Armed with our floggers, brown and gold crepe paper stapled together onto a sturdy stick and waved for every Hawthorn goal, Coo and I would arrive in time for the start of the reserves. We knew the numbers of every player and all their characteristics, idolising in particular, three or four of the first XVIII: ruckman Don Scott, rising rover Peter Crimmins, celebrated Tasmanian import Peter Hudson and half-forward Bob Keddie whose arms glistened with eucalyptus oil. 'It made it harder to tackle me,' he said. We also liked Kevin Heath and nicknamed him 'Canned Heath' after our favourite American blues band. Kids were welcomed into the rooms for the pre-game warm-ups and Scotty, invariably topless, would be at the front, sprinting furiously on the spot like he was about to run in the Stawell Gift. Huddo, never a hair out of place, would always be at the back smiling and waving to his mates and taking little or no notice of the drillmaster.

Hawthorn's coach was John Kennedy, a playing legend and the club's first premiership coach. He was renowned for his stentorian voice and his dark brown raincoat, which he'd wear on even the sunniest of autumn Saturdays. Kennedy would often stand on top of the coach's box on the member's wing and boom orders, negating any need for a runner. He insisted on contests, the tougher the better. Every player had to tackle hard and be fearless. 'Mouthguards in tonight boys,' he'd often say on a Thursday night, before conducting match practice at an intensity which allowed no leeway for anyone looking to hide an injury. Half-back Ian Bremner had a knee issue and told Kennedy at training one night he could run only in a straight line. 'That's all I want you to do Brem,' Kennedy replied. 'Straight lines.'

The arrival of Hudson heralded the club's most successful era, but Kennedy insisted on no favourites. Early one match, Huddo failed to chase his opponent and Kennedy called over his runner Norm Lord: 'Normie,' he said. 'Go and tell Peter that unless he chases, he's coming straight off.'

Jack McLeod, Hawthorn's selection chairman was sitting close-by. 'John,' he said. 'Peter has kicked six.'

'Has he?' said Kennedy. 'Normie... go and tell Peter to continue to do exactly what he's doing.'

Years later Kennedy agreed to address our 100-game club at Beaumaris and I asked Dulcie, his wife, how best we could show our appreciation. 'Well,' she said, 'he does need a new raincoat, Ken.'

MY FIRST EVER competitive game of cricket was in 1964. I was nine. I'd been pestering my Sunday school teacher and high-grade Beaumaris left hander Norm Armstrong[28] for months. 'Not today Kendrick,' he'd say. The Sharks fielded only one under-age team, at Under 16 level and I was too young. Finally, the club entered an Under 14 team into the Federal District CA. Maybe we were short, but I made the XI for the

---

28 Mr Armstrong's daughter Kerry, was to become a leading Australian actor, known in particular for her bouncy role in the iconic Aussie series *Sea Change*. She also was Best Actress for *Lantana*, in 2001 and a regular on *Neighbours* and *Dynasty*. Three years younger than me, she also attended Beaumaris High.

second match at Parkdale state school, a postage stamp of a ground, with little or no grass, just a hundred yards or so from where I'd been born, at Mordialloc hospital on Nepean highway. Told to stand at square leg, I duly marked my territory with an 'x' – and stayed there, not realising I had to change position at the end of each over. It would have taken me a couple of years to make double figures, but no one was keener. I'd filled-in in the opening round as 12th man for the Under 16s and learnt a brace of new swear words and came home stinking of cigarette smoke. About seven of us jammed into coach Dave Golden's car to Noble Park and back. No seatbelts or passenger limits then.

Soon I was scoring in the afternoon for one of our senior matting teams at nearby McDonald Oval in Black Rock. Bill Sheldrake, the captain, once drilled a drive over the largest eucalyptus tree on the fence at extra cover. It must have soared 75, almost 80 yards, despite the pencil-thin bats he and everyone else then used. Club president Roy Waters would waddle in off four or five steps and bowl hard-to-hit seam-up deliveries too good for most top orders. I'd bring my white shorts, just in case someone failed to show.

On Saturday nights, I'd be at Mrs Mac's local shop on the corner of Beach and Charman by 7pm waiting for the truck carrying the *Sporting Globe* to appear over the Cliff Grove hill. Tony Mac and I were school mates and would kick torps back and forth at lunchtimes. I shared his love of greyhounds. While Mum and Dad relaxed with the Avengers or the FBI featuring Efrem Zimbalist jnr, I would be poring over the District and sub-district first XI scores, game by game and would be thrilled when first cousin Richard Piesse was part of Kew's top-order.

Mondays and the start of the new school week were always lifted by the generosity of another of my school friends, Drew Payne, who would share large size prints of all the weekend's footy and cricket action courtesy of his Dad, Garth, a sub-editor at the *Herald*. I pasted mine into scrapbooks with full captions, pretending I was a sportswriter…

My school report cards were promising. 'A leader, alert and quick,' said my fifth grade teacher at Beaumaris state, Joe Bleeser. He had a crew cut like Sergeant Carter from *Gomer Pyle*. At the year end, he said: 'Near the top of the grade. A thinker. Has done a very good year's work. Well done Kendrick.' The following year, grade 6, I got straight As in mathematics, probably from my habit of adding up cricket scorecards. 'Some splendid work… has had a fine year… a capable lad,' were some of the comments. Mr Lundgren, our headmaster, was not as enamoured. He was on scholarship watch for Mentone Grammar and at a formal interview asked me to pronounce 'grotesque'. I answered: 'grotes-q'. Fail. If he had asked me to pronounce Ranjitsinhji, the Indian prince who played Test cricket for England, I'd have aced it. I would have been good for the Grammar school, but I would have hated having to wear a boater.

My whole week revolved around Saturdays. Back then I was an opening bat and wicketkeeper. The record books show I took five dismissals in one innings, four stumped off our legspinner Bob Howard. But one fateful day at Mentone Girls, while I was standing up to the stumps, a kid followed through after a pull shot and struck me with his bat flush on the jaw. I lost my appetite for keeping after that. I developed my leggies instead and in one game the following year took four for 2 and won the bowling trophy.

One of Dad's pals knew Val Holten, a sub-district legend and former Prahran and Victorian allrounder. Val lived locally and agreed to some one-on-one coaching on Sunday mornings. He so transformed my game that in my last years of Under 14s I won the batting average and the following season scored 50 in the semi-final and 65 not out in the Grand Final at Cheltenham's Shipston Reserve. I still smile each time I drive past Crawford Street which leads to the ground. On another day, a senior semi-final, I made 90 there. For years, Mum would practice her golf there.

Mr Holten would start at medium-pace, having me step back and across into my stumps like Ian Chappell just before he delivered. To his flighty spinners, he wanted me to be light on my feet and when attacking try and reach the ball on the full and hit it straight back down the ground with a vertical bat. 'Take them on Kendrick,' he'd say. Come Grand Final day, four or five of my boundaries came from cover drives against Mentone's off-spinner Trevor McDonald. We passed them eight-down and for years Mum spoke proudly of me carrying my bat. She was as thrilled as me.

BY NOW I WAS in outright cricket mode, keeping scrapbooks and detailing the Test and Shield statistics player-by-player in my VANA exercise books, just like Stan the Statistician from the Coodabeen Champions, the iconic, irreverent Melburnians who for decades so dominated the radio waves on Saturday mornings. Their host was Jeff Richardson, another Beaumaris boy.

During one set of holidays I'd take myself into the headquarters of the Victorian Cricket Association, then at the bottom of Exhibition Street near the old Phoenix Hotel and pore over the scorecards in their annual reports, copying the data, player-by-player of every major game. It took me the best part of a fortnight. My statistical researching went right back to 1948 and the Invincibles. Every Shield game. Every tour. Home and away. Jack Ledward was Association secretary and Bryan Cosgrove his offsider. A typist came in once, maybe twice, a week. Now, 50-plus years later, there is a cast of hundreds, operating at the Junction Oval in St Kilda.

That summer, 1966-67, almost all of Australia's best players were absent with Bobby Simpson's team to South Africa. Doug Walters was the only

Test regular missing, through National Service. His Army mates dubbed him 'Hanoi' – he was often bombed at night. The tour was one-sided, the Australians outclassed from mid-series, when the Springboks paired 20-year-old Durban rookie Mike Procter with No.1 paceman Peter Pollock. Procter's arm action was so witheringly fast many mistakenly thought he bowled off the wrong foot. He angled the ball at high pace into the right handers and away from the lefties and took 15 wickets in his first three Tests, including Bill Lawry bowled from around the wicket to one he left at Wanderers. Prockie was years ahead of his time. No one in world cricket could swing the ball so late at such Larwood-like speeds. Even then, he was bowling in excess of 90mph (145km/h). Denis Lindsay was the series star, with 600-plus runs and a South African record of 24 dismissals. Had he been allowed more scope in Australia three summers earlier, South Africa would have won that series, too. Test cricket was not to see a superior wicketkeeper-batsman until the headlining debut of mature-aged Adam Gilchrist in 1999. In the opening Test at Wanderers, Lindsay made 69 and 182 and took eight catches. He was remarkably gifted and humble. I interviewed him years later when he was an ICC referee.

Back home, Victoria won the Sheffield Shield under the inspired captaincy of Jack Potter. He used just three main bowlers: Al Pal Connolly who resurrected his career operating off a shorter run with wicketkeeper Ray Jordon standing over the stumps; the zippy, under-sized super competitor John 'General' Grant; and Bob Bitmead, who sent down slow left-arm in-swingers from wide of the far return crease off the wrong foot. His teammates called him 'La-La'. They reckoned he bowled a heap of poop. He was incredibly accurate and had a fabulous season.

Potter deserved to lead the Australian 'B' team to New Zealand at the summer's end but ignoring his leadership virtues and many of the most capable emerging youth, the selectors named Les Favell captain and granted farewell tours to seasoned quartet Norman O'Neill, Brian

Booth, Peter Burge and Peter Philpott, all of whom were 30 and over. The Don and his fellow selectors did a disservice to the youth of Australian cricket. O'Neill's troublesome knees were soon to hasten his retirement. He'd been a long-time pin-up boy of Australian cricket, a dynamic No.3 unstoppable at his best. In the monumental tied Test in Brisbane in 1960-61 he made an exhilarating 181, rivalling the majesty of even Garry Sobers. Somehow O'Neill survived the 'next Bradman' tag and became a champion in an elite team. His dashing batting and handy wrist spin was complemented by the power of his remarkable throwing arm which had initially alerted the interests of American baseball scouts. Years later, I spent a golden hour with him before a black tie baggy green gala event in Sydney. He reckoned all the talk about him being a nervous starter was 'rubbish'. Like any No.3 he often batted early when the bowlers were at their freshest. Sometimes he won. Sometimes they won. He signed a copy of his autobiography *Ins and Outs* for me: 'Best wishes Ken. Lovely talking to you, Norm O'Neill.'

The gentlemanly Booth had captained Australia in two of the previous summer's Ashes Tests and when he was dropped after Sydney, selection chairman Sir Donald Bradman wrote to him apologising: [29]

> 'Dear Brian
> 'Never before have I written to a player to express my regret at his omission from an Australian XI. In your case, I am making an exception because I want you to know how much my colleagues and I disliked having to make this move.
>
> 'Captain one match and out of the side the next looks like ingratitude but you understand the circumstances and will be the first to admit that your form has not been good. I sincerely hope that your form will return quickly and in good measure

---

29 *Booth to Bat*, Brian Booth and Paul White (Anzea Publishers, Homebush West, Sydney, 1983)

> *and in any event assure you of the high personal regard in which you are held by us all and our appreciation of the way you have always tried to do everything in your power to uphold the good name and prestige of Australia.'*
>
> *'Yours sincerely*
> *'Don Bradman'*

Booth included the Don's letter in his 1983 autobiography, *Booth To Bat*. He was grateful for his Test match opportunities, but by refusing to play on the Sabbath, he knew his representative days were numbered.[30] He absented himself from an end-of-season charity game between Simpson's South African party and Favell's New Zealand tourists in Melbourne to aid the Tasmanian Bushfire Fund – the third day of the match falling on a Sunday. In his Australian farewell, O'Neill made 0 and 74. An errant throw from Ian Chappell struck young NSW bat Geoff Davies under his left eye and forced him to retire hurt. The silky Melburnian Bob Cowper motored to almost 200 runs for the match without being dismissed. He was among the finest bats in the world, but business opportunities beckoned – he had a Bachelor of Commerce and was soon to be Monaco-based, working as an investment banker. He'd tired of being paid a pittance. And at 27, he left Test cricket altogether, before he'd even peaked. 'If the players before Packer were paid the same as they were in Bradman's era it would have been stupid to retire early,' Cowper said.

'In 1948, the Ashes tour fee paid was the equivalent of 75 per cent of an average cost of a Victorian house. In 1972 it was less than 10 per cent. Players were being asked to be committed professionals yet they were being treated as kids and being paid as amateurs. If it hadn't been Packer (challenging cricket authorities), it would have been someone else.'[31]

---

30   Booth's only appearance in his final first-class season, in 1968-69, was in the city of churches, Adelaide, which initially opposed cricket on Sundays.
31   Australian Cricket Society, Melbourne Branch, 1977 annual dinner

5

SOBIE AND THE STONES

'First-timer Joey Carew reckoned he'd never encountered such a friendly bunch. "They're always waving at me," he said. "That's the bloody flies," said his mate...'

JFK, Jezza and Jumping Jack Flash are forever branded in my memory. We'd only just purchased our first black and white television when the chilling news of the assassination of the American president was broadcast. Just as indelible is Alex Jesaulenko's spectacular snapped goal which buried Collingwood late in the 1970 Grand Final and Mick Jagger and the Stones powering into *Jumping Jack Flash* at the MCG in '99. We had only just returned from the Test cricket in the Caribbean. Boy, did we party that night. Air guitars, ouzo, the full shebang.

But equally prominent for me was the first, very bleak and overcast opening morning of the 1967 Melbourne Test over New Year featuring the Nawab of Pataudi's visiting Indians against the might of Australia's best. The boy from Cottesloe beach, Graham McKenzie, decimated India's top-order, taking six wickets before lunch on Day 1. Engendering near express pace with his wonderfully rhythmic, rocking action, he claimed wickets in each of his first five overs. It was so cold we sheltered under cover in the members' stand, just wide of the old open-air press box. We never normally sat that far back. It was 12 degrees but felt like six. Mum shared a second hand-warmer she normally used for golf. Everyone wore overcoats – and it was late December. After McKenzie's riveting opening, India was 5-25, his menacing bounce and fire with the new ball unnerving a set of batsmen raised on low and slow Asian wickets. Several panicked and self-destructed. It wasn't until Pataudi's arrival at No.7 that the innings was resurrected, but even then the tourists lost by an innings in under four days. On the final morning, Dad and I were running a little late and were in the queue outside the ground when there was a huge roar. 'Sounds like a wicket,' he said. Ajit Wadekar, 97 not out overnight, had succumbed to Bobby Simpson in the opening over and missed his century by one. Pataudi came in with a runner, having tweaked a hamstring and proceeded to blaze like he had an early seating at Pellegrini's, Melbourne's most iconic café.

With a two-eyed stance few of us had ever seen before – he'd lost sight in his right eye years earlier after a car accident – Pataudi unleashed some audacious on-the-up straight drives, against even the world No.1 McKenzie. One smashed into the member's sightscreen on the full. It was thrilling batting. In the rooms, Pataudi was in the habit of casually picking up the nearest bat within reach – and using it, brilliantly. One night Ian Chappell asked him what he did away from cricket.

'Ian,' said Pataudi. 'I'm a prince.'

'Yes Pat, but what do you do?'

'Ian, I'm a fucking prince.'

Noted critic Jack Fingleton called Pataudi a genius and a warrior. 'If more spectacular innings than Pataudi's 75 and 85 in the Melbourne Test have been played in Australia, then I have missed them,' he said.[32] Fingleton's articles appeared regularly in the Melbourne Age. If even one word was changed, he'd ring editor Graham Perkin, demanding an explanation and retribution against the sub-editor who had so dared to fiddle with his copy. For years he'd waged war on Bradman and even wrote a book saying Victor Trumper was the Don's superior on all wickets.

So perturbed was Bradman by India's lack-lustre series start, that he withdrew McKenzie from Australia's team for the final two Tests and when captain Bobby Simpson told the Don he wouldn't be making another Ashes tour later in the year, he was stood down and Bill Lawry immediately installed as the new captain. McKenzie was to finish with 246 Test wickets, two short of Richie Benaud's then Australian record. 'It was one of the most staggering decisions in postwar Australian cricket,' said McKenzie's biographer Ed Jaggard.[33]

Test cricket had been cheapened – and not for the last time. Australia should always select its best XI. Sir Donald's answer was that an Ashes tour beckoned and others must be tried. One of the newcomers for the third Test in Brisbane, fast bowling allrounder Eric Freeman from Adelaide, claimed a wicket with his third ball and his first scoring shot was a six. He was duly chosen for the '68 Test tour but played only twice. McKenzie figured in all five Tests and even today, into his 80s, his disappointment lingers at being denied two Tests he deserved to play.

Then an easybeat, India was beaten 4-0 and wasn't granted another tour downunder for 10 more years. Six decades later, India's Test team is now virtually unbeatable on home wickets, the depth of talent and

---

32 Jack Fingleton, *The Cricketer Winter Annual, 1969-70*
33 *Garth, the story of Graham McKenzie*, Ed Jaggard (Fremantle Arts Central Press, Perth, 1993)

mania for the game throughout the country unparalleled. Cricket administrations worldwide queue for matches against India home and away at red and white ball levels to boost their income streams. The monies made via lucrative media broadcast rights to a billion Indians and tens of millions more on the sub-continent is forever snowballing. The success of the Indian Premier League guarantees astonishing riches for the world's elite. Cricket's power base has changed forever.

LIFE IN THE '60s for this teenager was simple and uncomplicated. Dad bought a brilliant stereo system with huge speakers from Encels and we'd play the Kinks, the Byrds and Eric Clapton and Cream nice and loud after school. If I wasn't at home, Mum always knew where I was: McDonald Oval in summer and Oak Street in winter. I loved both sports and was always buying extra batteries for my transistor to tune into the match descriptions and summaries.

When the big cricket was interstate, Dad and I would listen to the broadcasts on the ABC and watch the final sessions on TV. Overseas commentators would inform and enliven. South African Charles Fortune came in 1963-64 and Englishman Arthur Gilligan in 1965-66. Gilligan was a man of many shades and memberships, including the British Fascists. Not that I knew that at the time. He and his old 1920s Ashes adversary Vic Richardson were the most amiable and happiest of companions. 'What do you think Arthur?' Richardson would ask.

'And what do you think Vic?' Gilligan would counter.

A tall, beautifully spoken Indian by the name of VM Chakrapani toured in 1967-68. He was a best known for his smooth-as-silk commentaries on Radio Australia. The doyen Alan McGilvray called him 'Chuck'. They shared a wonderful friendship.

Lindsay Hassett and our Beaumaris near-neighbor Colin McDonald were other regulars, on both radio and TV. McDonald had retired from internationals but continued to play Saturday afternoon club cricket with Brighton, on the proviso he didn't have to train. The MCG's broadcasting facilities were open-air and primitive and Col would invariably tote a large harlequin-coloured beach umbrella to shield the sun. He was on air one afternoon when an easy catch went up, only to be inexplicably grassed. 'Shit, he's dropped it,' said McDonald in amazement. Later I edited and published Col's extended memoirs in limited edition, autographed by five of his most illustrious teammates. A sixth, Arthur Morris, died before he could sign. It was a hardback and Col was so grateful. Few had been braver against the West Indian express Wes Hall in the celebrated 1960-61 Calypso Test series. When Australia was 'Lakered' at Old Trafford in 1956, he topscored in both innings with 32 and 89. In Australia's first innings, Jim Laker took seven for 8 in 22 balls. 'I had a good game,' Col was to write in a note to me later. 'But we still lost.' The wicket had been doctored but it was still extraordinary bowling. At tea on the final day, Australia was still a chance to force a draw and, in the rooms, an impassioned Ian Johnson gave a rousing speech saying 'we can still save this'. 'Betya 5/1 we can't,' said his vice-captain Keith Miller from a corner.

McDONALD STEPPED aside as Victoria's captain to help fast track Lawry's pathway to the Australian Test captaincy. Lawry was among Australia's best players and a batsman – always a high Bradman priority when anointing new leaders. Whimsical and humorous off the field, but dour and conservative on it, Lawry possessed little of the flair of his predecessors, especially Benaud. He played favourites and polarised many, including some of his own. Test aspirant, fellow left-hander Les

Joslin from Footscray would have loved more feedback, more coaching. Ashley Mallett felt almost unwelcome in Lawry-led XIs, especially on the hard-baked wickets of Australia. As his team's specialist off-spinner, he expected to bowl more than the part-timers. If he happened to concede a 4, he knew he was in trouble. Sometimes he was given only a few overs late in a session as an after-thought. John Gleeson was preferred as he bowled tighter, with a lower trajectory. 'I had little confidence in Bill as captain,' said Mallett.[34] 'He was too defensive and thought me useless on harder wickets. But one day in Brisbane, even with the wicket turning, I had just four overs before tea and they were in three different spells.'

Others, too, bridled at Lawry's attitude and intensity. 'He played for himself and didn't get the best out of his players,' said Ajit Wadekar, who succeeded Pataudi as India's captain.[35] 'And, unlike Simpson and Benaud, he cared little for the image he projected. He made rude gestures in public and had a hostile press...' *(Maybe Wadekar was talking about Indian journalists; in Australia Lawry was well liked, by most, even in Sydney.)*

Lawry won just nine of his 25 Tests as captain but did defend the Ashes in 1968 and went within five minutes of winning them, John Inverarity and co. lasting well into the final hour before the fall of the 10th wicket in the final Test at Kennington Oval. Months later, on home wickets, he piloted the crushing defeat of an ageing West Indian team. The Adelaide Test was a cracker, the tense ending reminiscent of Mackay and Kline from yesteryear. Outplayed early, the Windies scored 616 in their second innings and went within one wicket of squaring the series, the game extending through to 6.54pm with the need for 15 overs in the last hour. Australia's 10th wicket pair Paul Sheahan and Alan Connolly forced a draw by surviving the last 26 balls, most against the second new ball, Sheahan playing out maidens from Lance Gibbs and Charlie Griffith and

---

34 *Rowdy*, Ashley Mallett (Lynton Publications, Adelaide, 1973)
35 *My Cricketing Years*, Ajit Wadekar (Vikas Publishing House, Delhi, 1973).

No.11 Connolly facing a wayward over from Sobers. There was a late break in the TV coverage link, adding tens of thousands to ABC radio's Wednesday evening's audience. It was a riveting finish, the Australians finishing 21 runs short of victory, Lawry criticised for calling off the run chase after a late flurry of wickets.

In the final Test in Sydney – scheduled over six days – Australia started with 600-plus but rather than enforcing the follow-on, Lawry batted again and set the tourists 734. Pre-match he'd announced that he didn't care if it rained for four days straight as it meant Australia was guaranteed the Frank Worrell Trophy. Test umpire Lou Rowan was unimpressed and later wrote in his autobiography: 'Lawry sought only to inflict ignominious defeat on the West Indies; as part payment for Australia's sound defeat in the Caribbean three years earlier.'[36]

So magnificent was Ian Chappell that summer and during the Indian tour that Lawry ranked him the new No. 1 all-wickets batsman in the world – words he was soon to regret after champion Springbok pair Graeme Pollock and Barry Richards thrashed the travel-weary Australians in 1970.[37]

Doug Walters was also in the conversation among the world's best. Happiest on flint-hard home wickets – he'd averaged 38 in England in 1968 – he played with flourish and flair, finishing in Sydney against the Windies with 242 and 103, advancing his series aggregate to 699 at an average of 117. Even Lance Gibbs, the world's most illustrious off-spinner, couldn't shackle his brilliant advances. Anything flighted would be met with a full face and driven back down the ground. Sent into bat, the Australians lost 3-51 before Walters and Lawry added 336, peppering the boundaries and sprinting between wickets like teenagers.

---

36 *The Umpire's Story*, Lou Rowan (Jack Pollard Pty Ltd, Sydney, 1972)
37 Chappell made only 92 runs in eight innings in the Tests in South Africa, whereas Richards scored 508 at 72 and Pollock, 517 at 74.

Twelve months earlier, Walters' Army battalion was due to go to Vietnam. Being just six weeks away from discharge, he was welcoming a return to civilian life. He'd only just married. A superior suggested he sign on for another six months so he could stay with his unit. He claimed it would be better for his image to serve in Vietnam, rather than tour England with Lawry's 1968 Ashes squad. 'I told him he wasn't guaranteeing a return ticket (from Vietnam),' Walters said. 'And the Australian Board of Control was.'[38] He came out of the Army on April 10, 1968, eleven days before the team flew to England.

FROM MILDURA to Mackay and Loxton to Launceston, the 1968-69 Windies were sent everywhere maan. They were incredibly popular. First-timer Joey Carew reckoned he'd never encountered such a friendly bunch. 'They're always waving at me,' he said. 'That's the bloody flies,' said his mate.

After one practice session in Melbourne, I queued for Wes Hall's autograph. He was 190cm (6ft 3in) and looked taller. He was sweating from all his exertions. He was so black, he was almost purple. He signed for all of us kids. I floated home to Beaumaris that night.

On Test-eve in Sydney, Sobers was criticised for playing golf instead of practising. But he finished the tour with a rapid century and five wickets. Even at 32, Sobie was still a Rolls-Royce. Later we were to work together on a coaching column for Melbourne's *Sunday Observer*. Garry coached East Malvern and often would have a hit in the nets wearing no pads or gloves against the team's fastest bowlers. He married a local girl, Prue Forbes from Mentone. Everywhere he went he was treated like royalty.

Ian Chappell enjoyed the most prolific summer of his life, plundering almost 1500 first-class runs – two-thirds against the touring West

---

38 *The Doug Walters Story* (Rigby, Adelaide, 1981). The only Australian Test cricketer to serve in Vietnam was Queenslander Tony Dell.

Indies, average 96. I still have his scores, all neatly penned from my VCA recordings of the 1968-69 season:

A Combined XI (Perth)	23 & 188 not out
South Australia (Adelaide)	123
Australia (Brisbane)	117 & 50
South Australia (Adelaide)	180
Australia (Melbourne)	165
Australia (Sydney)	33
Australia (Adelaide)	76 & 96
Australia (Sydney)	1 & 10

Chappell's rapidly improving younger brother Greg was also making headlines at Sheffield Shield level. He was taller than his brother, more upright and preferred the front foot, playing classically straight, with a penchant for hitting wide of mid-on. Soon he was to surpass Ian as his country's premier batsman. Greg, then 21, should have been chosen for the extended tour of Ceylon, India and South Africa. He was furious when omitted from the XI for the opening Ashes Test of 1970-71. Once in, he was never dropped from the Test team[39] and was to surpass even the Don as Australia's most prolific Test batsman. He was also sublime in the slips. I don't recall him ever dropping a catch.

Greg contributed forewords to several of my books and addressed our Australian Cricket Society members, both 'live' and via Zoom during the Covid years. Few have been grander ambassadors for the game or been more influential and visionary in the advancement of young talent. And for those who like to rate the best since Bradman, he's right up there.

---

39 Chappell did miss selection in Australia's first two internationals against the Rest of the World in 1971-72. On return, he made back-to-back 100s.

6

SCARRED FOR LIFE

*'The gun salute started: BOOM, BOOM, BOOM.
Fearing for his life, Cowper dived for cover.
No one had ever hit the ground quicker...'*

Nothing compares to the dry heat of Adelaide in high summer. It was 100 degrees in the shade this early-February day yet 2000 were present for South Australia versus Victoria, most sheltering in the shade of the member's grandstand or in deck chairs under the formidable Moreton Bay figs at the far end. Almost all were in appropriate summer attire, t-shirts, shorts and thongs for the fellas and flowing summer dresses for the girls. One huge gent leaning against a downstairs post in front of the players' viewing area was impossible to miss. He was in lace-up Army boots and a full-length Army-issue Great Coat.

Bob Cowper, 29, was in his farewell season and captaining the Vics with Bill Lawry in South Africa with the 1970 Australians. Known to all as 'Wal' or 'Wallaby' after his famous father Dave, a rugby international,

Cowper had just began dating the love of his life, Dale, who'd separated from her husband.

Earlier in the morning, Victoria's fun-loving team manager Bill Jacobs had been informed there was going to be a 21-gun salute on the stroke of noon. Looking again at the big bloke at backward square leg, standing alone in the direct sun, Jacobs hastily scribbled a note and enlisted 12th man John Ward to run it out to Cowper.

'But it's almost drinks Faig (Jacobs),' said Ward.

'That's all right. Just get it out there. And hurry now.'

Ward rushed out to the centre at the over's end. It was just a minute or two before 12.

Cowper read the note, frowned and looked over towards the big fella in the conspicuous green overcoat, just 60 yards away. It was Dale's hubby, Jacobs said. Apparently he was none too pleased with Bob. And why was he wearing such a huge coat on such a stinking hot day? Could he be hiding a gun or a rifle under it?'

As Cowper re-read the note and again eyed the man mountain at backward square, the gun salute started: BOOM, BOOM, BOOM. Fearing for his life, Cowper dived for cover. No one had ever hit the ground quicker. Back in the rooms, the Victorians were screaming with laughter. 'Everyone was in hysterics,' said Ward, 'except for Bob. It was the funniest thing I've ever seen in sport.'[40]

In 2019, the Australian Cricket Society held a 50-year reunion for the team and Cowper and his vice-captain Graeme Watson were among the all-star attendees. Watson was known as 'Beatle' for his John, Paul, George and Ringo haircut. Years earlier, his coach at Melbourne FC,

---

40 *Bob's Boys, how Victoria won the 1969-70 Sheffield Shield*, Ken Piesse & Mark Browning, cricketbooks.com.au, Melbourne, 2019.

the legendary Norm Smith, had advised him to pursue cricket. It was a universal game which would allow him to travel. Football was played purely in the 'burbs. My Geelong buddy Mark Browning and I launched a tribute book, *Bob's Boys*, signed by 14 of the 16 players who represented the Big V that auspicious summer.

One of the old stars unable to attend was fast bowler Nigel Murch, a tall, deeply tanned blond fast bowler who was loud and verbose, the centre of most conversations. He and his wife Susie had been married for only four or so months leading into that title-winning season. They'd met at the Junction Oval during a double-wicket tournament organised by Bobby Simpson. 'She was sitting with Garry Sobers and I told her she was wasting her time with him and would have much better fun with me – and asked her out on the spot. Within the year we were married.' Years earlier, Nigel had dated British pop singer Dusty Springfield. They'd met during one of her gigs on the High Street in Northampton. There had been an instant attraction and Nigel asked if she would care to dance. 'Yes,' she said.

Afterwards he asked if she'd like to come home with him. 'Yes,' she said again, beginning a torrid three-month romance.

Victoria's matchwinner that summer was Alan Thomson, known to all as 'The Frog'. In Brisbane on a sporting 'Gabba wicket, he broke visiting international Tom Graveney's forearm with his second ball. 'Frog was too quick for him,' said teammate Peter Bedford. By day Thomson was a primary school teacher at St Albans North. At Fitzroy selection one night, his third XI captain Don Arnell, told of the kid with an unusual action who was rapid and could bowl all day. Within weeks, Thomson was playing in the ones and soon his mentor, ex-Stateman Eddie Illingworth had conceded the wind. Froggie contributed the foreword to *Bob's Boys*. With 49 wickets in eight games, he was pivotal in the success of the team.

'I loved playing under Bob (Cowper),' he said. 'He was the best, most-engaging captain of all. At our very first meeting approaching the game against Western Australia, Bob gave us a rundown on their players. He'd been in Perth for a year and played half a season in their Shield team. When it came to his appraisal of a young Dennis Lillee, he said Dennis was fast... but very straight. Back then, he may have been, but he sure wasn't in the end. What a bowler!'

Froggie was a folk hero at his beloved MCG. Before a one-day match against New Zealand, the crowd were singing: 'We love you Froggie, oh yes we do,' as he stepped out his 16 paces.[41]

My pal Coo Cowen and I rarely missed a Victorian home match that summer. In the closest, last pair Thomson and Blair Campbell added 50 or so in a slapstick 10th wicket stand against the might of New South Wales. It was like a skit from Benny Hill. Blair could bat but the Frog couldn't. Somehow, he made it to double figures – and in the second innings theatrically blocked three or four leg-breaks[42] from Geoff Davies to help the Vics to a one-wicket win. Soon he was touring and playing Test cricket for Australia. It had been a whirlwind, against-the-odds rise – one which makes sportswriting one of the happiest and most rewarding of professions.

HAVING BEEN humbled by South Africa, the Australians were to forfeit the Ashes to Ray Illingworth's touring Englishmen in 1970-71. Fast bowler John Snow mowed through the Aussies in mid-series in Sydney, taking seven for 40 in the most lethal spell of his life. One of his skidding bouncers struck Graham McKenzie in the face, forcing him

---

41 Ray Robinson, *The Cricketer Spring Annual, 1970*
42 Treating them like they were 'sticks of dynamite', according to Ross McMullin in *Pavilion* magazine.

to retire hurt. It was to be his final Test. Doug Walters was bounced all summer, ending in 'Queer Street', according to teammate Keith Stackpole.[43] And despite being his team's most reliable bat, Lawry was within weeks of being sacked.

Rockhampton's Ross Duncan had been included for the Melbourne Test, only to break down on match-eve at the final practice session at South Melbourne. But he played anyway, believing he may never again have the opportunity. He bowled just 14 half-pace overs for the game and concedes he let down his captain, his teammates and himself. He had a long-time ankle bone spur problem and it flared less than 24 hours before the game start. He and the Frog were the only two pacemen chosen. Alan Connolly had retired on the spot after being dropped a week earlier after the fallout from Sydney. He'd retreated down the Bellarine Coast and was uncontactable.

'All my life I'd wanted to play,' Duncan told me years later for *Fifteen Minutes of Fame*. 'I get the chance and then this happens. I probably wouldn't have played had I known what was going to happen.'

He had a cortisone injection just before the Australians bowled late on Day 2 and could hardly run-in, let alone bowl with purpose. 'I would have been better off putting up with the pain,' he said. 'The doctor consulted was expert in urology, not so much about cortisone injections and sports injuries.' Standing at mid-off, Lawry couldn't believe this was Australia's latest fast bowler. Veteran cricket writer RS 'Dick' Whitington likened Duncan's gentle speed to someone throwing paper darts. 'He was bowling on one and a half legs, at best,' he said. 'Whoever passed him as fit must have needed an overhaul themselves.'[44]

---

43   *Not Just for Openers*, Keith Stackpole (Stockwell Press, Abbotsford, Melbourne, 1974)
44   *Fifteen Minutes of Fame, Australia's 70 One-Test Wonders,* Ken Piesse (cricketbooks.com.au, Mt. Eliza, Melbourne, 2022)

The selectors were under siege and met via a trunk call: Sir Donald Bradman in Adelaide, Neil Harvey in Sydney and Sam Loxton in Melbourne. 'We're running out of quickies,' said the Don. 'Have you two seen anybody with any pace?'

'As a matter of fact we have,' said Loxton. 'Who?'

'A fella from Perth by the name of Lillee, Dennis Lillee.' 'Does he know where it's going?'

'No,' said Loxton, 'but neither do the batsmen.'

Duncan was out and Lillee, the 21-year-old Perth bank teller, in. One of the most illustrious and headlining careers was beginning. On debut, sharing the new ball with Thomson, Lillee took a 'five-for' and never again bowled into the wind. He was to become the most feared and feted fast bowler in the world.

NOT ONE LBW appeal was granted to English bowlers in 1970-71. In Brisbane, Australia's double-centurion Keith Stackpole was clearly run out at 18 by a direct hit from mid-on, but somehow survived. Cricket's DRS replay system was still light years away. A side-on photograph of Stackpole being 18 inches short of his crease exacerbated tensions. In the seventh Test in Sydney, so incensed was England's captain Ray Illingworth at Snow being no-balled for intimidatory bowling and subsequently manhandled by a spectator he led his team from the field. Detective Sergeant Lou Rowan from the Queensland Police drug squad was the offending umpire on both occasions.

Australia fielded nine newcomers for the summer, 35-year-old Ken Eastwood replacing the sacked Lawry for the decider. He'd hitchhiked to the ground on the opening morning after the team's taxis failed to arrive despite captain Ian Chappell's multiple phone calls. Given two baggy green caps to try on for size, he never returned the second. Sydney was to be his only Test.

Also new into the XI was Tony Dell, the 196cm (6ft 5in) fast bowler, little known outside Brisbane. Even Chappell was unaware he'd served in Vietnam and witnessed so many atrocities. Dell was scarred for life – and didn't know it.

Vietnam was the most divisive of wars, 60,000 Australians served, 3000 were wounded and 521 died. More than 20 per cent of Vietnam veterans suffer from Post Traumatic Syndrome, Dell among them. Tony and I became friends years later and we organised a luncheon launch of his book in Melbourne. David Hurley, Australia's Governor-General had agreed to attend before Covid stopped everything.

Just weeks before his return to Brisbane, Dell and a handful of his mates had lost their way in the blackest of jungles south-east of Saigon. A routine mission soon became their worst nightmare. Just as they were bedding down, having resolved to wait until first light to re-track their steps, a large enemy platoon marched directly at them. Any sound and they were dead. Dell held his breath paranoid that the Viet Cong would hear the thump-thump-thump of his heart beating. The Australians were hopelessly outnumbered. The enemy came within metres of the hideaways... and kept marching.

When it was finally safe to alert his superiors via their radio, Dell couldn't speak. He was so traumatised. 'We just had to shut up and hope that no-one spotted us,' said Dell of his near-death encounter. 'If someone coughed or the bloody radio had squelched, we were gone.'

His time in Vietnam left monumental scars, his weeks in the jungles triggering decades of torment. He saw a bullet blow an enemy soldier's brains out. Another enemy soldier was shot in the chest and his whole back exploded with the exit wound. 'A couple of years in Vietnam changed my outlook on everything: life, cricket and people,' Dell said. We did an extended interview. It was chilling. No wonder he had become his own worst enemy. Originally, he'd viewed his two years of National Service as a Boy's Own adventure. His name had been plucked out in Queensland's National Service lottery. 'I didn't mind it one bit,' he said. 'We were going to play real soldiers...'

Known throughout his teen years for his amiability, wide smile and considerable cricketing ability, the atrocities and horrific violence he witnessed left him sour and insufferable. Haunted by the vision of the dead and disfigured and jolted by flashbacks of enemy fire whistling overhead, rarely could he sleep for more than two hours each night. It wasn't until he was in his mid-60s, living alone in his mother's garage on the Sunshine Coast that he learnt the truth of his own painful self-destruction and the reasons behind all the dramatic mood swings and marriage breakdown. A diagnosis of Post Traumatic Stress Disorder emanating from his active service allowed him to finally piece together the ruins of his brooding, troubled life and find some answers.

Ironically, without his time in Vietnam, he would never have opened Australia's bowling alongside Lillee in an Ashes Test. Always regarded as a gentle giant – known for his bounce rather than his pace – he returned fitter, fiercer and more focused.

Now almost 80, the former Army signaler said there was no repatriation for those returning to civilian life. A generation earlier, my Dad and his Commando buddies had a similar experience. 'One day I was in the jungle shooting at people. Two days later (in March 1968) I was walking down Queen Street in Brisbane looking to get back to work,' Dell said. 'There was no counseling, no time to decompress. I didn't talk about Vietnam. None of us did.' Cricket was his distraction and for a time his savior. With Australia plunging to a series defeat against Illingworth's Englishmen, Dell, 23, was called into the deciding Test match in Sydney to open with Lillee, who had debuted just a fortnight earlier. *The Age* newspaper, a little optimistically, referred to Dell as 'the cyclone from the north'. The Australians lost but Dell impressed with five wickets for the match. He out-bowled even Lillee, who took three... not that he remembers anything about the game. 'It has gone,' he said. After just one more Test, his big-time career was over. Crankier and increasingly irrational, his dark moods and flashes of anger were to be constants as his life raged out of control, costing him his marriage and turning friends and family against him.

AS SOCIETY WRESTLES with a growing global mental health crisis, Dell's own private internal war lasted a lifetime. It wasn't until he'd hit absolute rock bottom that he was able to find some answers to his inner torment. He had little or no money and was living just above the breadline. Baked beans on toast was a staple and chicken nuggets in chicken noodle soup a once-a-week treat. 'I was living off the smell of an oily rag,' Dell said. He had always shunned the hoopla associated with being a military veteran. He bypassed the annual Anzac Day parades and ignoring invitations to reunions. He'd never wanted to return to Vietnam, as so many had done, to revisit old haunts and try to heal old wounds. His war service seemed like a lifetime earlier.

Until that winter of 2007, Dell had no idea that he was the only Test cricketer to have served in combat in Vietnam. The man who told him, a retired colonel, thought that piece of history made Dell the ideal guest-of-honor at the inaugural International Defence Cricket Challenge that summer. Teams from the Australian Army, Navy and Air Force were due to compete in Canberra with defence forces from New Zealand and the United Kingdom. Dell duly flew to Canberra, made some speeches and was preparing to leave again when he was asked if he had his 'fifth' Medal, the Vietnam Medal. He didn't have even the first four he'd been issued. 'My kids had wrecked them over the years, tearing the ribbons off. There was nothing left.'

Told he could request replacement medals from the Department of Defence, he nodded and said he would, before flying home and promptly forgetting all about it. 'I got a call a month later. "Have you been back to get your medals?" I said no. They called again in January. "Have you been back?" I again said no. I thought to myself I'd better do it otherwise they'll just keep on calling and it'll drive me nuts.'

Tony Dell had initially viewed the opportunity to serve in Vietnam as a Boy's Own Adventure. 'We were going to play real soldiers,' he said. The experience left him scarred for life. He lost his friends, family, almost everything.

Dell finally sought out the veterans' drop-in centre in Caloundra. As he began to explain why he was there, looking for information on applying for replacement medals, the old volunteers wanted to talk about cricket instead. Over a cuppa, the conversation flowed, the veterans exchanging anecdotes. After half an hour of chatting, one said to Dell: 'You've got PTS.'

'Bullshit,' he said.

Despite his circumstances, like all old soldiers he'd always regarded himself as bulletproof. He thought his fading and jangled memory was just bad luck. He could recall only flashes of his cricket career, yet Vietnam and *that* incident on the trail to Hoa Long was still incredibly vivid. Until that meeting, Dell had never heard of Post Traumatic Syndrome. Fellow veterans were weakies turning to drink and drugs.

Born in August 6, 1945, the day Hiroshima was bombed, he'd been christened Anthony Ross Hiroshima Dell. At 21, he dropped the 'Hiroshima'. He didn't like it.

MY BOYHOOD HERO Geoff Skinner from Beaumaris was also conscripted among a band of almost 1500. Like Dell, he was also incredibly excited. Six weeks into training he was told he'd be among a dozen selected for officer training in Queensland. The night before heading north, he had a bad toothache, slept poorly and ended up having the tooth out. Just as he was leaving the medical room, a doctor asked him why he was wearing wrist bandages. 'I wear 'em for footy,' he said, 'but by the end of a game I can hardly hold a pen.' X-rays found hairline breaks in each of his wrists and he was immediately discharged. No Vietnam. No war. Geoff was devastated. He was 19. He so wanted to serve his country.

One of his sporting mates from Beaumaris, Gary Forster, did serve and was next to his best mate when he was shot. He told Skinner once how his mate's brains were spattered all over his hands. He broke down in tears, inconsolable. Skinner now knows he was one of the luckier ones.

7

DEMOLITION MEN

'One short of a length delivery zipped throat-high and almost knocked him off his feet. Turning to Chappell at slip, Marsh said: "Hell that hurt, but I love it."'

It was a bombshell, cricket's biggest news story for years. Bill Lawry's sacking as Australia's captain just days before the deciding Ashes Test was insensitive and callous and triggered fresh volleys of condemnation and vitriol towards Sir Donald Bradman, in his last turbulent days as head selector.

Melbourne *Herald* cricket writer and colleague-to-be Ken Davis was packing his gear at the Travelodge in Adelaide ready to return home after the sixth Test when he tuned into 5AA's news bulletin right on 10am and listened in disbelief at the lead story: 'South Australia's champion captain Ian Chappell has been appointed captain of Australia.' Buried halfway through the radio bulletin was a single sentence: 'He replaces the Victorian Bill Lawry'.

'Back then, everyone stayed and travelled together, the writers and the cricketers,' KD said. 'I dropped everything and made a beeline for Bill's room. His was on the same floor as mine, just down the corridor. 'Redders (Ian Redpath) and Stacky (Keith Stackpole) were already there. They'd heard the same bulletin. Phanto (Lawry) told us he'd also heard it, but he actually hadn't. Braddles (Sir Donald), (Alan) Barnes (the Board secretary) or any of the selectors hadn't even bothered to give him a call.

'I immediately returned to my room, dialed 9292 2000 (the number for the Herald), asked for a copytaker and armed with my exercise book complete with clippings and stats, spent the next half an hour dictating everything I knew. Back then there were no computers. No internet. Everyone carried their files and reference books with them. Bill had gone nine Tests without winning. My story made the front page and stayed there. It was big.

'Bill was such an icon of the game. But he'd been critical of the Board (of Control) just months earlier after the crazily elongated tour which took in Sri Lanka (then Ceylon), India and South Africa with hardly a breather. His cards had been marked. What really hurt was when he was also omitted from the '72 Ashes tour. The bloke they picked ahead of him, Bruce Francis, played three Tests and barely made 50 runs in five hits. Freed of the responsibilities of captaincy, Bill would have made a huge difference.'

Lawry had been one of only three to average 40 against Ray Illingworth's Englishmen. When some in the top-order were unnerved by the skid and bounce of John Snow, Lawry played him with rock-solid efficiency. Even at 33, he was still indispensable, a champion of the game. His dismissal was another glaring example of Australian cricket's shoddy public relations and lack of care for its own. The reaction was savage:

* 'They'll never get me like that...' [45] (Ian Chappell)

* 'Heartless, one of the worst things I have seen in cricket...' [46] (Bobby Simpson)

* 'Disgraceful, unprecedented...' [47] (Ian Redpath)

Stackpole reckoned had Lawry played in Sydney in the final Test a week later, Australia would have won the game and squared the series. 'His replacement Ken Eastwood was in his mid-30s and too old to be playing his first Test against England,' he said.[48]

Out of the chaos and controversy, however, a vibrant new Australian captain emerged, the best of my time. Chappell was to rival Richie Benaud as the game's headlining talisman. He was an outstanding No.3, an inspired, spirited and strategic leader and unfalteringly loyal. Few led with his dynamism or passion. He won 15 and lost only five of his 30 Tests as Australia's captain, revitalising the game and making it attractive to fresh bands of youthful followers. He wore jeans, swore like a sailor, smoked cigars and in later years, rocked cricket's conservative castle. At Kerry Packer's insistence, he, rather than brother Greg, Australia's incumbent captain, led Australia during the tumultuous years of World Series Cricket.

He had the enduring support of almost all his players and was calm under fire, unless Glenn Turner or Ian Botham were in his orbit. 'I trusted my players,' Chappell said. 'They knew when they'd had enough to drink or when they should go to bed. I was never aloof from them. I always thought I was exactly the same as the rest of them. I don't feel a player ever let me down in an important match and that's all that ever worried me.'[49]

---

45 *Chappelli, Ian Chappell's life story* (Hutchinson of Australia, Richmond, Melbourne, 1976)
46 *Simmo*, Bob Simpson (Hutchinson Group, Richmond, Melbourne, 1979)
47 *Always Reddy*, Ian Redpath (Garry Sparke and Associates, Melbourne, 1976)
48 *Not Just For Openers*, Keith Stackpole (Stockwell Press, Abbotsford, Melbourne, 1974)
49 *The Chappell Era*, Ian Brayshaw (ABC, Sydney, 1984)

One of his favourites Doug Walters always enjoyed his nightlife to the full and was prone to sleeping in and even missing the start of a game. When he finally appeared 20 minutes late one morning for a Test in the Caribbean and waited at the player's gate to come on, Chappell deliberately ignored him, so Walters jogged on anyway.

'You,' said Chappell, 'Fine leg.'

At the change of overs, Walters was again dispatched to fine-leg and for the next half an hour was made to jog from end to end. Eyeing a bike perched against a fence, Walters momentarily wondered if he should borrow it, before finally being called back into the infield.

'You won't do that again, will you Doug?' Chappell said.

'Ian,' he said. 'I can't promise that...'

Chappell could be abrasive, specially if he felt some were coasting. At a cocktail party in Kingston during the WSC tour of the Caribbean in 1979, Chappell went one-on-one with fast bowler Len Pascoe, questioning his commitment and suggesting he'd be sent home early unless he did some hard yakka in the nets, rather than resting under shade trees talking to the locals. So incensed was Lenny that he grabbed Chappelli by the front of his shirt and lifted him off the ground, like he was a marshmallow – before they were separated by teammate Bruce Laird. Pascoe never missed a net session for the rest of the tour and was particularly full-frontal and fast whenever Chappell was in.

Chappell hated losing or conceding. Eyeing defeat at Port-of-Spain in Trinidad in 1973 – the West Indies needed just 66 with five wickets in hand – he looked around a hushed room at lunch and delivered a tirade as fiery as any from the hot gospelling Melbourne football icon Ron Barassi.

> *I can't believe you guys are fuckin' down and out and already fuckin' beaten. All we need is another fuckin' wicket. We're*

not fuckin' giving this up... no fuckin' way. Let's fuckin' well get into 'em.' [50]

Max Walker delivered with a wicket first ball after the interval and within an hour, the Windies had collapsed from 3-219 in mid-afternoon to 289 all out, giving Australia a stirring, unexpected victory. Three local steel bands booked for the after-match celebrations were sent home. Kerry O'Keeffe took the last wicket and a Test-best four for the innings and six for the game. He also made 37 at an important time in Australia's first innings. Afterwards, tears streamed down his face. The blond leggie from Bradman's club St George never thought he'd be good enough to play for Australia, let alone be so influential in a Test match win. It was a remarkable team effort – one of Australia's finest overseas – triggered by a century-in-a-session from Walters and Chappell, the fruity orator and master leader.

Chappell's two bowling champions from the '72 Ashes were both absent: the tearaway Dennis Lillee with stress fractures and swing specialist Bob Massie on form. He'd lost his ability to bend the ball both ways. Lillee's back injury was one suffered by gymnasts, trapeze and trampoline artists.[51] His run-up was wild and woolly and he subjected his body to incredible stress in his desire to be the fastest man alive.

Fresh responsibility fell to the whole-hearted Walker, who had initially moved to the mainland to play football before realising he could swing the ball around corners. His new ball partner was the fast and willing South Australian Jeff Hammond. Some thought Bomber could be as quick as Jeff Thomson, who had played an initial, unimpressive Test when injured against the Pakistanis in 1972-73.

---

50 *TJ Over The Top*, Terry Jenner with Ken Piesse (Information Australia, Melbourne, 1999)
51 *The Cricketer* magazine, July 1973

In Georgetown, where Australia clinched the series, Hammond captured seven wickets for the game: Roy Fredericks, Geoffrey Greenidge, Alvin Kallicharran (twice), Clive Lloyd (twice) and Rohan Kanhai. It was an early example of Chappell's Midas touch.

It was the happiest of tours. Walters and his roomie Terry Jenner set up 'Club 9' in their Kingston hotel room after local sponsors Red Stripe delivered two large kegs of beer and positioned them conveniently on their ground floor balcony. 'I didn't think my Test career was going to last long,' Jenner told me. 'I liked to have a beer and a good time and reckoned I had two options: follow Phanto down the road to the pictures eating an ice block, or join Ian, Dougie and Johnny Gleeson at the pub for a beer. I wanted to make the most of all the fun which went with both international and interstate cricket while I could.' Life after cricket was to be complicated for TJ. He spent time in the Big House and his autobiography, which I ghosted, went into multi-editions.

Jenner, O'Keeffe and the Novocastrian John Watkins were the three specialist spinners chosen after Ashley Mallett joined Paul Sheahan in saying he needed to concentrate on a real job which paid properly. Watkins hardly played a match all tour but most mornings would shuffle five or six laps in his Grosby Shipmates, just in case he was needed. He was not to add to his career tally of one home Test when he bowled a set of the widest wides ever against the Pakistanis at the Sydney Cricket Ground. Few at the highest levels had ever been so afflicted and overcome by nerves. But the touring team to the Caribbean had already been chosen; he was in. Australia's 14 was really only 13. 'When you lose your confidence, you don't want to bowl again,' said Wok.[52]

---

52 *Fifteen Minutes of Fame, Australia's 70 One-Test Wonders*, Ken Piesse (cricketbooks.com.au, Mt. Eliza, Melbourne, 2022)

THE CATALYST FOR Chappell's snowballing success in the mid-'70s was the fast bowling pair of Lillee and Thomson. Their furious pace and ferocity triggered nine Australian wins in 12 home soil Tests in 1974-75 and 1975-76. They were the most menacing set of speedsters since the Bodyline era and triggered an exulted status for Chappell and co. Across those two much-celebrated home summers, Lillee took 52 wickets and Thommo 62.

England was blown away in the 1974-75 Ashes, its only win coming in Melbourne when Thomson was absent and Lillee injured early. The crowds were at record levels, 77,000 attending Day 1 of the Boxing Day Test, now a feature on the cricket calendar. In Sydney's New Year Test, England's stand-in captain John Edrich was struck in the ribs first ball by Lillee and forced to retire hurt. The crowd were yelling 'KILL-KILL-KILLLL' as the two expressmen bowled faster than anyone my mates and I had ever seen. We sat on the old Hill, partaking in a Toohey's or two. When in Rome...

Several times Thomson bouncers soared over the heads of both the batsman and wicketkeeper Rod Marsh. Another struck Keith Fletcher directly on the badge on his cap. 'Blimey,' said teammate Geoff Arnold, 'he's just knocked St George off his 'orse.'[53]

A storm was fast approaching, huge black clouds dominating the southern sky. A Roman coliseum could not have been as atmospheric.

In the opening Test in Brisbane after Lillee bowled the first over, Chappell initially opted for Walker to share the new ball, coming up into the wind. But on the spur of the moment, he changed his mind. 'Tang, hang on,' he called. 'Thommo, have a go this end.' His first over was witheringly fast, Marsh acrobatic in his saves. One short of a length

---

53   *Dynamic Duos, cricket's finest pairs and partnerships*, Ken Piesse (The Five Mile Press, Melbourne, 2012)

delivery zipped throat-high and almost knocked him off his feet. Turning to Chappell at slip, Marsh said: 'Hell that hurt, but I love it.' No one had ever been faster, or as lethal into the wind.

Marsh stood back 27 paces and was still taking the ball shoulder high.[54] Greg Chappell said Thomson was two yards quicker than anyone of his time including all the mighty West Indians. He was glad that he and Thommo had both moved to Queensland and were in the same state team.

In one of the most spectacular of all Ashes debuts, Thomson took nine wickets including a sandshoe crusher which scuttled Tony Greig's boot and shattered his stumps. He'd made a hellraising century in the first innings. Psychologically, the Englishmen never recovered. Pre-tour they had under-estimated Lillee's near express pace in his comeback season and some thought the 'Thomson' in Test contention was my old mate the Frog, the windmiller from Melbourne.

One well-credentialed UK journalist, Tony Pawson, had described Lillee as a 'dying meteor'[55] in the lead-up to the summer; a giant faux pas. 'Test cricket was changing,' said England's veteran opener Brian Luckhurst. 'To look at us walking out in those pre-helmet days to face two of the fastest and most dangerous bowlers the world has seen – on lightning-quick and bouncy surfaces – provides an almost ghoulish fascination.'[56]

For Luckhurst, 35, it was one tour too many. His opening partner Dennis Amiss had been one of the form batsmen in the world, averaging 75 in six home Tests in 1974. But he had his thumb broken in Brisbane and had little impact.

---

54 *The Cricketer*, September 1975
55 *Cricketer magazine, Ashes special*, 1974
56 *Dynamic Duos*

'Thomson and Lillee ran in like madmen,' Amiss said. 'They were frightening. Three bouncers only just missed my chin and because the light was poor, one of the umpires warned Thomson to pitch the ball up. Thomson was not having any of that. The next four balls whistled by my face and off we went for bad light.'[57]

Lillee had rebuilt his upper body, re-fashioned his action and honed his approach, working with former world sprint champion Austin Robertson snr. His spirit for the contest and ability to swing the ball away from the right-handers at high pace was to make him Australia's most prolific Test wicket-taker.

Thomson was faster again and amazingly athletic with a superb arm, every bit as strong as Paul Sheahan's before his collision with teammate Alan Turner in Adelaide several years later. In the lead-up to the summer, Thommo had told Sydney cricket writer Phil Wilkins ('Redcap' of *Cricketer* magazine) how he loved to see blood on the pitch and if he hurt somebody, so what. With his slinging, javelin-style action, he bowled at close to 100mph (160km/h).

The pair's success triggered one of Australian cricket's immortal catch-cries:

> *Ashes to Ashes, dust to dust*
> *If Lillee doesn't get yer, then Thomson must.'*

EVERY CAPTAIN would have loved to have access to the pair. A batsman had 0.47 seconds to react from the time the ball left Thomson's hand. Asked to describe his action once, Thommo said: 'I just shuffle up and go wang!'[58] Chappelli was in the right place at the right time. So much he touched turned to gold.

---

[57] *Dynamic Duos*
[58] *Chappelli, the Cutting Edge*, Ian Chappell (Swan Publishing, Nedlands, Perth, 1992)

8

'WHAT'S THIS SHIT TOLSTOY?'

'What should I say to Mr Perkin?' I asked, changing into a collar and tie. 'Smile,' said Dad, 'look him in the eye and shake his hand like you're Teddy Whitten.'

The Piesse family has always flowed with writers, scholars, lawyers and larrikins. My great-grandfather Frederick William Piesse was a member of the first Australian Federal Parliament in 1901. And my grandfather Edmund Leolin Piesse was Australia's Director of Military Intelligence during the Great War. In 1935, he penned a visionary booklet *Japan and the Defence of Australia*,[59] six years before Pearl Harbour.

'ELP', or 'Par Par' to family, had a Christian-based Quaker education. He was a lawyer, a gentle, shy man who preferred not to drive. Often,

---
59 Under the pseudonym of 'Albatross'

he'd take a country train and, with his youngest son Dick, get off at one station and walk to the next, 20 and more miles away. Dick was captain of football, cricket and the school in his last year at Carey. A noted environmentalist, he was a long-time editor of *Walkabout* magazine and also taught at Melbourne High, working under one of his heroes, Australia's Bodyline captain Bill Woodfull. He'd always worried about reaching 87 years of age, believing it be a devil's number.[60] He and my aunty Joan possessed an auspicious library housed at Glen Lyon in magnificent floor-to-ceiling oak bookcases which had originally been at the family home, Merridale. Another of my uncles pioneered electric fences and encouraged me to pursue some Indian outlets for my books. Another was a jazz pianist. If he happened to visit unannounced and we were away, he'd pin a note to our clothesline: 'Does anyone live here?'

OUR DAD'S WAR experiences coloured his life. When his commando unit went missing for several weeks in Timor, my grandmother's hair turned white. His buddies were his extended family and years later, shortly after Dad's death in 1982, I edited their memoirs *Commando, From Timor to Tarakan*. They had shown outstanding bravery under extraordinary duress to help repel the Japanese after Singapore had fallen. All the men lost someone close to them. They witnessed atrocities the human brain is not meant to experience. It affected them all. Deeply. Yet they were supposed to return to civilian life as if the war had just been an aberration. I asked Dad once what he would have done had he seen a Japanese man in the street immediately after the war: 'I would have kicked him in the balls,' he said.

In the early '60s, when Des, one of the 2/4thers became so ill he was unable to support his wife and family, everyone rallied, donating food

---

60 Uncle Dick never did make it to 88.

and monies, taking his children on holiday and over several weekends, painting his house inside and out. The boys had so much fun that they formed their own Independent Painting Company and for years would paint each other's houses – and party afterwards, when the weekend's 'awards' would be boisterously bestowed, from the best to the messiest painter. Somehow the boys all made it home safe and sound. There was no .05 law until the mid-'60s. One who always drove an impeccable straight line was Charlie Black, a VFL boundary umpire, who drank only Schweppes pelato. His preferred ground was Glenferrie Oval where Hawthorn played. He didn't have to run as far there. It was always an exciting weekend when the boys gathered at 26 Deauville Street armed with paintbrushes and extension ladders, plus chips, Twisties and soft drinks for all of us.

The comradery and love among them resonated. Years earlier, at Wilson's Promontory where they trained before heading to Darwin and the islands, one of them was about to be cut, but his buddies rallied and told their superiors that for all their mate's deficiencies, he was incredibly gifted in signaling and might one day save some lives. And he did in Timor on a day when time stood still and without him, a whole unit would have been jumped and exposed.

Another of Dad's mates was Creighton Burns, the associate editor at the Melbourne *Age* and like Dad, a Scotch College old boy. They'd often catch-up at the MCG for cricket and footy matches. I'd wanted to go to Scotch, too – for the sport. But with four children, a stay-at-home Mum and Dad initially working a second job to supplement our finances, there wasn't enough money to go around. I was drifting through high school, living for the weekends, when Dad attended one of his few parent-teacher interviews and was told by my American history tutor Mr Livitsanis: 'Mr Piesse… your son… he's bludging'.

'WHAT'S THIS SHIT TOLSTOY?'

Never had I seen Dad so furious. He worked so hard and here I was, his youngest son, going at half pace. I loved history, especially cricket and football, but couldn't quite warm to the Battle of Gettysburg and why tens of thousands had died such bloody deaths. It was a turning point for me. I didn't ever want to disappoint my father again... and never did.

French was another of my least-liked subjects, but our teacher Mrs Borenstein liked me. She invariably dressed in snappy leather miniskirts and was so patient and understanding with all of us. In mid-class, a spoilt kid named Colin blew up, said something coarse and headed for the exit. I was nearest to the door and blocked his path, telling him to go and sit down again – and apologise... immediately. Mrs B was blushing near the blackboard. Colin did what he was told and said he was sorry. Never before had I received a 'B' in French.

Most teachers were militant back then. One would line all the boys up at the start of class and use his thumper on us. 'That's for what you're going to do,' he'd say. I was daydreaming one afternoon and he told me I wouldn't be able to play sport that afternoon. Talk about hitting me where it hurt most.

One sports day was remarkable for a 1500-yard match-race between a kid called Ian McGorrie, who was pencil thin but could run like the wind and one of my older footy pals Jeff Angelo who was big with a barrel chest. After two laps, McGorrie led by almost 150 yards, but Angelo began to wind up. He had an incredible tank and a rare will to win. He halved the margin with a lap to go and with McGorrie slowing and looking back over his shoulder, Angelo kept coming and caught him right on the line. It was so brave. And an example of what you could do, if you truly believed.

Angelo was later a bouncer at the Bowie hotel and would always look benignly upon our crazy, high-spirited behavior. One Thursday night, right on 10pm closing, one of our lads Ronnie got banned for life after a fierce argument with the proprietor. It was the first of three such life bans. Ronnie kept coming back and the proprietor kept on throwing him out.

DEAUVILLE STREET, at the Mentone end of Beaumaris is noted for its huge Tudor castle. We used it as a landmark when walking back from state school across the paddocks. One Christmas Eve I was heading for my pal Rick's place and just inside the castle's front gate were a dozen long necks intended for the garbo's. We drank them that night and returned them with their lids on and included a special note, thanking them for their lovely gesture.

At 17 and in my last year of school, I didn't have steely ambitions but loved going to the big sport, especially the 'G and the Junction Oval where the peanut man was famous for his catch-cry, which he continued well after the introduction, in 1966, of decimal currency: 'Peanuts, shilling a bag.'

My match reports of our cricket games were regularly published in our Year 12 Beaumaris High newsletter under the nom de plume *Spinner*. One of the teachers, Mr Mooney, told me one day I was becoming too big for my own boots. I reckoned he was an old grouch.

One set of holidays I worked in the mailroom franking letters for Coles & Garrard in Bourke Street. My boss was a Mr Ray Verity. At the interview I asked him if he might be related to the famed Yorkshireman Hedley Verity who singlehandedly had beaten the might of Australia at Lord's in 1934!

Most of my school pals wanted to be teachers. Slowly but surely journalism was becoming part of *my* conversation. *The Herald's* Bob Coleman lived in Beaumaris. His daughter Lesley was in my year level at school. I liked her best friend, Jane, but was too shy to tell her. I met with Bob and he encouraged me to apply to both the two major Melbourne newspapers and use Creighton and himself as referees. Mum says David Syme & Co., longtime publishers of *The Age*, received 407 applicants for cadetships that year and I was one of just seven to be successful. The final, decisive interview was with the paper's editor-in-chief Graham Perkin, one of the most dynamic and visionary journalists of his, or any era. He was making The Age great again by championing inspiring and innovative investigative journalism of the highest quality. He had specialists in every area: finance, education, the Town Hall, medical, business and sport. His team was young, ambitious and highly capable – a little like Hawthorn's elite footy sides of the '80s.

Dad picked me up from my school holiday job stacking fruit boxes into carriages at the Kensington railway yards. 'What should I say to Mr Perkin?' I asked, changing into a collar and tie. 'Smile,' said Dad, 'look him in the eye and shake his hand like you're Teddy Whitten.'

I started in January 1973, the first of four fun-filled and satisfying decades in journalism. The Age's offices were on the corner of Spencer and Lonsdale Streets. All the reporters and photographers were housed in one huge room, on the third of five floors. Everyone could see everyone else. The dynamic vibe and a pursuit for excellence was a constant. We were all encouraged to be inquisitive and instinctive.

No Australian paper possessed our depth of editorial riches. Saturday's paper was so heavy with advertising you almost needed a small forklift to pick it up. Greg Taylor was editor, a young Les Carlyon among a score of erudite and expert feature writers, Les Tanner a gifted cartoonist and Bruce Postle and John Lamb star photographers, who vied each day for page 1. Now in his 80s, Poss was one of a dozen headhunted in 1969 by Taylor from Brisbane's *Courier-Mail*. At his interview he brought some of his best news and feature images with him. Taylor smiled, shook his hand and didn't bother to even look at the prints. 'I know what you can do Bruce. You're hired,' he said. Having settled his affairs back home, Poss again flew to Melbourne and was on his way to the city from Essendon airport on his first working day when a big fruit truck went through a red light in the inner-north causing mayhem. He asked his taxi driver to stop so he could take photos of the crash. Introduced later to Mr Perkin, he said: 'And by the way Graham, here's your frontpage picture for tomorrow!'

Ben Hills led the Insight team and would bark coffee orders to his offsider Graham Willingham. Hills was the Nick McKenzie of the '70s, bright, ambitious and fearless. Michael Gordon, Jennifer Byrne and Margaret Gee were fellow cadets, just a year older than me. Mike was a son of a gun, his father Harry another of Australia's most-decorated journalists. Neil Mitchell was beginning a great multi-media career. Tim Colebatch, the economics editor, also dabbled in tennis writing and had been a ball-boy at Kooyong. Paul Heinrichs smiled as he typed his stories. He so loved what he was doing. He and the others were all inspirational for tenderfoots like me. They wrote with clarity, simplicity and rhythm. Only a couple of university graduates had been part of our intake. It's different now. Most of us were straight from high school, learning the job as we went. We were reporters pure and simple, not show ponies or influencers with agendas.

In 1974, Frank Sinatra held a press conference for a much-anticipated comeback tour downunder, his first in 15 years. His PR people told us nothing was off limits. We could ask what we liked. But Mr Sinatra was soon miffed by one questioner, a girl and within minutes called all the women present 'a pack of whores and hookers'. An immediate blanket ban on any Sinatra publicity was imposed coast-to-coast, across TV, radio and the written press. The trade unions also blacklisted him and within days the cranky old crooner was forced to apologise. Rock 'n roller Lou Reed, was another to be temporarily banned, after he made an obscene gesture and comment towards my music-loving pal and fellow cadet, Helen Thomas. Helen and the rest of us enjoyed a genuine fraternity, often partying together on a Saturday night and sharing the delights of The Doobie Brothers through to Motown headliners Gladys Knight and Smokey Robinson.

My main focus was always towards the sports desk, where Percy Beames, Ken Knox, Ron Carter and rising cricket writer Peter McFarline were among the most profiled. Peter walked with a stoop, mimicking his hero, cricketer Slasher Mackay. In 1977, he was to break the news of Kerry Packer's rogue World Series Cricket troupe. He toured a lot and in his early, travelling days had more marriages than most. Pulled up by the police one Sunday morning close to the office, he was asked for his name and address: 'Peter McFarline. No fixed abode.' Asked again, he repeated the line, this time with more intent. 'Peter McFarline. No fixed abode… look, I'll bloody well prove it to you.' Jumping out of his car, he opened his boot and showed the officers his only possessions: six shirts, some slacks, shoes and a folder of Red Smith essays.

'Knocker' Knox was 199cm (6ft 6in) and had been a top swimmer. So long were his legs he could hardly swing them under his desk. He wrote beautiful long-linking sentences, which were hard to cut – he'd been paid by the word when he'd first started years earlier at *The Argus*. Dawn Fraser was his all time favourite. He wrote her book, *The Dawn of Swimming*.

'Ronnie the Rat' Carter had upset the legendary Blueboy John Nicholls on one interstate trip, 'Big Nick' telling Ronnie he'd scrub him forever. 'I'll never give you anything again Carter,' he said. 'Well,' said Ronnie, undaunted. 'You never give me anything anyway Nick.' Ronnie called me

'Ken-babe'. I was young and raw – but I was keen and willing to get my hands dirty.

Perc had captained Victoria at both football and cricket and had there been a 1942 Ashes tour, he probably would have made it. On his first night as a teenager down from Ballarat to play footy, he stayed at an apartment building on Jolimont Terrace and was amazed how many pretty girls were about and how much fun everyone seemed to be having. No one told him it was a house of ill repute. Perc was at work late one Sunday on the rest day of a mid-'50s Ashes Test when an old footy buddy and member of the MCG ground-staff rang and tipped him off about stand-in curator Jack House illegally watering the pitch square in mid-match. 'I'm going to put a bit of fizz back into it,' he told his mates. Perc sat on the story of his life for 24 hours, double checking his source, before his world scoop was published on the Tuesday.

Perc would carefully cut out the first paragraph of every major story he wrote and date and paste it onto a thick wedge of paper sheets clipped onto a large A4-sized board. On Friday nights he'd flick through his leads to see if there was anything from the past that could be used for his previews the following morning. 'What's Perc doing?' I asked Mike Sheahan, a star to be, who'd also just joined The Age from *Newsday* and the Hobart *Mercury*. 'He's getting tomorrow's lead,' he said. We both laughed. In hindsight, it was incredibly smart. Perc was totally self-trained. He wrote crisp, short sentences, rarely missed a story and built an enviable arsenal of contacts and mates. He was also very competitive and one night complained to the sports editor after I'd submitted a stats snippet about an in-form Doug Walters which ran beside his Test match report.

Cricket's Centenary Test in Melbourne was the game's greatest birthday event of all and I was able to interview many of the visiting greats from the oldest, 84-year-old Percy Fender and Trevor Bailey through to Godfrey Evans and the charismatic but absent-minded Denis Compton, who'd only just made the chartered jumbo jet, having left his passport behind at a rugby international in Cardiff. Fender's eyesight had so deteriorated that he could no longer see the players on the field. 'But there was no way I was going to miss out on the celebrations,' he told me.

Two women were a part of the racing staff at The Age. One international cricketer of renown rang the desk one night looking for one of them, promising as much sex as she could take, all night long. 'Hang on a minute,' said the answerer, known to bat for the other side. 'You must be wanting so-and-so.'

In 1976, Geoff Hunt, Australia's squash champion, won The Age-Caltex sports star of the year. The Governor Sir Henry Winneke presented him with the trophy. It was the backpage lead and I was given the privilege of writing the story and interviewing Geoff. I was particularly pleased for him, as he like me, had attended Beaumaris High. His record was incredible. In 98 tournaments he'd reached the final 93 times and won 80 titles.

Journalism could be a tough gig, with hard-bitten types drinking long into a night in the pursuit of leads. Many of the sub-editors kept their grog under their chairs. Once our first edition had been printed, they'd all congregate in the sub's room drinking and smoking like it was a footy after-match. Part of my brief on police rounds was to bring the first edition of the *Sun* back to Spencer Street, just in case there was something we may have missed. The midnight smoke haze in the locker room was guaranteed to make you cough.

Police rounds was an education. Our brand-new, high-powered Ford Falcon was stolen out of the police carpark one night and ended up in Kyneton. Our habit was to leave the car unlocked and wedge the keys under the front sun-visor for whoever was on the next shift. Very late one Saturday night I thrashed it down the South Gippy highway to Cranbourne to see my girlfriend-now-wife Susan. Reckon it took about 25, maybe 26 minutes: Russell Street to Ballarto Road. If there was a red light, I didn't see it. On Sundays all the roundsmen would go to a tiny little Carlton milk bar known for its incredibly generously freshly cut ham and pineapple sandwiches. They were chunkier than David Warner's cricket bat and kept you going all day. We were competing against each other – but we were also close mates.

One of my police rounds buddies, tall and good looking, was known for his roving eye – and for spending days away from home, 'on assignment'. One night he returned to his own house to find it totally empty. Everything had been taken: the furniture, food, appliances, drapes, even the carpet. On the mantelpiece was a tiny card, with a message: 'I've left you'.

The Age was published Monday to Saturday, but never on Christmas Day or Good Friday, when we'd all have the Thursday off and play golf, about 100 or so David Syme employees from all floors vying for the Jim Power Cup. One year I won it, shooting in the low-80s at Victoria, where Mum was an associate. I'd been practicing all week and arrived an hour early to warm-up. I was in a four with Perc, who even into his 60s was very capable. On the ninth, our long drive hole, my ball finished 30 yards ahead of his but trickled just a few inches off the fairway. Perc had a distinctive owl-like laugh: 'Hoo-Hoo-Hoo... pity, young Ken. You're just off the cut stuff... mine's in play.'

Almost everyone called me 'Tolstoy'. They reckoned my lengthy District cricket reviews rivalled War and Peace. My very first byline, in 1973, was short and sharp: a review of a Slade rock concert at Festival Hall, just a few high and mighty Doug Wade torps from our office. It was incredibly loud. The band's lead singer Noddy Holder wore these huge platform shoes and on the encore song, *Get Down and Get With It* had to tap the fella playing bass guitar to join in. I phoned through my copy by the 10.30pm deadline and it made page 2.

Every day was different. Nick Nolte was in town with underwater cinematographer Al Giddings promoting their new Hollywood movie *The Deep*, co-starring Jacqueline Bisset. I would have much rather interviewed her, but Nick and Al were charming and the movie a hit.

Another afternoon, at Yarra Yarra Golf Club, Gary Player, the iconic South African golfer, gave a clinic and kept drilling sublime six irons 160 yards one bounce into a bag his caddy was holding. He didn't have to move even a yard left or right. 'The more I practice the luckier I get,' said Gary, using his signature quote. As always, he was dressed in black. He was a picture of quiet determination. Having won his first Masters (in 1961), he returned to Johannesburg, with the green jacket. The chairman rang him and said it was tradition for the winners to always leave their jacket at Augusta. 'You'll have to come and get it,' said Player.

I visited Cerberus one Sunday where Hawthorn was finishing a preseason camp. I was so awestruck about seeing so many of my idols, I could barely talk. Don Scott came and introduced me around and I was away.

On one Melbourne Sun tour, Victoria's cycling classic, we saw one of the riders illegally hanging onto a truck for at least a kilometre or two on one of the high stages. I spoke to him at lunchtime and he admitted his guilt. He'd had an early tumble and was just trying to maintain his place in midfield. The Sun's veteran cycling writer Jack Dunn approached me later in the day: 'Are you trying to scoop me son?' I was – but Jack's arsenal of cycling contacts always kept him informed.

My first page 1 picture story featured Yarraville's man mountain recruit Bruce Riches from Geelong, who was 29, 199cm (6ft 6in) and weighed around 125kg (20st) depending on his pizza intake that week. There was no bigger ruckman in Australia. He had this amazing round face and double chin like John Candy and dwarfed everyone, being known to all and sundry, even his mother, as 'The Frog'. Editor Taylor loved the picture and the words. One of his offsiders Geoff Barker adored footy and we'd often go down to Como Park with Mike Sheahan and I and have a kick. Kevin Sheedy often joined us. No-one lived football every day quite like Sheeds. The following year he began his amazing coaching stint at Essendon.

The Age sent us to journalism school at RMIT twice a week. If we happened not to be in class, we could always be found in the Oxford red room across the road. It was fantastic to be paid going to school. To gain my Dip J, my Diploma of Journalism, I completed a thesis on the history of Australian cricket annuals and magazines, Carlyon my mentor.

As the sport cadet I was responsible for VFL, VFA, District cricket news and general sport. I also had to keep the scrapbooks up to date. McFarline made sure of that. I didn't bother telling him I'd been compiling them at home since I was 10. Peter could be gruff but he rated my cricket writing, in particular. Once he met some of my mates who told him how much I liked to party. 'Me too,' he told them.

There were some huge names in the VFA, none bigger than Bob Johnson the Melbourne legend who was captain-coach at Oakleigh. One day Bob called Howard Leigh and I into the rooms. 'Come and hear my speech,' he said. 'Just stand over there so everyone can see you.' He went into overdrive immediately, as coaches could do back then, urging his players to win no matter what it takes. 'And do you know what?' he said. 'Those blokes there,' pointing at Howard and I, 'those blokes… THOSE BLOKES. They don't think you can win. Let's stick it up 'em.' There was a roar of approval and plenty of dark looks for us as the players ran up the race. Big Bob winked at us on his way through. 'Thanks boys,' he said. 'See you after the game.'

One night at the VFA tribunal, the elderly chairman Freddie Hill asked me what I thought. Was the fella guilty? Some of those charged came in suits with shiny leather shoes, spoke beautifully and were invariably exonerated. Others wore scruffy jeans, t-shirts and runners. Having received two weeks for something fairly innocuous, Kevin Goss from working class Port Melbourne erupted, called the tribunal members a pack of wankers and was promptly given two more weeks. Another night, at board level, Councillor Alec Gillon, the Association's long-time president, advocated his clubs 'pirate' as many League stars as they could afford. With Sunday TV revenues about to dry up, it sent many clubs to the brink of extinction. Few were as committed as Cr Alec, but he had gone one term too many.

Initially, before working on sport, I'd been given Saturdays off and continued to play footy and cricket with my teenage buddies. I won Beaumaris FC's senior best and fairest in 1975 and was runner-up in 1977, to Mal Smith, who played League footy, as did his 200-game son Nick. In 1976, covering a League game every week, I played only once, but trained one night a week with the Under 17s, mentoring the likes of Michael Roberts and Michael Nettlefold who were both to play lots of top-quality League footy. Another of the boys, Chris Dennis, still likes to quote me: 'What's the use of having one beer if you can have 100.' I was only joking Bones. Mick's father Neil had won the 1958 Brownlow Medal. Both were tanned and good looking, so much so that Molly Meldrum rang Mick at home in Beaumaris one night wanting him to trip the light fantastic with his mate Elton John. Mick's Mum answered. 'Tell him I'm asleep,' said Mick.

The basic working hours at The Age were 2pm to 11pm, allowing me mornings free and I'd spend half an hour most days doing series of sprints on the wide-open sandbanks opposite the Beaumaris Yacht Club. I liked the responsibility of being our No.1 ruckman and wanted to be at my fittest so I could jump and counter the taller ruckmen we inevitably opposed. I was our vice-captain and one of the few over 182cm (6ft). In 1977, we won a South-East Suburban open-age premiership under the Williamstown legend Gerry Callahan, known throughout footy circles as 'The Monster'. Afterwards Gerry said our win had given him as much pleasure as any of his many flags at Willi. In the final minutes of the second semi, which we lost, I was shirtfronted and was so badly winded, all I could do was lie there. I can still hear Gerry yelling from the boundary edge: 'KENDRICK... KENDRICK... GET UP...'. So sore was I that my mates went clubbing without me that night.

A fortnight later we beat them in the play-off. It was one of those magic days; a boilover. Chadstone sung their victory song at half-time. They were three goals up. They had us, so they thought. We had a titanic third quarter and in the last were just a point up with barely a minute to go after a late flurry of goals from their fat full forward. Eddie Melai, the Dandenong legend, was 36 and had rucked one-out most of the match after his younger back-up had been suspended for seven weeks earlier in the year for striking me behind play. I couldn't attend but signed a stat dec, saying exactly what happened. Eddie had belted me in the same game. I was wary of him, but this was a no tomorrow situation. There were just four allowed in the circle. I'd never contested a more important centre bounce. If he wins it, Chadstone surges forward and most likely kick the winning goal. I win it, the flag is ours. The bounce was just a little skew-whiff and luckily for me, hovered over the top of Eddie, allowing me extra momentum and time I needed to jump a little higher and knock the ball to my rover David Nicholson whose bullet-like left foot pass almost knocked over our leading forward Peter Linton who kicked the sealer. Nothing beats a footy premiership with close mates. Those first five minutes after the siren were as exhilarating as any I ever had in a lifetime of sport. At our reunions, I always ask Linton to show us his chest just in case TW SHERRIN is still emblazoned on it.

That Grand Final morning I'd learnt my mentor and old coach Ted King was in intensive care after a heart attack. I played for him that day. I'm still proud I was one of his boys. Five years earlier, just before joining the Age, we'd won an Under 17 flag against-all-odds. I rucked against Steven Smith who was to play 200 games at Melbourne. Ted, our coach, presented him with an award for being Ormond's best player and Steve promptly jumped on the trophy. I still ask him now whatever did happen to that presento…

We were total outsiders that day, but when I assess our list now, we had five or six who played VFA footy while Marty Lyons played at Sandringham and at Melbourne. Ted was so excited with us leading at half time that he smashed a trestle table with his hand, losing his false teeth and upending all the cordial and three-quarter time oranges. One night at training he made me oppose Linton, our star open-age full-forward in a series of one-on-one marking duels. Finally, at about the 10th kick, I outmarked him. 'See Kendrick, you can do it,' said Ted. He had unshakeable belief in me. I can still hear him now encouraging his son, Eddie, 'Run straight at the ball Edmund.' Ted had white liner fever like few I know, but he championed the youth of Beaumaris. He made us all stand tall in any company. I loved that man.

BEHIND EVERY SUCCESS story are caring, kind and talented mentors. You can't beat experience. One of mine at Beaumaris was Peter MacGeorge, who at 36, was the oldest player afield in our memorable flag win against Chaddy. We got to 19 points up with time on approaching in the last quarter and one of the boys, Peter Whitty, jumped into Peter Mac's arms, saying, 'We've got it, we've got it.' 'Not yet Whitt. Not yet,' said Peter Mac. Chadstone kicked three goals in as many minutes and suddenly it was anyone's game again. Peter was my first captain-coach out of juniors. Boys being boys, we never needed an excuse to convene at the pub and on one hot, pre-season training night I kept tripping over the cones which he'd arranged in a small circle. 'Henrick,' he said. 'Go home.'

At Spencer Street, I had two outstanding and encouraging mentors in Eric Beecher and Geoff Poulter at a small office next to the Age's reporter's room. They wrote and published Cricketer magazine and Inside Football weekly, according to the season, for Newspress, the Age's magazine division. Both were just a few years older than me and recognising my keenness and passion gave me immediate scope and opportunity. I began to submit country and VFA stories in football season and cricket interviews and features in summer. Beecher had started *Australian Cricket* magazine as a schoolboy in Sydney in 1968 and *Cricketer* upon his move to Melbourne in 1973. When he became less interested in cricket and joined the Age as a general reporter, his human-interest stories regularly made page 1. He was to influence and inspire so many during his long and distinguished media career. The boys had fun with me, using a picture byline: 'Ken Piesse's Hot VFA Flashes'. The following year it was 'War and Piesse'. I never had trouble filling my page. Poult remains one of my best mates and even allows me to sit on his Tasmanians-only table on his birthdays at The Emerald – as my grandmother Christina was raised on Maria Island.

Back in the Age reporter's room, during one Christmas week, I spent three days compiling the leading District first XI averages, batting and bowling, for each of the 16 clubs and proudly presented them to my sports editor Dave Austin – just as he returned from a round of reds at

The Golden Age. 'What's this shit Tolstoy?' he said before throwing the copy high into the air. 'About 5000 thousand pieces of copy paper landed all over the floor,' said Sheahan.

Memo Ken: do not try and sell a story to the sports editor on a Thursday night after he has been to the pub.

CADET REPORTERS were deployed to multiple areas as part of our fast tracking. By 1978, my 12 months on sport had ended and I was switched to police rounds, covering a myriad of news stories and features from Nappy Ollington's illegal two-up school in Franklin Street to the shenanigans of the after-dark bandit and several Yarra River rescues after canoeists had been caught in snags. The most tragic story of all concerned Essendon family man Sam Gulle who one mid-winter night returned home to 55 Matthews Avenue, just minutes after a twin-engine light plane taking off from nearby Essendon airport clipped power lines, exploded into flames and plunged nose first into his lounge room, killing all six, including his wife and four children. The family was sitting together watching TV and didn't have a chance. It was our lead story for days. The frontpage byline featured five of us, headed by chief police reporter Lindsay Murdoch. So moved was Taylor that he initially withheld publishing the picture of a stunned Gulle being consoled by neighbours.

Susan and I were about to be married. We already had a child, James, and I approached our chief of staff Pat Boyce and asked if the paper could possibly pay me a little more as we were buying a house. He acknowledged my hard work and yes he could assist. I went from a grading of 'D-minus' to a 'D-plus' – an extra $20 a week. It was a wake-up call to start specialising. Sport was my forte. I needed and wanted to write it, each and every day. Fortuitously, the 'pink paper', the Sporting Globe across town in Flinders Street was seeking a young writer. Jimmy

Robb was moving to public relations and there was an opening. No one was more ambitious than me. Ron Reed was filling in as editor. We were midweek cricket teammates at the Plastic XI, where famously Ron had once taken the new ball ahead of Ian Botham. The Globe was offering a 'C' grade with the opportunity to tour.

My farewell night from Spencer St was out of control. It was the disco era, flared pants, wide ties and body shirts unbuttoned to the navel. The Bombay Bicycle Club in the heart of the city was the club of choice for many where Brett Goldsmith the DJ was known to play *Stranded* by Chris Bailey and the Saints at full tilt and immediately re-play it because he wanted to dance too.

After the BBC, we continued to party back at our third-story bayside flat. It was a warm night, the music was super loud and we were all MC Hammered. Around 1.30am, maybe later, there was a THUMP-THUMP-THUMP on our front door. It was the cops. 'Mate' said one. 'We can hear your music on Elwood beach.'

'Yeah,' I said. 'Magnificent sound system. You've gotta love the Stones… ' None of us had a stitch on. It was the Seventies, the era of sex, drugs and nude rock and roll.

9

LESSONS FROM THE LEGENDS

'Curvy girls would jig and gyrate without their tops. When one chubbier one also dispensed of her bra one night, she was bombarded with tomatoes...'

My dream had always been to write sport and I thrived at The Globe, loving the immediate responsibly and the environment. There were multi-pages to fill twice a week. Finally, I was writing sport fulltime, competing against the best and utilising my knowledge, enthusiasm and passion for my favourite two games. On Day 1 at Flinders Street, Greg Hobbs, the doyen of football writers, blew me away when he told me I was the paper's new chief football and cricket writer. I was just 22 and filling a role held by so many of the notable and multi-skilled from Ernie Baillee and Jumbo Sharland to Hec de Lacy and Ian McDonald. 'What about so-and-so?' I asked, pointing at one of the senior reporters.

'Don't worry about him,' said Greg, before suggesting I go down to Middle Park and chat with Laurie Nash, the South Melbourne immortal. 'You'll like him,' he said. 'He'll tell you how good a footballer he was and he played a couple of Tests, too, for Australia.'

I spent a golden afternoon with LJ. I asked just one question, maybe two and hours later he was still talking himself up. He was Victoria's outstanding footballer in 1934 and 1935. Back then, the Champion of the Colony was more prestigious than the Brownlow. LJ would take a shot from 50 yards out and say to his opponent, 'Which foot do you want me to kick it with? Left or right?' And spiral it through post high. He kicked 18.2 in a state game for the Big V one day and said he would have got 22 or 23 had the rovers Percy Beames and Haydn Bunton 'not been so selfish'.

'And Ken,' he said, 'I played full-forward for only three quarters that day. I started upfield but Billy Mohr went down and I took his place.'

He was of only average height at 177cm (5ft 10in) but could outleap the ruckmen. No one of his era matched his kicking skills on both sides. He played at either end of the ground and was just as lively off the ground, a raconteur supreme, rivalled by only Neil Roberts and later Sam Newman. I asked him how friendly he was with his high-profile teammate, the acrobatic Bob Pratt, South Melbourne's high-flying full-forward – one of only two to ever kick 150 goals in a season. 'I never saw much of him,' said Laurie. 'Only ever saw the studs of his boots flying over the top of me!' Just as I was leaving, I said to him: 'Oh Laurie… Hobbsy back at the office passes on his best – and he asked me to ask you… who was the best player you've ever seen? 'Son,' he replied, grinning broadly. 'I look at him every morning in the mirror when I shave.'

Laurie's home-away-from-home was the Cricketer's Arms in Clarendon Street, within a few of his old booming torpedoes from the Lakeside Oval where he'd been so dominant in the '30s. He camped himself on a huge throne of a chair, probably bought from Franco Cozzo, Brunswicka's favourite furniture shop, exchanging signature stories tall and true with the Whale, Brian Roberts, the publican and dual premiership ruckman. The only time they were ever silenced was when Keith Miller entered with a cheery, 'Hello boys'. Even LJ bowed to royalty.

The Whale had his own set of old chestnuts. He almost won a Brownlow when traded to South Melbourne. A huge man with a heart of gold and a happy knack of making everyone laugh, he was forever playing practical jokes on his long-time coach Tommy Hafey – and leaving his 'guess who?' notes at the scene of the crime. Tommy lost count of the number of times he found his whistle buried deep in the mud in the centre cricket wickets at Punt Road, with only the lanyard showing.

One October, Tommy's Tigers were in the Australian Championship Final in Adelaide and the Whale was having a shocker. Richmond trailed at half-time and instead of joining his teammates in the rooms he immediately veered into the medical room looking for the team's doctor. 'Doc, Doc,' he said. 'I haven't gone near it. Tommy is going to hate me forever. Doc, you've gotta give me something. I need a lift. I don't care if it's illegal. Please Doc, please…'

'I'll see what I can do Whale,' he was told.

Just as the players were about to run out again, having been given a suitable serve by Hafey, the Doc nodded solemnly to Roberts, called him into a corner and quietly handed him three red tablets and a half-glass of water. 'Don't tell anyone Whale,' he whispered. 'If I get caught, they'll throw the book at me…. do you promise?' 'Yep Doc… and thanks.'

'Swallow 'em straight down now. Whatever you do, don't crunch 'em.'
'Yep Doc… yep.'

Roberts bounced out of the rooms and had a golden second half, dominating the ruck, taking some strong grabs and helping Richmond to a massive comeback win. Rarely had he been on such a high. 'I was floating out there Doc,' he said, before burying him in a bear-hug. The Doc didn't have the heart to tell him the pills administered were red smarties.

MOST THURSDAYS, in season and out, I'd have a morning coffee with the VFL's chief executive Jack Hamilton, discussing footy news, past, present and future. Jack was one of the leading full backs of his time, tough and unrelenting. As an administrator, he was cool, canny and genial. He always had time for the young ones. He had been a VFL office boy, too, in his first years at Collingwood. Among his clerks, all sitting side-by-side, were teenagers Dermott Brereton, Peter Tossol, Geoff Iles and big Hughie Rumph. When Grand Final seats for the reclusive ex-Brownlow Medallist Peter Box were returned, 'ADDRESS UNKNOWN,' Dermie gave them to his parents, beginning a September ritual.

The League's media manager Ian McDonald would often have him run errands and toss him his car keys with a 'hurry up now Derm'. Dermie was in Flinders Lane, one of the city's busiest one-way streets and this day found an immediate park. It was his lucky day. He threw his car door open directly into the path of a small delivery truck. On return to Jolimont, Dermott said: 'Here's your keys Macca. And here's your door.' Dermie was Hamilton's favourite, but sometimes if he happened to make a blue, Hamilton would yell from his office: 'DERRMMMOTTTT'. The Kid would pop his face around the corner of his door and say: 'Do I have to call you Mr Hamilton now, Jack?'

League president Allen Aylett juggled his full-time dentistry practice around his 40-hour footballing week. He kept a supply of freshly ironed shirts at VFL House and would often have a five-minute powernap in a taxi between appointments. No one was keener for football to go national and to be played on Saturdays and Sundays. In February 1979, my frontpage lead banner in the Mid-Week Globe was: 'Sunday footy – new VFL plan', Aylett keen to break the state government resistance and allow more fans to attend matches all weekend. The League hosted all the working media at its official Saturday matchday luncheons, Aylett using the forum to share his vision for a national competition. A who's who of celebrities would always be on our table, from disc jockeys to rock stars like Shirley Strachan from Skyhooks. Daryl Timms and I would always partake in extra Irish coffees. Geoff Poulter was more of a bread rolls man, his personal Waverley record 15. *(At our engagement party, Geoff positioned himself right next to the oven and had 26 of my Mum's homemade sausage rolls. 'Great sausage rolls, Mrs Piesse,' he kept saying...)*

One of the biggest stories Hobbsy and I broke was the news that Hawthorn had pledged an unprecedented $40,000 a year to re-contract champion rover Leigh Matthews. Matthews had won six best and fairests and was still only 25. The next best paid player was the club's captain and No.1 ruckman Don Scott, on $23,000. Forty grand was a small fortune, worth upwards of $200,000 now – and footy was not even semi-professional. Like everyone else, Matthews worked Monday to Friday. He was a sports store proprietor at Brandon Park. It was the scoop of the 1979 summer and came straight from the Hawthorn boardroom. Melbourne had been chasing Matthews as its new captain-coach, a job which was to be taken by the tall, intimidating man-mountain Carl Ditterich.

I wanted to be the first to conduct a feature interview with big Carl. He was forthright, bright and entertaining. Telling him that his ex-teammate

LIVING THE DREAM

Trevor Barker and I had been mates for years, I arranged to speak to him before one of Melbourne's summer sessions at Dendy Park, but he was late, arriving only a minute or two before 5pm. Seeing me in a suit and leather shoes, he said he had to do a few warm-up laps. 'You can run with me if you like,' he said. I did and halfway through the first lap, he stopped and said: 'So… you and Barks are mates, are you. What do ya want to know?'

When opponents dared rough him up, Barks merely had to look in Ditterich's direction, nod and within minutes his opponent would be seeing stars. With only one field umpire and little video, football in the '70s was brutal. And no one was tougher than Ditterich, known as 'The Shadow'.

Barker was the ultimate high-flyer who would take Mark of the Year most weeks. With his flowing blond hair and good looks, he was everyone's favourite, drove a racy two-door Datsun 200SX and had an incredible black book of glamorous lady friends. Even visiting superstar Cher took a liking to him one night. One afternoon he rang me from his Dingley home. 'Guess where I am Master?' he said. There was splashing and lots of giggling. 'Yes, I'm in the spa.'

'Has anyone got any gear on?'

'Nah.'

Barks died young, at 39, from cancer. Months earlier I'd chatted with him in the rooms at St Kilda. His clothes were too big for him. His last words to his father Jack were: 'I tried (to beat it), Dad.' Five thousand attended his funeral at the Moorabbin Town Hall. The majority were pretty girls in black minis.

HOBBSY AND HIS photographer Ray Jamieson would travel for weeks all around Victoria, into the Riverina and down to Tassie engaging leading sports stars of the past for Greg's column *Bushwhacked*. It was nostalgia at its most delightful, a path I was to travel often. One of his biggest coups was tracking down and interviewing Footscray's mid-'50s hero Box, who he found shearing deep in the southern Riverina. Box was the Howard Hughes of football. He hadn't given a meaningful interview since his early VFL exit. But he spoke to Greg. Years later, back at the Melbourne *Herald*, Greg was tipped off that Ross Oakley was to become the new chairman and chief executive of the Victorian Football League, ahead of the favourite and long-time media ally Alan Schwab. He rang Oakley first thing one morning, finding him, err, still in bed. Oakley categorically refuted the story, telling Greg his name would be mud forever if he went ahead and printed it. His London-based boss from Royal Insurance was arriving that very day; Hobbs could be sued if he went ahead.[61]

Greg paced up and down the Herald reporter's room, debating with himself. 'Do I or don't I?' His source was impeccable. 'Bugger it,' he finally said. 'I'm going with it.' It was the backpage lead. And, within a year or so, Oakley was to hire him as his media manager.

FOOTBALL WAS KING at The Globe, especially when Collingwood won. The best footy clubs had quality lists and administrations with an emphasis on PR. At Arden Street, a plate of freshly cut sandwiches and a half a dozen Courage long necks would invariably arrive in the press box just before half-time, compliments of North Melbourne's astute and affable marketing manager Barry Cheatley. When Ron Barassi came to North Melbourne, Cheetah went into overdrive, signing up virtually every retailer up and down Errol Street. It was the era of long lunches and having started early, Cheetah would find an extra gear between 4pm and 5.30pm as even the big bosses would have to come back to their

---

61   *The Phoenix Rises*, Ross Oakley (Slattery Media Group, Richmond, 2014)

businesses sometime. North was so lucky to have him. His successor Francis Trainor was similarly dynamic, North's Grand Final day breakfasts unparalleled for its wealth of politicians and celebrity guests.

At Princes Park, Carlton coach Alex Jesaulenko would invite us into the boardroom for a chat immediately after a game, the beers again flowing. We always attended the post-match celebrations where umpires, players, past and present, could all be interviewed. At Victoria Park one year the press box could only be reached via a 30-yard trek across a corrugated iron grandstand rooftop. One time it was really windy but there wasn't a safety rail in sight. The do-gooders would never allow that now. Magpie legend Harry Collier acted as an ambassador to all of us young ones, taking us into the locker room and introducing us around. Years later, Jack Jones would host us at Essendon's Saturday night dinners. Sarah Jones, of Fox Sports fame, is his granddaughter. Jack had played alongside John Coleman and was like a God to us. If there was a nicer bloke in the world than Jack, I never met him. He introduced me to the triple Brownlow Medallist Dick Reynolds, the youngest 70-year-old of them all who lived six months up north and the other six down south. In 1994, Dick was among a host of ex-greats to share with me some of his favourite stories in *Just for Kicks II*. Norm McDonald, Essendon's livewire indigenous flanker, loved a beer and as penance after a very late night out, Dick insisted Normie run extra laps after training at Windy Hill. Having completed four, Normie stopped and told Reynolds: 'It was only beer I was drinking the other night Dick. Not rocket fuel.'

Geelong was always among the most hospitable clubs, inviting key writers to their committee-room luncheon on matchdays at Kardinia Park. Bobby Davis and I became instant friends. He loved to 'surf' his old Ford Galaxy V8 on two wheels through the main gates into the Kardinia Park carpark. He was Geelong royalty, having coached the '63 team to the premiership. Weeks earlier he had called Geelong's Grand Final opponents Hawthorn 'the roughest, dirtiest side that (he) had ever seen... any time they want to play football, we'll give them a hiding.' And they did on Grand Final day when TV celebrity Happy Hammond played his harp in the rooms pre-match and even ran out with the team. Davis was like another father to all his players, particularly the Twins (Alistair and Stewart Lord), the Fatman (Doug Wade) and Shadda (John Sharrock). Every second year I'd take my Frankston Peninsula third XI to Geelong for a Saturday-Sunday fixture and we'd stay at Bobby's motel, the Parkwood in North Geelong. He'd shuffle out in his slippers and want to meet all the lads, who all knew him via TV: League Teams on Thursday nights and World of Sport on Sundays.

SATURDAYS WAS OUR time to shine at the Globe. All six games started at 2.10pm. I was responsible for the page 1 lead and the feature match of the day. Each of us had a phone man. Mine was John Fisher, the ex-Hawk, who would dictate to a copytaker the starting line-ups and the goals, behinds and misses, quarter by quarter. Within seconds of the final siren, I'd provide a punchy 'top' to the story, an extra 100 or 120 words. My police rounds training at The Age where I had to make so many late-night deadlines was a blessing. We'd print by 5.30pm and the papers would be in the milk bars by 7. On Sundays we needed to be finished by lunchtime for the mid-week paper to go on sale Victoria-wide from first light Tuesday.

Greg was big on person-to-person interviews and I'd do at least two a week, from 86-year-old Wells Eicke, born pre-Federation who'd played League footy at 15, through to Fred Fanning, still the only man to ever kick 18 goals in a match and Dickie Harris Richmond's champion goalkicking rover, a star in both the VFL and the VFA.

Eicke had made a massive contribution on and off the field at St Kilda but quit the club's committee when it insisted on leaving the Junction Oval for Moorabbin in 1965. He was silver-haired and self-sufficient, living in a small upstairs flat off Balaclava Rd. and still loved football with a passion.

Fanning possessed the biggest pair of hands – like Neil Mann or Stewart Loewe – but like so many League stars of the time, quit the bigtime prematurely at just 25 to go bush to Hamilton FC which had promised him 20 pounds a week, almost seven times his wage at Melbourne.

So deadly was Harris in front of goal that ruckman Jack Dyer would turn and walk back to the centre even before he torpedoed the ball through. Harris crossed from Richmond to Williamstown in 1945, the year Ron Todd kicked an Australian record 188 goals. 'I was on nine quid a match. Richmond paid me only three,' he said. 'Ronny approached me halfway through the year and told me how Bill Dooley the bookmaker was also paying him a one-pound bonus for every goal he kicked. "Dickie," he said. "I'll give you five shillings for every goal you give me." Five bob was pretty good money in those days. Every time I got the ball I'd pass or flick it to Ron. Things worked out well.'

One Sunday, just as we were going to press, I took a phone call from Collingwood's lovable wildchild, Ronnie Wearmouth asking that my feature on his scheduled 100th game be 'put on hold' for a few weeks. He'd broken his wrist jousting at the Bear's Cave, home of the Caulfield VFA footy club, one of the few places in the inner suburbs where beer was freely available on Sunday nights. He admitted he was smashed and had fallen down off a mate's shoulders. This was the free-spirited, swinging '70s and hedonistic behaviour celebrated. There was dancing, boozing, cavorting and Cave sex – lots of it. When the DJ played Patrick Hernandez's huge disco hit *Born to Be Alive*, curvy girls would jig and gyrate without their tops. When one chubbier one also removed her bra one night, she was bombarded with tomatoes. Amorous couples kissed and cuddled in the carpark and in the darkest areas of the grandstand. There was a constant stream of couples coming in and out of the front and side doors.

The club also ran an annual porno night, attended by hundreds of people, many high-profile. Sentries would be stationed with walkie-talkies in case of a raid. Halfway through one show, the police arrived unannounced and everyone was told to freeze. The local Glen Eira mayor was one of those present. 'I can't be caught here,' he said, ignoring the constable and bolting for the nearest door. The explicit blue-rated cassette was hastily buried among some cricket equipment.

'What's in there?' said one policeman, pointing to a nearby cupboard.

'Belongs to the cricket club. We don't have a key.'

'Oh… ok.'

MY FIRST CRICKET column was published in the Globe on October 11, 1978 – just a week or so before the arrival downunder of Mike Brearley's Ashes tourists. Champion left-hander David Gower and I shared the same wild, wavy blond hair and a happy snap was taken of us with a pretty girl from Cricket Victoria trying to identify the real David Gower. It made our frontpage under the heading, 'Confessions of a Test star's twin'. On England's next tour, my wife Susan and our just-born daughter Melinda, were with me at the Crest Hotel in Brisbane and David asked if he could cuddle our new little bubba. We remain mates all these years later.

In the lead-up to the Test series, the first at Ashes level without all the big-name stars who had signed with Packer, I rang one of the national selectors Neil Harvey and asked him, confidentially, if there was anyone from left field in consideration. Like everyone else, I knew him as 'Nin'. His best mate Sam Loxton had been my chairman of selectors at Prahran. 'Yes Ken, we've picked the team,' said Harvey, 'but it won't be released until the weekend.'

'Fair enough Nin,' I said, 'I understand… may I throw you some names? Pause if I'm half right.' I asked about Rodney Hogg, the firebrand fast bowler who had hit Clive Radley in the head and knocked him onto his stumps in Adelaide. 'He could be (in) mate,' said Harvey. 'What about Clark, Wayne Clark?' He'd dominated alongside Jeff Thomson just 12 months earlier against the Indians.

'Nah,' he said.

I had my frontpage: 'Axe for Clark in Test Shock'. In the absence of all the big-name World Series Cricket defectors, Clark was out and the mature-aged Hogg in, for the first time. A self-confessed wildman in Melbourne, Hoggie had shifted states, become a morning milkman and was scaring the daylights out of most batsmen with his skidding bouncers aimed right at the melon. He thrived on Adelaide's bouncy run-ups, believing they allowed him extra momentum at the crease. He was to take 41 wickets that summer at an average of 12.75… better than Thommo, better than just about anybody. I asked Hoggie if he was still a milko. 'No,' he said. 'I slept in one morning… and got the bullet.'

The Globe sent me to all six Tests and there I was working alongside my old *Age* colleague Peter McFarline, Rod Nicholson from *The Herald*, Tom Prior from *The Sun* and a host of interstaters including Phil Wilkins and Alan Shiell, who'd taken a double-hundred off the Poms in the mid-'60s. Sir Donald Bradman suggested Sheff change his grip on the bat to widen his repertoire of strokes. He refused and was soon out of South Australia's No.1 team and into full-time journalism.

Neil Hawke hosted the entire Australian and English cricket writing troupe out at Westlakes one night, his old pal Freddie Trueman holding court with an array of stories and all of us taking turns to hit golf balls into the Lake, like Happy Gilmore. There was a great fraternity amongst us all. Jimmy Woodward from Sydney's *Daily Telegraph* could do a head stand while singing Good King Wenceslas and Mike Coward from Adelaide's *Advertiser* was a brilliant baritone.

I'd just released my first major book, Prahran CC's centenary history and Prior quipped how he was up to chapter five – where Loxton's Mum, Annie, was making the cucumber sandwiches on Saturday mornings for all three grades. 'Now I know why they call you Tolstoy,' he said.

In Adelaide, Hogg told Graham Yallop to meet him behind the grandstand after play. 'He didn't have a tennis match in mind,' said Yallop, who had chased him into the rooms after Hogg refused to bowl an extra over.

A YOUNG IAN Botham was dominant that Ashes summer. We'd played several mid-week games together for the Plastic XI two years earlier when he had a season with Melbourne University CC and famously blued with Ian Chappell at the Hilton Hotel. We'd batted together at Monash University one day. He made 60 and me 2. We collaborated in mid-series for an exclusive column:

> 'There's nothing second rate about this English cricket team, including me... I'm out to firmly shove that not-good-enough tag firmly down your throats. I'm no sub-standard bowler. Seventy wickets in 13 Tests speaks for itself... after we finish with your lot this weekend, you'll need a completely new side.'

Beefy's run-up was longer then and he bowled at genuine pace. Later he slowed down, relying on swing and seam. He cornered more headlines than most and there were few restraints on what he and others could say. Australia was humbled 5-1 and Yallop soon stood down as captain. Hogg was never again as menacing but fashioned a highly successful after-dinner speaking career revolving around his '41 at 12.75'. Later, in *Truth* newspaper, he predicted that St Kilda's rolypoly leg spinner Shane Warne would not only play Test cricket, he predicted he'd take 300 Test wickets. He was sacked on the spot. 'Wish I'd said he'd take 700,' he told me years later.

Bill O'Reilly and Norman O'Neill were among many former greats following the Ashes series from city to city. Normie succeeded Lindsay Hassett at the ABC and he and Alan McGilvray would sip scotch long into a night at their motel room. We'd come back from dinner and be invited in for a nightcap.

O'Reilly and Hassett had been inseparable during their auspicious playing careers and remained the closest of buddies. Each day, Tige would watch the first hour of play before hopping up, saying 'it's time to stretch the legs'. Within minutes he'd be found with Lindsay in the nearest watering hole. Tige had a magnificent writing hand and having drafted that day's story neatly into his VANA notebook, he'd dictate it sentence by sentence to a copy typist and resume his yarn-telling out the back with his little mate.

Twelve months earlier, I was in Sydney for the Test and to interview Bishen Bedi, India's visiting captain for *Cricketer* and accidentally sat in Tiger's seat in the front row of the SCG press box. I was among the first arrivals, only just ahead of Bill.

Seeing me, Tiger said to Ernie Cosgrove the scorer: 'How long Ernie have I been sitting in that same seat here at the SCG?'

'Thirty-one, maybe 32 years Tige.'

He asked me who I was and where I was from. 'Ken Piesse, Mr O'Reilly. I'm from Melbourne.'

'Melbourne,' he said. 'That figures.' Then he smiled and said: 'Bill O'Reilly. Pleased to meet you.'

I shuffled over one seat and sat next to one of Australian cricket's immortals for the entire Test, beginning a habit at most Tests we attended. It was an education. He'd originally been a schoolteacher and as a young man in White Hills had even met Henry Lawson. It was impossible not to take to Tiger. He was a living treasure. He particularly loved sharing stories about his old spinner partner, the tall, dark and handsome Chuck Fleetwood-Smith who had been expelled from Xavier College for getting a girl into trouble. Few were as popular in England in '38. Don Bradman was also a conversational point. 'He wasn't the most popular though, was he Tige?' I ventured one day. 'You don't piss on statues young Ken.'

One year, during an Adelaide Test, Tiger uncharacteristically slammed the bowling of Geoff Lawson. Henry replied with a two-page letter which Tiger read before marking with a red pen all of Lawson's misspellings and syntax errors and sending it back to him, with a '4' out of 10 in the top right-hand corner.

The Globe covered both the official Tests – at length – and the Packer Supertests. On a fast and true drop-in pitch at VFL Park, Lawrence Rowe made a classical century, treating even Dennis Lillee with contempt. But for his eye operation early in his career, Rowe might have emulated at least some of the feats of fellow West Indians Viv Richards, Gordon Greenidge and Dessie Haynes. He was a glorious shotmaker, noted for whistling to himself as a bowler approached to aid his concentration. He also batted with just one contact lens, in his left eye.

Another night in the rooms at Waverley, I met the big boss Kerry Packer. At that stage I hadn't joined the Globe. 'Where are you from son?' he asked. 'Cricketer magazine, Mr Packer.' He turned on his heel. Conversation over. My editor, Eric Beecher had been critical of WSC, one front page banner heading proclaiming: 'The Great Packer Yawn.' Packer had an elephant's memory and he wasn't going to waste his time bothering with a young whipper-snapper like me. Yet, he was to change cricket like no-one before or since. By pirating the best 30 cricketers in the country, plus a who's who of the world's best from overseas, Packer's World Series Cricket Supertests became epic contests on an-impossible-to-match level. We saw Barry Richards open with Gordon Greenidge with Viv Richards at three. It was remarkable cricket played at a stellar standard. Packer's winner-take-all one-dayers were also fiercely fought, helmets a necessity with even the fast bowlers firing bumpers at each other.

For the first time viewers were able to see the action front-on at Packer's insistence for cameras at both ends of the ground. And his passion for night cricket became a staple on which today's Twenty20 tournaments are based worldwide. The whole venture cost him tens of millions but it also bought Channel Nine the rights to the cricket, which it held for 40 years.

Without Packer, the charismatic David Hookes insisted, professional cricketers worldwide would have remained paupers for years. 'When they say their prayers each night, they should all bless Kerry Packer,' he'd say.

Fringe fast bowler Mick Malone had been working as a primary level teacher in Perth, supplementing his modest take home pay with $25 a day when playing state cricket. His WSC wage was worth five times his school and Sheffield Shield salaries combined. Signing with Packer for him and dozens of others was a no-brainer.

10

COMPETING LIKE THERE'S NO TOMORROW

'Barass shook my hand and grabbed my abdominals. "Where's your six-pack?" he asked. 'Back at the pub cooling down Ron.'

I have always embraced challenges. I'm driven. Everything is done at pace. I hate wasting time. I'm full-on on everything, whether it's a story I'm chasing, a batsman I'm trying to deceive, a little old lady I'm racing to the supermarket checkout or keeping up with Belle my champion swimming Chesapeake each morning at Canadian Bay. Susan says I create chaos in the kitchen because I'm always in a hurry. She hides many of her most treasured family possessions to guard against breakages. She's right. My focus is often diverted. I'm often thinking about how to compete – and how to make the next sentence sing.

One of my primary school teachers at Beaumaris State, Mr Sweeney, doubled as our football coach and at the end of each session would roost a left foot torpedo high into the air for one of us to mark. This day there was maybe 15 in a group and he called my name: 'Kendrick, you get this one... no matter what... get it.' And I did.

Once our third XI at Frankston was humbled in a one-dayer by Prahran and immediately afterwards I ordered ten 100-metre sprints, telling the kids they were squandering their opportunities. I ran them all, totally outpaced but urging them to go harder. Ex-Test opener Julien Wiener was coaching Prahran ones and afterwards he laughed: 'Ken Piesse... behind that calm, smiling exterior,' he said, 'is a real competitor.'

It was Test match time in Adelaide and North Melbourne FC had scheduled a pre-season camp, with running and footy drills on Saturday morning and basketball on the Sunday. As a publicity stunt, Greg Hobbs asked me to join them, a request coach Ron Barassi readily granted. Just back from a study tour in Germany, Barass shook my hand and grabbed my abdominals. 'Where's your six-pack?' he asked. 'Back at the pub cooling down Ron.'

He called the players into a circle and introduced me. There were stars everywhere: Greig, Schimmelbusch, Blight, Dempsey, Dench, Johnny Murphy from Fitzroy via South Melbourne and 'The Galloping Gasometer' Mick Nolan, North's No.1 ruckman who tipped the scales at around 115kg (18 stone). 'Let's start with something different this morning lads,' said the super coach, smiling broadly. 'Grab the bloke next to you and piggyback him around the oval. Piesse... you take Nolan.' I staggered 100, maybe 125 yards before Barass called us all back. Everyone was laughing. Big Mick weighed a ton. But Terry Phelan's picture was a beauty and my feature ran the entire back page of the Globe, under the heading: 'Ouch, never again!' 'You're a bit stiff,' said Nolan. 'My Mum has been away and I had to take over the running of the pub at Wang (Wangaratta) for three weeks. Reckon I've added a stone, maybe more since Christmas!'

While in Adelaide I spoke with Dennis Lillee, then 30 and still menacing, despite having lost a little of his spitfire pace from his youth. 'The days of charging in and getting all fired up are over,' he said. 'It's terrific to bowl fast. I'd love to still be able to do it but I realise my limitations and I save the odd quick one for when I need it now.'

Lillee had been intimidating batsmen for years. Psychologically he had many beaten even before they took guard. Dare hit him for four and you could expect the next at your throat. He said once he'd gladly die on the pitch if it meant Western Australia winning. We believed him.

In March 1976, Victoria named five first-gamers for its final Shield match of the summer, against WA. I organised a picture of them in their batting stances for *The Age*; four were in the starting XI and Tom Cullen 12th man. It was a dark, murky Melbourne autumn morning, the pitch green and Lillee lethal. Opening batsman Doug Rolfe was struck in the head and carried off, his replacement Dav Whatmore, also in his first game, marking centre in a pool of blood. Talk about an initiation. Five Vics made ducks on the way to a declared score of 9-44, the match finishing in well under two days.

Lillee and I always shared an easy rapport. He often came to Melbourne to speak, several times to the Kingston Saints CC where I acted as emcee. He didn't possess the conversational skills of a Dougie Walters or a Freddie Trueman. But he didn't need to – he was DK Lillee, the greatest fast bowler of them all.

While promoting one of his five autobiographies, we recorded a radio interview for Sport 927, now RSN, with whom I have worked for 20 years and more. His schedule was hectic and I was told to keep it to five minutes, but it went 10. I knew my subject backwards and bounced off his answers. Afterwards Lillee shook my hand warmly and said: 'I really enjoyed that'.

In Dean Jones' testimonial game at the MCG, a 17-year-old Brad Hodge was opening up against Lillee, then in his mid-40s. Charging at his first ball just as he was releasing, he smoked the delivery high over the top of point for four. The next one was two yards faster and straight at his left armpit. 'No one charges the great DK,' said wicketkeeper Rod Marsh, laughing.

I asked Hodge later why he had treated Lillee so cavalierly. Wasn't Dennis his hero? 'Didn't think I'd ever get another chance,' he said.

BEFORE THE SYDNEY Test of 1979-80, we played a 'Press Test', England versus Australia, 40 overs aside on a good turf wicket at Waverley CC. Having witnessed Bobby Simpson and I sharing a decisive half-century stand, visiting British comedian and cricket lover Ronnie Corbett named me man of the match. Ronnie was tiny, barely 5ft (154cm). He was very chatty and affable, just like on TV. My 36 included one downtown six from Scyld Berry's gentle slowies. Earlier I'd taken a reflex one-hander from the bowling of Mike Coward – a particularly proud moment as Dad and Mum, on holidays in Sydney, were at the game. I saw the ball off the bat, threw myself to my right and somehow it stuck in my outstretched right hand. Ronnie shook my hand. 'Is this the hand that took the catch of the match?' he said. Simmo aside, we all were strictly club standard. He'd only just retired coming off a second stint as Australia's captain and had qualified to play via his feature writing in the Sydney press. Twelve months earlier, in a similar friendly, we'd been opposed by Ken Barrington, England's manager and he smashed us – particularly me. 'The men who write about the game of cricket lose their expert status when they come to play it,' wrote John 'Darkie' Edwards, Australia's affable team manager, next day in *The Age*.

The birth of Melinda, our eldest daughter, made for the happiest of New Years, the Globe kindly making me 'Sportsman of the Week' – with a Michelin-class dinner at the famed Old Melbourne Motor Inn, run by

Alan Johnson, one of North Melbourne FC's key corporate backers. Years earlier, at breakfast at the OM, Barassi had said 'yes' to coaching North, an agreement signed and sealed in bright red pen on a table napkin. Barass was like the Pied Piper. He had myriads of followers everywhere. Tough, talented, caring and affable, his death late in 2023 stopped a nation.

My stories had a wider reach with the *Sunday Press's* liaison with the Saturday night *Sporting Globe*. I was also editing *Cricketer* magazine and needed a 25th hour in the day to complete everything. Susan was stoic, never once complaining. I've never met anyone as generous, positive or sensible. She allowed me the scope to excel. It meant long hours away but I always had time to read stories to the kids at bedtime.

At the season-end, crosstown rivals the *Sunday Observer* approached me to become its sports editor. They were offering an 'A' grade salary *and* a company car. I took it. I'd be continuing my lead cricket and football writing roles and organising the paper's 20-page sports section. One of the head honcho's at the Herald & Weekly Times said I was being groomed to cover the 1981 tour of England for the group, but there were no guarantees and the extra monies were welcome after all my years working for peanuts at *The Age*. The prospect appealed going head-to-head against Scot Palmer, the high-profile sports editor at the *Sunday Press*. We didn't make it to England in '81 but we made up for lost time with all our tours from 2001 onwards.

Mike Worner was a most supportive editor and we had a small, expert and dedicated team of freelancers, including Ken Davis, Howard Leigh and Daryl Timms who scooped everyone when Hawthorn players went on strike over pay demands during the 1980 pre-season. It was one of the biggest stories of the summer and we enjoyed an immediate readership spike. Within months, when another football-dominant edition saw our circulation reach 100,000 copies for the first time, the paper's managing directer Peter Isaacson, hosted us all at a restaurant in Glenferrie Road. An old war hero who had once flown a Lancaster under the Sydney Harbour Bridge, Peter was genuinely thrilled.

Each Saturday night, we'd print the paper on site in Prahran and by midnight would have copies and be looking to do updates for a second and even third edition, especially when Wimbledon and the Ashes cricket was scheduled.

St Kilda's big-name import Garry Sidebottom was our feature footy columnist and on Mondays would drive to our house in Seaford and spend an hour with me on his column 'Saints & Sinners' for the following weekend. I covered the match-of-the-day in football season, attended the Tests and the interstate football matches. We were there the year the Victorian bus was caught in a traffic jam approaching Westlakes. That most vibrant of personalities, Teddy Whitten, flagged down a motorcycle policeman, told him who was on board and within minutes a police escort had been arranged, sirens blaring, with the Big V bus following on the opposite side of the road all the way to the stadium.

Early into my tenure, our soccer expert Fred Villiers, who was also on World of Sport, joined Truth and took umbrage at me, a 25-year-old, daring to question his ethics. I expected loyalty from my team and would have liked Villiers to have at least phoned me to say he was going. Instead on Truth's back page was a headline: 'Mr Soccer Joins Us'. Our conversation was short, but he got the message. His replacement, Peter Desira, was twice as good as Fred, caring, engaging and loyal.

My War and Piesse and Memory Lane sports columns were a mix of current news and nostalgia, ideal reading for a lazy Sunday afternoon. One early feature revolved around my teenage idol, the champion Tasmanian Peter Hudson who had been wooed by all 12 mainland clubs, including at the 11th hour, Richmond. 'Graeme Richmond, the Godfather of recruiting, came into our house carrying an old Gladstone bag,' Huddo recalled. 'Halfway through our discussions, somehow it fell open and all these pound notes cascaded onto the carpet. 'How much is there?' I asked. "1500 pounds (approximately $10,000) and that's just the start." I learned later that Graeme did it all time: the old kick-the-bag trick.'

Hudson thanked him but confirmed he was committed to Hawthorn and wouldn't be able to live with himself if he played anywhere else. On his first night at Glenferrie, Hawthorn president Ron Cook addressed the players and said Hudson, 21, was going to be the highest paid player in club history – and with him, the Hawks could win a premiership. And they did, four years later, in 1971. They might have gone back-to-back in 1972, but he badly injured his knee in the opening round and missed the rest of the year. 'We would have given it a shake,' said Don Scott, Hawthorn's captain at the time. 'The day he got injured he'd kicked eight and was lining up for his ninth and it wasn't even half-time. He said he was feeling so good that year he could have broken Bob Pratt's 150-goal record. It's all hypothetical of course, but we were on fire that day against Melbourne. We would have gone close again for sure.'

I loved all the conversations with the past greats. There were no recruiting zones or player drafts back then. On the way to Tooleybuc to sign a teenage John Sharrock one year, Geelong's coach Bob Davis and secretary Leo O'Brien stopped off at Horsham for a kick-to-kick with a local prospect. Bob wasn't enamored, but at the other end of the ground this fat kid was roosting torpedoes post high through the goals.

'Who's that?' asked Bobby. 'Oh, that's a kid called Wade. Doug Wade. Not sure if he's going to be much good… but he can kick.'

By the time 17-year-old Doug Wade had walked around the corner to his house in McPherson Street, Bobby was already onto his second cuppa. 'Would you like another party pie Bob?' said Mrs Wade, Doug's Mum.

'Don't mind if I do.'

Wade became the second player to kick 1000 goals in League football. He also figured in two premierships, one under Davis in 1963, a team which also included maybe the greatest of them all in Graham 'Polly' Farmer, wooed from Perth for a small fortune. Davis had been chatting with O'Brien in the club's offices in Moorabool Street. 'Wadda we need to win the flag Leo?' he said. When Bob was excited, he'd talk fast, like a kookaburra.

'We need a ruckman Bob, a good ruckman,' he said. 'Who's out there? Who's available?'

'A fella in Adelaide by the name of Kerley, Neil Kerley, but he'll never come across. He hates Victorians.' 'Ok, who else?'

'Well of course there's Polly Farmer in Perth (who'd again dominated at the Australian championships, in Brisbane).' 'Ok, get 'im on the phone.'

'I haven't got his number Bob.' 'Just ring the Perth exchange. They'll know who he is…'

Within five minutes, the phone rang: 'It's Graham Farmer, Bob… in Perth.'

'Arr Poll, great to speak to you,' said Davis, going into immediate overdrive.

'We've been discussing our team and reckon we are just one player short of winning a premiership… only one. And that's you Poll. We want you. We think you'll make the difference. We want you to come and play with the Geelong Football Club.

'Oh Bob,' he said. 'That's very kind of you. I'm truly flattered. But I am very committed here. I love Perth… always have.'

'Ok, we've got our trip away to Surfers Paradise next week. Would you like to come, as our guest?'

'Yes, that would be lovely, thanks Bob.'

Farmer had the best week, hardly paying for anything. 'Well Poll, what do you think of us?' said Davis on the last day. 'Will you come?'

'I have had a great time and the boys have been wonderful… but of course Bob, if we are to come I'm going to need a house, a car, a job, moving expenses – and naturally, a sign on fee.'

'Leo,' said Davis, calling O'Brien to his side. 'Write 'em all down, Leo. Car, house, job, expenses… keep writing 'em down Leo.'

When Geelong agreed to a 15,000 pound signing fee – the equivalent of more than $100,000 today, an extraordinary sum for the times – Farmer committed. Yes, he'd switch states. Luckily for Davis, he had a most-generous patron, the well-heeled Geelong timber merchant Alex Popescu who agreed to finance the lot, even the 1500 pounds East Perth wanted for their champion ruck.

Farmer was an exceptional talent, an indigenous boy raised in an orphanage who was to dominate Geelong's 1963 premiership, play in another Grand Final in 1967 and also coach the club. It was an incredible privilege just to be in the same room as him, as he shared his wisdom at the after-match press conferences. Other than my brother Jim, I have never met a kinder, more caring man.

RECRUITING IN THE '60s was hit and miss, club secretaries often relying on tip offs from past players and friends of the club. The appointment of specialist, paid talent scouts was considered an American thing. Hawthorn's Bill Newton would often arrive at the house of a budding recruit armed with a two-tiered box of chocolates and present it to his mother. For the very special ones he'd plant a five-pound note under the first layer.

I loved all of the recruiting stories and the weird and wonderful names of the country towns where many of the boom youngsters had first played – like Jim Wallis (at Quambatook), 'Turkey Tom' Carroll (Ganmain), Nolan (Tarrawingee) and Peter 'Crackers' Keenan (Wilby).

Brendan Edwards, the Chris Judd of the early '60s, hailed from Sandhurst, where the great Graham Arthur had started. No one was in higher demand as a teenager. He was ahead of his time, a fitness fanatic who could run all day, gather the ball in close and on the outside. Word trailed back to Hawthorn this mid-week afternoon that North Melbourne's charismatic coach Les Foote was in Bendigo looking for him. Foote had been a champion player and was one of the game's biggest and most-recognisable faces. He was camped out at his hostel waiting for Edwards to return from his teaching round. Several of North's committee were with him. Ex-Hawk Kevin Curran had coached a young Edwards at Sandhurst and fielded an urgent call from the Big Smoke. Curran met Edwards at the tram stop in the heart of town, just minutes from his digs. 'I've got 50 quid here Brendo if you sign this form four right now,' he said. Fifty quid was the equivalent of a month's wages back then and Edwards signed on the spot. Turned out that North's offer was four times Hawthorn's...

St Kilda's Ian Drake spent so much time in Hobart and Launceston chasing the likes of Baldock, Bonney, Bingley, Stewart, Howell and Lawrence that he'd go in disguise complete with dark sunglasses and wig. Once, on a trip to Terang in the western districts, he was asked to wrestle for the signature of the young champion Daryl Griffiths. 'His Dad Alec was a shearer. It was the end of the season and this night he returned home pretty merry,' Drake said. 'He was wearing just a pair of socks and an old Footscray jumper. We were necking warm beer out of bottles and Alec suddenly said to me: "If you want my son's signature, you'll have to wrestle me!"

'He was a big bloke and very wide across the shoulders. He started to stalk me around the dinner table. Luckily I was able to produce some more beer, he laughed, threw himself back into his easy chair and we signed Daryl that night. He played every game of '66 including the Grand Final.'

Football's best-known early recruiter Percy Page broke years of silence to speak with me. He was 81. 'I don't give interviews,' he'd initially said. 'I don't like publicity.' Known in his heyday as 'The Prince of Secretaries', Page was a tough and successful businessman, rating 19 lines in the Who's Who in Australia. I found an old Big V picture which included him as team manager and sent it to him, fully captioned, with my compliments. He rang and thanked me. Miraculously, he didn't possess the picture among his own memorabilia. All of the stars of the day were there: Syd Coventry, Geddes, Leeta Collier, McCormack and Moriarty. 'Do you take shorthand young man?' he asked me. Thanks to Mrs Travers back in my cadetship days at The Age, I could truthfully say 'yes'. 'Come Wednesday,' he said.

Years later, Jack Dyer told me that one matchday Page refused to allow a Richmond player a new pair of socks. 'Take them home and get your wife to darn them,' he said. The player ripped them up in Page's face and said he was withdrawing from the game. 'Please yourself,' said Page. 'No play, no pay.' He ended up playing, ripped socks and all.

We spent an absorbing few hours together, Mr Page talking about some of his biggest signings from coach Checker Hughes through to his most significant player signing of all, Melbourne's goalkicking colossus, Jack Mueller who is in almost every footballing Hall of Fame:

> 'I got a call one morning from Hughie Dunbar, an old Melbourne player at my printing business in Queen Street. Hughie said he had seen this kid playing with Echuca Imperials. He reckoned he was going to be a champion.

'I was that impressed by what Hughie told me that I rang my mother immediately and said: "I won't be home tonight Mum. I'm going to Echuca".

'I went up by bus and arrived at the Mueller house around midnight. Mr Mueller, a solicitor was throwing a card night. He apologised to me saying that Jack wouldn't knock off work at the local flour mill until 2am. But if I cared to wait, I could sit down and play cards.

'When Jack came in he was just a boy, tall and thin and covered in flour.

'Mr Mueller wasn't keen to see his boy go to the Big Smoke. But Mrs Mueller called him into the kitchen and said: "Franz, this just might be Jack's chance."

'He signed a form four that night and you wouldn't believe it, at 8am the next morning, Hawthorn officials were knocking on the front door. You had to be quick.'

MULTI-SKILLED DES Fothergill was another on my interview wish-list. He'd won the first of his three Copeland Trophies as a 17-year-old at Collingwood in a Grand Final year and represented Victoria at cricket, even playing overseas as a professional in the Lancashire Leagues. I rang and wrote to him without joy. Finally, unannounced, I visited him one mid-afternoon, knocking repeatedly on his front door. It was a cold winter's day and initially there was no answer. But his car was in the driveway, so I persisted. Finally, a voice came from deep inside the house: 'I'm in the bath, keeping warm. Go away.'

'Mr Fothergill,' I said. 'It's Ken Piesse from the Sunday Observer. I've been ringing you. I love football and cricket, just like you. I've so wanted to talk to you. May I wait.' There was a silence and then an 'all right, I won't be long.'

He opened the front door in his winter pjs and dressing gown, smiled and said: 'Come in'.

He kept his best and fairest medals in a hanky in his sock draw. Like many of the old stars he'd also had a stint in the VFA, where the pay for the standouts was often treble what they earnt in the VFL. Fothergill was proud of his achievements and his eyes sparkled when I mentioned the 100 he made against a South Australian team which included Don Bradman in Adelaide just after the War. It was his only three-figure score for Victoria. I'd always warmed to those who played both football and cricket at the highest levels. At 173cm (5ft 7in), Fothergill was Bradman's height and played his football effortlessly, at an exulted level to most of his opponents. In 1940 he tied for the Brownlow Medal. It was great to shake his hand. Hobbsy would have been proud of me.

THE SUNDAY OBSERVER'S six-figure circulation was built around show business, entertainment and sport. TV celebrity Bert Newton made more front pages than anyone. In Perth, when Test fast bowler Terry Alderman dislocated his shoulder tackling a pitch invader, we had all the words we needed via me, but no pictures until assistant-editor Antony Cheesewright told the local wire service we were the Observer and the pictures were meant for us, rather than our London equivalent. Cheeky but effective.

There was little stability at the top, however, and in the next seven years, I had seven editors, all with different ideas on how to accelerate our roller-coasting sales figures and match the Sunday Press. One wanted the paper to go 'up market' with page long features and words few of us could understand. He totally misread the market and was soon sent packing. We competed when we concentrated on the basics: football, meat pies, kangaroos and Holden cars… as the popular jingle of the time went.

Mr Isaacson backed my request to publish a cricket annual and we released four very comprehensive editions from 1980 until 1983. They were produced 'scrapbook-style' with the stories being cut and pasted onto pages alongside headings and picture bromides. In the first edition, released in 1980, we included a who's who of Australia's 300 or so Test cricketers and allowed six or seven pages for it. Close to printing, I asked the compositor, Timmsy's mate Johnny Handley, how it was going. 'Fitted like a glove, Master,' he said. It wasn't until I read the printed product I realised half the 'W' entries were missing. Johnny had simply pasted the overmatter under the bench.

The '81 Ashes series triggered late nights for us all. At Headingley, Australia so dominated the match that bookmakers Ladbroke's offered 500-1 odds against an English victory. Australia had won the first Test and drawn the second. Victory at Leeds would ensure the Ashes. Our midnight banner was emphatic: 'THE ASHES ARE OURS'. Enter Ian Botham who made an inspired century and Bob Willis, who took eight wickets as Australia lost the unlosable match on the way to a 3-1 series defeat.

JOURNALISM was cutthroat as reporters chased exclusives. It reminded me of Billy Wilder's classic *The Front Page* starring Jack Lemmon and Walter Matthau, where ethics and integrity was often ignored. I'd built an arsenal of trusted contacts and rarely upset anyone, though I did question the commitment of Collingwood's bulky journeymen Rene Kink, who had a constant weight battle and suggested tennis ace John McEnroe should take his brattish ways back to the USA.

We ran some big stories, including the time (in 1984) Richmond's David Palm confessed to deliberately biting his St Kilda opponent Robert Elphinstone on his forearm at the MCG one day in retribution for a rough tackle. 'I Bit Saint' was the frontpage headline. 'I was punched and lost my mouthguard,' Palm claimed. 'So rather than get reported for hitting him back, that was my plan of attack. It's not a regular thing.'

'Calls to Sack Dennis Lillee' also made page 1 after his 1981 Headingley bets were exposed years later with the launch of his life story. Bradman Invincible Neil Harvey was among many old Test stars bewildered by a champion current player deliberately betting against his own team. 'It's a stupid nonsensical thing to do,' he said. 'It's bottom of the barrel. We must stop these fellows.' Australia's oldest living Test cricketer, Stork Hendry, 87, said he'd rub out Lillee and Rod Marsh for all time.

Kelvin Templeton won the Brownlow Medal and the Observer's Footballer of the Year award in 1980 and shared some of the secrets of his success, including his habit at half-time of re-reading his reminder cards: 'Am I getting to every possible marking contest? 'Am I kicking through the ball?' 'Am I chasing?' How many tackles have I had?' He wasn't a champion by accident and remains one of the few forwards to ever win the game's most coveted individual award.[62]

In 1983, he and Collingwood's Peter Moore crossed to Melbourne in an incredible summertime recruiting coup, Mike Sheahan's biggest ever story and there were dozens. While Templeton's injuries were to cloud his final years, Moore won a second Brownlow Medal, in 1984. His best was electrifying and his son Darcy is just as idolised now.

---

62 St Kilda's Tony Lockett, the 1987 Brownlow Medallist was an out-and-out full forward. Forty years earlier, South Melbourne's Ron Clegg also won the Medal having played 11 games at centre-half forward and five at centre-half back. Delighted South officials presented him with a deluxe set of golf clubs, but within a year when finances were tight, asked for half of them back!

11
BACK TO KINDERGARTEN

'Your mates,' she said. 'They're mongrels!'
'He has just kicked eight. He's on a high...
it's the greatest day of his life.'

You can take the boy out of Beaumaris but you can never take the Beaumaris out of the boy. It was September 1980 and we'd just committed the *Sunday Observer's* footy final's edition, my first, to print. It was party time at 46 Porter Street, Prahran and everyone was happy. George, our intern, was really letting his hair down and unfortunately was sick all over the fax machine. Exit George. Having found a tennis ball and unscrewed a leg off a flimsy table out the back to use as a bat, Daryl Timms and I were playing an impromptu game of corridor cricket, on the main floor, in-between desks. He kept blocking, refusing to play a shot. 'Must be a two-dayer,' I said. We'd had a few beers and grabbing a small pot plant, I said, 'See if you can hit this.' With a left-hander's natural swing to leg, Timmsy bunted the pot plant over about six desks. It disintegrated and there was a helluva mess. If we tried to clean it up, we weren't terribly successful and a terse memo was sent to the entire Saturday night staff the following Tuesday by the second-in-charge, our news editor Antony Cheesewright:

> 'During the past year we have worked hard to get rid of the kindergarten element that once ruled the Sunday Observer before it became a newspaper.
>
> 'I thought we had succeeded in this aim but in the early hours of Sunday morning the children came out to play once more. In the process a pot plant was hurled across the office and a telephone smashed.
>
> 'Therefore new security arrangements will apply from this week.
>
> 'In the future, when I leave the building, the first floor will be cleared of late-night revellers and access to it locked. The only exception to this will be when Alan Burrows and/or David Maguire (the two chief sub-editors) are left in charge.
>
> 'From now on, all casual staff will vacate the premises as soon as their work for the day is completed. Any recurrence of the behaviour that took place at the weekend will result in alcohol being banned from the premises.
>
> 'I sincerely hope those responsible for the vandalism are well satisfied with the results of their efforts. – AC.'

We took our Saturday night partying off-site into town and often would meet with Susan and her sister at the Underground, our new club of choice, having moved on from the Bombay Bicycle Club. Its very late liquor licence suited us. The Fitzroy boys were invariably there and always multiple drinks ahead of us. We were good mates with them all, particularly Matt Rendell and Scotty Clayton and would have early-morning drinks back at Matty's hotel, the Highbridge in Prahran. They introduced us to the Blues Brothers and we were always exchanging one-liners from the show, or singing the opening lines of Tammy Wynette's 'Stand By Your Man', one of the movie's classic tunes: 'Sometimes it's hard to be a woman….'

One 1983 mid-season Saturday was particularly memorable as Fitzroy (second) defeated North Melbourne (first) by 25 goals, Matty kicking eight. So dominant was he that he deserved to get all six Brownlow votes: the 3, 2 and the 1. I went off to buy a round and on return, Susan's sister Linda was almost purple with rage. Matty had asked her downstairs for a kiss and a fondle – and they'd only just been introduced. 'Your mates,' she said. 'They're mongrels!'

'He has just kicked eight. He's on a high,' I said. 'It's the greatest day of his life.'

'I don't care. They're mongrels. All of them.'

Years later I had a spare ticket to a cricket dinner at Kooyong featuring ex-Test captain Kim Hughes and asked Linda if she'd like to join us on the head table. 'I'd rather slash my wrists,' she said.

MATTY RENDELL was a fine, athletic ruckman, as good as almost anyone in the game. Like star Hawk Dermott Brereton, his habit was to return to training heavy, giving him an immediate incentive in the tough weeks of pre-season which occasionally included even 100 100-metre sprints. So luxuriant was his tummy on return to summer training in 1983-84, his mates dubbed him 'Bundy' after the wrestler King Kong Bundy. He was huge.

In the first game of the new season, Matty opposed Peter Moore, Melbourne's star import ruckman, in his second year. Moore had a picnic and Matty's summer of excess showed. At half-time Matty was red-faced and exhausted, with his jumper and boots off and there was still an hour to play. He simply couldn't keep up with Moore, who was to win another Brownlow Medal that year. That night, big Peter bounded into the Underground, full of vim without a hair out of place. Seeing Moore standing at the bar, Clayton elbowed big Matty: 'There he is. Here's your chance. Go and stand next to him!'

IT WAS EXCITING seeing so many top-notch teenagers such as Richard Osborne (Fitzroy), Michael Voss (Brisbane), Adam Goodes (Sydney) and David Neitz (Melbourne). All were emerging champions. At Princess Park, Vossy must have had 10-11 possessions in the first quarter, nine of them handballs to grateful teammates streaming past. Like Greg Williams, he was fearless and would bore in and under, opening gaps for others. He was a leader from Day 1. After some inglorious opening years, Brisbane became a force, equally as good as the star-studded Melbourne teams of the '50s and my Hawks from the '80s.

No player was off limits in the rooms immediately after a game. There were no media managers to herd you into corners or behind ropes. Reporters could flick here and there asking all sorts of questions. The greenhorns would bowl up to Tony Lockett while he was still changing and he'd see red, telling them to nick off. It helped if you knew the player. At the Western Oval one day, Graeme Allan was in the carpark staring at the ground cursing his mistake in kicking across goal in time-on. Footscray's Simon Beasley had intercepted the ball and kicked the winning goal. Gubby spoke honestly and emotionally about his shame in costing the Magpies the match. It was an unexpected exclusive. He and I had known each other for years since he was a teenager at Sunshine. One day against Port Melbourne he took nine bounces running through the centre. 'Was it only nine!' he said.

At Gerard Healy's encouragement, I began an interview with Warwick Capper one day. He spoke so incredibly fast, I couldn't understand even one word and soon called off the exercise. A more satisfying chat was with Silvio Foschini, a League debutant at 17 who had just joined St Kilda, having refused to move to Sydney because of his close family ties. Three generations of Foschini's all lived in the same Clayton street. He was a freakish talent who had mixed soccer with Aussie Rules as a young man. His highlight reel was as good as anybody's at the time. He had seven TVs, one in virtually every room. He slipped several bottles of home-made, very alcoholic Italian grappa into my hands as I was leaving. 'Put it in your next spag bol,' he urged. The kids reckoned it was delicious, especially our eldest James.

In 1984, my feature 'Big Boys Play at Night' won the best feature award in the VFL's Sterling Cup competition. I led on teenage debutant Geoff Parker who kicked a pivotal goal in Essendon's semi-final win, the match played in freezing two-degree temperatures, the coldest footy night I'd ever known. Geoff was also a considerable teenage cricket talent, hitting me for four 4s in an over one day at the Punt Road Oval.

While football and cricket was pivotal to our back pages, the spring racing season was always fun and a chance to dress up. At Caulfield one day the old grandstand roof almost lifted as everyone's favourite, the champion gelding Kingston Town came from almost last at the turn and powered to the finish, only just beaten. The roars for the horse rivalled anything I'd heard until the 2000 Olympics in Sydney when the Thorpedo and the Australians won relay gold in world record time. Swimming the third leg, William Kirby was almost lifting out of the water, so loud was the clamor for him to beat the Americans to the wall first. The force and fever of hometown crowds can never be underrated.

SPORT OPENS DOORS. Every day was an adventure. At a golf dinner one night, Bruce Devlin introduced me to the 'Golden Bear', the champion American Jack Nicklaus, winner of so many majors including the 1986 Masters at Augusta – still the most exciting nine-hole charge I've ever seen. He was linking up with Jack jnr, his caddy. We shook hands and within minutes he was asking me about my family. By then we had four children, with the arrival of two more girls, Tori and Jessie. It was extraordinary that such a major sports celebrity would be asking me about my kids. Tori's birthdate, incidentally, was always the easiest to remember: 2-2-82, the day Allan Border made a century to save Australia. AB's heroics also made the birth notice.

One cold, very grey afternoon, I was at the ABC Studios in Lonsdale Street to promote the latest *Cricket Year* annual. Hollywood icon James Stewart happened to also be in the green room, waiting to be interviewed. His hair was silver grey and his handshake firm. In that familiar drawl of his – straight out of the movies – he said: 'Pleased ta meet ya'.

I also spoke with Shane Gould, the champion swimmer, living as Mrs Neil Innes, on a small farm just outside Margaret River in country Western Australia. She'd made a one-off return to swimming in a charity river race at nearby Bridgetown. Ten years earlier, as a 15-year-old, she'd won triple-Gold at the 1972 Munich Olympics and now was the mother of three children, all under four. She said her comeback was a one-off, purely to support the town and a local charity close to her heart. She'd been overwhelmed years earlier by her gold medal publicity and was amazed how interested the media was in her life after swimming. 'Sport is king in Australia, Shane,' I said.

'Don't I know it,' she replied.

12

ENTER AB

'If Lillee was challenged by authorities, I didn't hear about it. Too often DK was a lawbreaking maverick. Too often he was to be thrashed by a feather.'

It was the most extraordinary of Grand Heists. News of Australia's elite 30 cricketers defecting to Kerry Packer's Supertest circuit somehow remained secret until Greg Chappell's team was a fortnight into its 1977 Ashes tour. Had the selectors known that 13 of the 17 had gone rogue, they would have sent an entirely different squad. 'We should all have been sent home there and then,' said David Hookes, the youngest signing.

Tony Greig was hosting a Saturday night party at his home in Hove for the Aussies, his Sussex teammates and the touring press. My ex-colleague from *The Age*, Peter McFarline had heard whispers about a rival cricket troupe being established for some 'TV matches' in the coming Australian summer. So had Alan Shiell, representing *The Australian*. They pooled resources and during a rain delay earlier in the day, visited the Australian rooms and asked Chappell for comment. 'Sounds interesting,' he said. 'I'd like to know more about it.' [63]

Seventy days earlier, Chappell had signed a $175,000 five-year contract with Packer. Most of the others were also on significant salaries four and five times in excess of their previous earnings. As important as the money was for Chappell, he believed the Board intransigent and was irritated by their continuing refusal to listen to the players, who were increasingly being asked to be more professional, without the accompanying rewards.

It was the sports story of the decade – 'the best kept secret in sporting history'.[64] The headline in The Age was: 'Nine plans greatest cricket show on earth'. To McFarline's disbelief, it was buried on an inside page, next to some racing chat. It wasn't the sports editor's best day. Shiell's version made the front page.

In Sydney, Packer said he hoped the Australian Cricket Board would co-operate and if they didn't, they'd 'run into a meat mangler'[65]. His aim was to secure exclusive TV rights to Test cricket for the Nine Network which had televised the '77 Ashes, using the BBC feed. He wanted more. 'Everyone is a harlot,' he told the ACB's Bob Parish and Ray Steele in a meeting at Jolimont. 'What's your price?'

At the Centenary Test in Melbourne, World Series recruiter Austin Robertson had been mingling with the players in the rooms, handing out sign-on cheques. 'Here's your theatre tickets boys,' he said smiling. Parish and Steele were amazed at the easy rapport between Robertson and the players. They knew little about him, other than he hailed from Perth, had played football with South Melbourne and managed Dennis Lillee.

---

63 *The Cricket Revolution*, Eric Beecher (Newspress Pty Ltd, Melbourne, 1978)
64 *A Game Divided*, Peter McFarline (Hutchinson of Australia, Richmond, Victoria, 1977)
65 *The Cricket Revolution*.

When the Board confirmed long-time partners the ABC as its immediate broadcaster of choice, Packer created a breakaway league and spent tens of millions in the process. He wasn't used to being rebuffed and rarely ran second, in anything. He was preparing for a third rebel season, too, before a meeting in Adelaide with Sir Donald Bradman, then 71 and retired from almost every board, but still the most revered and important personality in world cricket.

World Series was to be a blessing for the game, the leading players and the freshmen, who were fast-tracked into Baggy Greens. Twenty-three newcomers were chosen in 16 months. While many were to play just once or twice, one of them, Allan Border, the slimly built left-hander from harborside Mosman proved to be a generational champion, one of the greatest of his or any era.

Skilled, committed and ambitious, Border was never out of an Australian XII after debuting in Sydney in 1978-79. His headlining efforts in the Christmas Test in Melbourne in 1982-83, when he shared a 70-run 10th wicket stand with Jeff Thomson, stopped a nation. Using a bat borrowed from England's Ian Botham, Border all but clinched what would have been one of the greatest Australian victories downunder of them all. Instead, England won by three runs.

So secure was England's position overnight, with Australia still needing 37 runs with only one wicket in hand that none of the Australians bothered to change for their normal warm-up. But Border could sense the anticipation of the crowd. 'They were streaming in and it was still only 10.30am,' he told me for the Melbourne Cricket Club's sound archive. 'Their mood, even pre-start, strongly suggested that they expected something out of the ordinary.' After a string of failures in the earlier Tests, the 27-year-old was playing for his immediate career. He admitted the odds against an Australian win were '1000/1' when

Thomson had ambled in at No.11 late on the penultimate evening. He'd self-destructed in the first innings, playing an unsightly slog against Geoff Miller. He'd tried to hit it to Richmond station and was bowled. There was a reason why he was batting at 11. Yet 18,000 Melburnians turned up to see the last rites. 'They were the good judges,' he said. 'It could have been over in one ball.'

Walking with Border onto the field to a standing reception, Thomson said to his mate: 'If it's good enough for all these people to come along, we should attempt the impossible and give it our best shot.'

It was thrilling to be there live. It was a Thursday workday and I had my column to write – as well as assorted features. Just five runs came in the opening half an hour. To concerted applause, Thomson playing out one maiden from Norman Cowans and then another. This time everyone was out of their seat cheering like it was VFL Grand Final day. Cowans had taken eight wickets for the game. He was zippy and menacing.

England's fast bowling captain Bob Willis called for the second new ball and when Thomson punched him forward of point for three to register their 50-run partnership, less than 25 were needed. It was gripping cricket, the crowd either deathly silent or wildly exuberant as each ball was negotiated. To delirious cheering, substitute fieldsman Ian Gould collided mid-pitch with Allan Lamb and Border stole a cheeky single to keep the strike. An against-all-odds victory loomed. Eighteen to tie, 19 to win. 'We inched towards our target,' Border said. 'The Englishmen were clearly unsettled; some were panicking.'

Willis set a deep field to Border, conceding singles, but saving boundaries. There was no inner rope; the ball had to make it to the steel pickets to be four. England's whole concentration was on Thommo, the vulnerable one. Less than 10 were needed when Botham was reintroduced from the southern end and Border drove him firmly through mid-off. They could have run four but settled for three with Border again cornering the strike. The bowling was tight and directed at the top of off. But when Willis overpitched on middle and leg, Border glided him backward of square and to screams of encouragement, sprinted back for two. He was now 62 – three to tie, four to win.

Thomson was on strike to Botham, coming from the southern end. One bounced more than he expected and nipped away and Thommo nicked it. Backing-up at the non-striker's end, Border initially thought it was ballooning over the slips for the winning four. 'Then I thought, it's in Tavare's hands,' said Border. 'But it bounced out. Beauty, I thought. Then all of a sudden Miller (at second slip) was there, taking the rebound. The old heart jumped into the mouth about three times. So close… yet so far. I was associated with having saved so many Test matches for Australia. I would have loved to have actually won one, but I was at the wrong end.'

It was an unforgettable match, one of the closest in Test history. My column for the Sunday revolved around the 'clean-skin' bat with which Border had rejuvenated his career. Afterwards, in the rooms, Border confirmed the bat he'd been using had been borrowed from Botham after the only two bats he was carrying both broke. His replacement was a Duncan Fearnley. He'd taken the stickers off, so as not to break his contract with Harry Solomons at Symonds. He'd signed two years earlier for a then-record $12,000 a season. Solomons reckoned the 'D' and the 'F' could still be clearly seen on the back of the bat. Border hoped to keep it. 'This one has a nice middle to it,' he said, smiling at Botham.

WITH THE retirements of the 'Big Three', Greg Chappell, Dennis Lillee and Rod Marsh at the Sydney Test the following summer, Australian cricket went into free-fall under Kim Hughes, Australia's new fulltime Test captain. In Melbourne in the 1981 Christmas Test, he'd made the most exhilarating Test century I'd ever seen against Roberts, Holding and co. after Australia had lost 4-26 in the first hour on a spiteful wicket. His dare-devilry square of the wicket that day will never be surpassed. Kim's best was electric, but there were too many troughs and soft dismissals for him to be ranked alongside Lawry, Simpson or the Chappells. True champions don't average 37. Many were irked by his confidence and strut. Opposed to a young Craig McDermott in a Sheffield Shield match one day, he took 20 runs off an over and after one boundary, he said, 'Shot Claggie. That's four young fella.' [66]

In the nets Lillee would often unleash a stream of high-speed bouncers aimed straight at Hughes' throat. He'd so wanted his mate Marsh to be Test captain. If Lillee was challenged by authorities, I didn't hear about it. Too often DK was a lawbreaking maverick. Too often he was to be thrashed by a feather. But without his obstinate streak, he would have been only half the bowler. You can't have genius without warts.

Under Hughes, Australia opposed the West Indies in back-to-back series home and away and was thrashed both times. In Port-of-Spain, Border batted 10 hours and survived 535 balls without being dismissed, scoring 98 not out and 100 not out as Australia forced an unlikely draw. The next highest scoring Australian was Hughes with 24 and 33. AB's unbeaten 98 was his finest solo moment in a distinguished, long-lasting career. For courage and gallantry, it rates alongside Stan McCabe's Bodyline 187 not out and Dean Jones' 216 at Madras among the bravest of all Test innings by Australians.

'The state of the game was disastrous,' he said. 'The pitch wasn't good for batting and the opposition bowling was hell of a standard. My technique was as good as I have ever produced. It's a war of attrition

---

[66] *Golden Boy, Kim Hughes and the bad old days of Australian cricket*, Christian Ryan (Allen & Unwin, Crows Nest, NSW, 2009)

against the West Indies. You really don't have any option but to tough it out against them. The trap a lot of players fall into is trying to fight fire with fire. I tried to wait for them and score off the bad balls.' He didn't offer even one chance and at the conclusion, the congratulations from even the West Indies were warm and heartfelt. He'd battled across three days against the likes of Garner, Marshall and Daniel – as menacing and furious a set of flamethrowers as almost any in history. Entering on the first morning at 3-16, he provided the immediate mettle which allowed Australia to force play into a fifth day and then deep into the final session when Viv Richards, conceding the Windies could not win, walked over to Border and shook his hand. He'd only just reached his 100, he and last-man Terry Alderman safely negotiating the final 100 minutes before being cheered off the ground by Trinidadians, recognising the enormity of Australia's achievement. They had just witnessed one of Test cricket's greatest escapes. 'It was quite moving,' Border said. 'West Indians are fiercely parochial and regard the other team as villains. Yet here they were greeting us like hometown heroes.' [67]

Border had traditionally floundered against the 'Big Bird' Joel Garner who was 203cm (6ft 8in) in his socks and capable of extracting disconcerting bounce from even the most docile of surfaces. Pre-tour, he incorporated into his daily routines skipping and stair running to quicken his feet and enhance his evasion skills. He knew he'd need to be as light on his feet as possible. Few balls were going to be pitched in his half.

Garner threatened to run through Australia's top six, taking four early wickets. The pitch was damp and two-paced and Border struck several times, once over the heart. The thump could be heard from the Queen's Park pavilion. It was a fearsome blow. He refused to buckle, his

---

67 *Simply the Best, the Allan Border Story,* Ken Piesse (Newspress, Melbourne, 1993)

concentration relentless and fast feet a feature. He was Australia's rock – and soon was to be its new captain.

MONTHS LATER, IN Australia's home summer, the first Test lasted just 10 sessions and the Australians mauled again in the second. The angst between Hughes and Channel Nine's on-ground interviewer Ian Chappell was ballooning. Chappell had little or no respect for Hughes and Hughes refused to talk to him at the toss.

We were in the Queensland Cricketers' Club for the after-match captain's conference when Hughes hurried in, spoke briefly about the game before saying he had an announcement to make. Unfolding a piece of paper, he told us he was resigning as captain. No longer could he handle the pressure. He broke down halfway through and handed the note to Australia's team manager Bob Merriman, who finished reading.

The Test had again finished early and after completing my radio commitments, I went downstairs to the club's bar with Tiger O'Reilly and one or two others. The Tiger was adamant about Hughes' replacement. 'There's only one who it can be,' he said. 'Allan Border.'

Their deadlines met, everyone else gradually started to drift in, forming a big circle. It was Tiger's turn to buy. 'How many is it boys?' he asked. 'Thirteen?' No wonder we so loved him.

13

A SECRET COMEBACK

'Fellas would come in with contraband hot off the wharf. One would take off his coat and he'd have seven watches strapped down his forearm. "Which one do you want Guru?"'

Late in my time at the *Sunday Observer* we were recognised by the VFL for the Best Finals cover of any print medium. We'd beaten all the big boys, all the dailies, even Scot Palmer's *Sunday Press*. In extraordinary 30-degree heat[68] on Grand Final day 1987, Carlton knocked over my Hawks. I duly attended Carlton's premiership celebrations and right on the deadline, dictated 400 words with quotes direct from the event. It made all our city editions. There was great fanfare and also a $500 cheque which I hoped could help to make our office Christmas party even merrier in early December. This was a big deal, but my editor said no. His communications skills were poor and he

---

68 The temperature reached 30.7 in mid-afternoon, the hottest recorded September day in Melbourne since 1928. The average temperature in September is 17.3.

had little idea about teamwork. 'Okay,' I said, 'can all the footy writers who contributed all September… can they be invited to the party? Everyone can pay for their own drinks.' Again, no.

The best man managers reward achievement. Good things happen when you work with inspirational go-getters, people who share your drive, zest and vision. Work is fun and every day an adventure, like it was at *The Age*. But if you're unhappy at work and have little respect for the boss, what's the point of being there? I just shook my head and did an about face. Maybe he was under the pump, but from that day I started widening even further my freelance bases across multi-mediums, realising it was line-in-the-sand time.

For 12 months and more I'd secretly been on the cricket comeback trail, playing at an elevated new level in Port Melbourne CC's first XI. Previously I'd also had a half season back at Beaumaris, making two or three 50s and taking my first 'five-for' in senior cricket. We'd made it through to a semi-final at my old favourite, Shipston Reserve in Cheltenham. I made 90 but we still lost. I'd tired of the editor's intensity and unsmiling ways and was so desperately missing playing. I shared my secret – and Saturday afternoon whereabouts – with only one other, Peter, our chief sports sub-editor, from Cumberland newspapers, where we produced *Cricketer* magazine. I'd play my game, leave immediately afterwards and be back in the office by 7pm, ready to write the backpage lead. One of my mates was on the same plane to Brisbane as Hawks legend Peter Knights. He was about to be announced as the new coach of the Brisbane Bears, a scoop we published, despite vehement denials from a prominent Bears' official. He never did apologise for his blatant untruths. Maybe he didn't trust me. Hundreds of others did. We went with the story anyway.

My desire to play again had been fueled by regular Friday night training sessions on the way home from work at Dingley and some mid-week matches, initially with the Plastic XI and then most Wednesdays for Swan Richards' Crusaders. Swanny invariably recruited some internationals for the games against the private schools. One day at St Bedes, I batted with Sri Lanka's Aravinda de Silva and he struck a ball over the school's main building into a quadrangle just short of the tennis courts. It was huge. At Geelong I bowled in tandem with ex-international George Tribe. Afterwards, Phil O'Meara, a friend from Gray-Nicolls and Port's playing coach, said Billy Masterton, the club's No.1 spinner was moving on and invited me to take his place. Phil asked me how I'd gone in my last game at Beaumaris. I'd taken two-for, but been expensive, conceding 50 or 60 runs. 'How many catches were dropped?' he asked. 'Three, maybe four.'

He told me how Port had had 19 run outs before Christmas the previous summer on the way to winning the 28-team Championship. Everyone had a specialist position. Everyone had to hold at least 100 catches each Tuesday and Thursday. The catches dropped at Beaumaris would be taken at the higher level. I was honest with him. I didn't think I'd be good enough. Subbies cricket was just one level below Premier cricket. But I was so elated to be asked. Every one wants to be wanted. 'Yes,' I said. 'Thanks. I'll try.' It was like being born again. Twice a week, I'd knock off work around 4.30pm, drive to Port and the big, wide, white practice wickets would all be set up at the far end. It was an incredibly encouraging and positive environment. I loved it from Day 1 and was soon dubbed 'Guru', the spin guru. We were a mature team with lots of footballers from Port and beyond, characters like Stretch Aanensen, Graeme Anderson, Bunker Tinsley and in the twos, Greg Dermott, known to all as 'Biff'. One tumultuous afternoon at Brighton, big Stretch had shirtfronted Brighton's Danish international Ole Mortensen in mid-pitch. He wondered what a Beaumaris Liberal, sportswriting poofta prick (I think that's what he said) was doing at his club. 'Blame Phil,' I said. I worked hard and earned their respect and come the semi-final at Camberwell took a four-for, including the last from a catch by Stretch at square leg. 'You're still a Beaumaris Liberal, sportswriting poofta prick… but I love you,' said Stretch.

One Saturday-Sunday match, at Williamstown, I was so keen not to be late to the ground that I forgot to take off my make-up from my pre-recorded World of Sport cricket segment. Stretch took one look at all the rouge on my face and started abusing me all over again. I took four for 10 and two for 22 that afternoon and we all but won outright. Stretch reckoned the competition standard must be slipping.

Thursday nights pre-Christmas were hilarious. Fellas would come in with contraband hot off the wharf. One would take off his coat and he'd have seven watches strapped down his forearm. 'Which one do you want Guru?' he'd ask. Another had perfume and remote-control racing cars. For four years I did my Christmas shopping for Susan and the kids almost exclusively at the club.

One year during the spring racing carnival, we played on Melbourne Cup day and I said to everyone how I'd see them all on the Thursday. We were playing the top team and needed to be at our best.

'Did you say Thursday, Guru?

'Yep.'

'Nup,' they said. 'It's Blokes Day. We're in the members.'

'All right then, we'll train first thing and you can go off to the Oaks afterwards.' They all fronted by 9am before having their Big Day Out.

We all had nicknames. There was Bunk, Ted, Crock, Mac, Fab, Arms, Beva, Eggie, Shecki, Nuffy, Cocky, Dusch, The Fireman, Luigi, Ecka, Rig,

Suds and Marty the Brain. Never have I played with a closer bunch. We were thick-as. Still are. The Fireman had so much ink one night that he couldn't find his way home – and he lived 400 yards away!

In my one-and-only seconds game – penance for going to a Test match in Perth – Cement-Head, in at No.11 and I batted for almost two hours at Yarraville to all but avert an outright defeat. 'Just block and keep 'em out here, Cement,' I said. 'They're not as good as they think they are.' I'd arrived early on Day 1 already in whites ready to go. But our lads didn't rock up until 15 minutes before the start. It was the first time I'd ever seriously thought about joining the opposition for their warm-ups. The boys in the seconds weren't quite as motivated as the ones. I took two for 95 from 25 or 26 overs, but had the same left-hander dropped three times in three overs by Cocky at mid-wicket, who received a roasting afterwards from our skip, Colonel Denis Byrne: 'Git down to training McFarlane,' he said, 'and do some catchin' practice.'

One of our older lads, a long-time bachelor, was known for his penchant for porno movies. He met a young lady and announced his intention to marry. That was cause for drinks all round. The following Thursday he brought all his cassettes down to the club and shared them out with the boys. 'Can't be caught with these,' Denbeigh said. Phil took four or five, shoved them in an old cupboard near his TV and his teenage boys found them during school holidays. 'Best sex education we've ever had Dad,' they said.

On Phil's arrival from St Kilda, he asked who opened the batting. 'One's in the nets right now,' he was told. 'He has played 49 games.'

'Well,' said Phil, having seen two or three balls. 'He's not going to make 50.'

On the way to the finals one year, we knocked off the top team, Mount Waverley. We'd always be changed and ready to go an hour before a game. On arrival this day, their captain-coach Dave McClean, was revving them up like Killa Killigrew, the last of the hot gospellers. They were already practising when we got out there for a warm-up lap. Normally we'd veer wide of the batsmen hitting up. 'Let's run straight through the pricks,' said Stretch. And did. They had us five-for early, but we still beat them by 100 or more runs, Arms Anderson and I adding 90 when we were five for not many.

Lew Coyle joined us as an opening bat from Elsternwick and we won the first four games. 'It took us four years to win four games at Elsternwick,' he laughed. One day, against Werribee, we chased down 283, Robert Bevilacqua making the hundred of his life. He had this big bat and kept lifting full deliveries high and handsome over mid-off, like Aaron Finch at his exuberant best. Our curator Johnny Normal was seen rolling our wicket and drinking longnecks at midnight on the Wednesday and Thursday nights. The wicket was an absolute road, the best in subbies by far. And on Day 2, Johnny was still cutting the outfield just minutes before we began our chase. It was all legal. We passed them four down. It was the best home-and-away win I'd ever been associated with. Johnny joined the huddle for our victory song.

We won the group final against Sunshine at home and I said to the lads, 'One more to go. Just one more.'

'No,' said Arms. 'It's a final. We've won the flag. Get into it.'

I tried to match Stretch ouzo-for-ouzo and was seeing stars after seven. He was on a high, having taken seven-for with his little wobbly outies. I caught two of them, including Lee Perussich the footballer having suggested to Phil between-overs that he might just glide one to me if I moved a little squarer close-in on the legside. 'Go where you want Master.' I shifted two yards to my right and Stretch's very next ball was firmly clipped straight into my hands.

I dismissed Oakleigh's Robert Harvey, the dual Brownlow Medallist first-ball one day at Port but couldn't get his Dad, Jeff out. He kept running at me with brilliant footwork. The same day, Geoff Van Vugt, a big-hitting left-hander, shaped up to a leg break and smashed it right out of the screws like he was the Louisville Slugger. Following through, I said, 'that's just a slog pal.'

'Hang on a minute Guru,' said Stretch at slip. 'Have a look where it has gone.'

It had all but sailed into the local soap factory.

Ormond had one good bat and he top-edged one of my leggies to deep square to my outrider Macca, who not only missed the catch, but it bounced off his head and over the pickets for six. The boys laughed later. They knew how much I hated being hit for six. I never did ask Mac how he was…

So hot was it at Melton one day, with a northerly wind blowing directly down the wicket, that Phil told the fast bowlers they'd have to bowl into the wind and I'd be coming with it. No prizes for guessing their reaction! I went off several times that day, to ring through the latest golf scores from Huntingdale for 3MP…

One Thursday night I lost $80 in about five insane minutes of poker with Crock. Twos were wild. I'd doubled him and he doubled me back. I needed Dustin Hoffman from *Rain Man* next to me to count the cards. 'See you next Thursday, Master,' said Crock. 'Bring your wallet.'

Another night, after our Saturday night edition had been put to bed, I came back for Port's talent quest. My version of Gerry Humphries' *The Loved One* received polite applause but everyone joined in the chorus for my encore, an old ribald RMIT drinking song my mate Rick Erickson had taught me, beginning with, 'My name is Giavanni…' Bunk still reckons I deserved first prize.

In my first two comeback seasons at Port Melbourne, I'd averaged only nine or 10 overs an innings. It was a tough school. If you got hit, you were off. We won the Group Final in 1986-87 after I shared an important 80-run stand with Darren Duscher, after we were 5-100. It's still the best 30 of my life. I have it on tape. Dusch kept on saying to me, 'Play straight, play straight.' You want to contribute at the pivotal times and I did.

In 1987-88, my bowling responsibilities doubled and I took my first two five-fors for the club. I would have got six against Moorabbin at Port but the square leg umpire, a mate of mine from Beaumaris, was watching me bowl instead of the batsman on-strike. The fella missed the leggie, lifted his back foot and Arms made the stumping. My mate Jan shook his head and said, 'Sorry lads, I wasn't looking.'

'You're bloody kidding,' said Arms, throwing his gloves to the ground. He was furious. Arms became the club's most prolific runmaker, ahead of Tommy Lahiff late in the season. He was such a fine player, almost unbowlable. In my four years opposing him most nights in the nets I can't remember dismissing him even once. He won 13 batting averages at the club, to go with his three Grand Finals for Collingwood.

I batted mainly at 7 and bowled second change. As soon as Stretch was hit for four I'd start warming up at mid-wicket. 'Phil, Phil,' Arms would say. 'Have a look at Piessey. He reckons he's on next.' And invariably I was. One year at Port we played the eventual champions Werribee. Peter Cox and Graham Ross, two Victorian players, were their stars. I took four wickets including Cox from a full toss miscued to mid-on. So disgusted was he that he threw his bat halfway to the pavilion. I was opening up late in the day and Cox, at gully, was still furious, saying I was no good and never would be. I took guard and he was still trumpeting. Backing off, I said to the umpire, 'As soon as he shuts up, I'll bat.' The abuse started all over again. The more abuse he hurled, the more determined I became. Ross's first over took about 10 minutes and we made it through to stumps unscathed.

In winning the bowling award in my fourth and final year, I took 30 wickets, including the Twenty20 matches we again played, going through all the way to the Twilight final against Gary Cosier's St Kilda at Caulfield. The trophy was named after one of the club's most distinguished, Tony Bogdanoff and he'd keenly watch my progress most nights. He liked my energy at the crease.

Our last game of the season coincided with South African cricket's Test centenary in faraway Johannesburg. Everyone who was anyone was invited and the Melbourne contingent was flying out on the Saturday morning. I wanted to play and asked Ali Bacher if I could delay our travel for 24 hours. 'Sure,' he said. 'I'll pick you up on the Sunday.' And did. We had our suitcases with us, ready for a custom's check, but Ali just took us through a side gate. 'Follow me,' he said. We visited game parks, Soweto, played golf at Sun City, went to the Currie Cup final and to a black-tie banquet dinner to which every living South African, English and Australian Test player had been invited. In the April edition of *Cricketer*, delayed a week to accommodate my travels, I wrote about the amazing inroads cricket was making with its encouragement of black sportsmen. Within just a few years, South Africa was back on the world stage.

MY FOUR YEARS AT Port Melbourne were incredibly happy and satisfying. I'd never worked harder or played better. After training, if we weren't having Luigi's signature hot dogs with mustard, we'd be at Topolino's in Fitzroy Street eating pizza. We won a Championship and went through the next year undefeated only to lose the semi, having been dobbed on a wet wicket. What should have been a two-day final became a one-dayer, the match being decided on the toss. We made only 81 but fought back and Altona was eight-down when they passed us. The rules were changed immediately, the subbies executive realising we had been badly wronged.

Having joined Frankston, purely to lessen my travel time to town and back, we played a one-dayer back at Port. I walked into the rooms and everyone was lined up at the bar sniggering. Stretch had stuck white tape over my name on the bowling averages honour board. Call it Karma, but I was run out for a duck and he walked me all the way back to the dug-out, questioning my Beaumaris roots and saying how 'you should never have left us'. Within the hour, our game was washed out. 'Beauty,' said Arms. The boys were already inside playing cards. They loved it when it rained. They made it through to another Championship final the following year and I trained with them on the Thursday night leading into the play-off, Phil delighting in dancing at me and hitting even my best leg breaks past cover. 'You're playing him into form Guru,' said Nuff, our fast bowler. Phil top-scored in the final against Caulfield but the boys lost on the whim of an umpire – a blatant caught behind against the ex-Victorian Graham Matthews being given not out, immediately after a break. He'd taken two steps towards the Pavilion and the umpire still shook his head. It cost us another flag.

MEANWHILE, BACK AT WORK, on the day of our 1987 staff Christmas party, I left early. The editor hadn't even bothered to attend. He was still at his desk. He seemed genuinely surprised when I said I was resigning. 'You're taking a great risk, aren't you?' he said. I just smiled. There was so much I'd wanted to say, but I kept it all in, like Warnie years later when he played cards for a living. Never show your hand. At 32, I was a full-time freelance and it was the best business decision I ever made. *Cricketer* magazine, which I'd first edited in 1978, was now a staple. I rejoined *Inside Football* as a virtual full-timer, contributing columns on behalf of Dermott Brereton, Tony Shaw and my buddy from Aspendale, Gerard Healy, who was to win the '88 Brownlow. I also submitted colour stories to the Australasian Post on a range of friends from Shirley Strachan and Warnie through to Leo O'Brien and the Duck, Wayne Carey. Susan and I had five children, so work was always important. Windows open and close so quickly. I'd say 'yes' to everything, not knowing if the job would still be available a month later.

The very week after my last byline in the Observer, from a Saturday night match at Waverley, I had my first 'By Ken Piesse' story published in *The Times on Sunday*. I ghosted Don Scott's column and soon afterwards they asked me to work in the office co-ordinating their Saturday sport. But I wanted to stay on the road, meeting and greeting, cementing friendships and chasing news. It also allowed me Saturdays off in summer. When The Times was discontinued, I joined the *Sunday Press* and worked for years alongside Scot Palmer, my long-time rival.

Scotty would always send me to St Kilda matches, on Tony Lockett watch. He knew we were friends. I'd rung Tony at his farm at Devon Meadows saying that Peter, Dermott Brereton's hairdresser in Frankston, was looking for an apprentice. Would Vicki, Tony's girlfriend and now wife of four, care to apply? Tony was rapt. We became instant mates. Rarely would a Saturday pass without the volatile full forward making headlines. Unlike the rookies, I'd give him some space. He'd nod and come over in his own time, speaking only to me.

Darrel Baldock, Tony's coach at St Kilda, was always apprehensive about Tony's white-line-fever ways. Only 'King' Carey got angrier on the field.

Once, at Moorabbin, Tony threw an elbow at West Coast's Bluey McKenna. From memory, McKenna might have finished in the Animal Enclosure. A seven-week suspension followed and Baldock was aghast, worrying about how the Saints would replace their champion and also how big Tony was going to control his weight. He only had to walk past his local pizza shop at Cranbourne to put on an extra stone. 'You've got greyhounds down there at home Tony, haven't you?' Baldock said.

'Yes Doc.'

'What about get your best one and give him an extra k's walk morning and night. That'll help you both.'

The following Tuesday, Tony reappeared at training, clearly puffier in the face and around the middle.

'Haven't you been walking that dog, Tony?'

'Sure have Doc. I just put him on the walking machine, press the button and away he goes!'

Later, in his time with the Swans, Tony tired of a loudmouthed fan sitting in the front row, directly behind the goals. He'd been abusing him all day, saying he was fat and past it. Tony ran into an open goal, got as close to the goal line as he could and with venomous intent powered a low torpedo which zeroed straight at the fella. It tipped the point of the picket fence and veered past his ear. I'd never seen Tony so furious. Like the time he threw a crutch at the young Channel 10 reporter Eddie McGuire, he really wanted to hurt the guy.

14

TRACKING OLD BERT

'Bryce would organise our golf days for us, including the riotous Sunday when we had a nude tee-off just behind the church on the 12th at Flinders Golf Club...'

It wasn't until my 52nd birthday that I conceded my dream of playing Test cricket was over. Bert Ironmonger had been Australia's most senior representative. He told his mates he was 50 when in fact he was 52. Old Bert couldn't bat or bend in the field but bowled left-arm spin and swerve beautifully from the stub of a finger severed in a farming accident. His action, however, was considered too faulty for him to be taken to England. Cricketers were ambassadors, too, and Bert, a common mower man for the St Kilda council, was not to be trusted, so the conservatives on the Board of Control said, much to captain Bill Woodfull's ire. He wanted him in 1930 and again in 1934.

Famously, Ironmonger assisted the boy wonder Don Bradman to

his only century of the Bodyline summer in Melbourne in 1932-33. Approaching the young Don in mid-pitch, he said, 'I won't let you down son'. Playing and missing at his first ball, he didn't see the second which somehow shaved the stumps. Back on strike, Bradman went from 97 to his much heralded hundred with a powerful pull shot through mid-wicket.

Having hardly played in my 20s, through work, it was fanciful to think I could wear a baggy green. The only time I did was when Dean Jones handed me his for a picture opportunity after a coaching clinic at the Albert Ground. 'You might never wear one of these again Master,' he said with a smile. We'd been mates for years. He used to open the bowling and bat at No.3 for our mid-week competition team, the Plastics. Few could strut like Deano, but to be the best you have to believe you *are* the best. He would be bowling to some top-level District players and following through and mouthing at them like he was Dennis Lillee. If only I had his confidence levels, inner belief and even a fragment of his skill. At Dav Whatmore's indoor nets at Mt Waverley, I sneaked a dipping leg-break past Deano's outside edge one session. 'What was that one?' he said. He didn't allow the next six to land. Suddenly I was defending all over again, trying to limit the damage.

In another session, shortly after we'd been in Darwin for a winter carnival – I struggled with the bat but bowled okay – I was playing nicely against Simon Davis and co. and danced at one of Dav's spinners and hit it past mid-off at pace. 'Why didn't you play like that in Darwin?' he said.

One time at the MCG I caught Bob Hawke at cow corner after he tried to lift the Liberal Party's Tony Street into the Brunton Avenue trainyards. 'As he walked off, the Prime Minister muttered: 'First time I've been caught out by a journo in 25 years.' (Street, incidentally, was a very fine leg-spinner who had played several 'bush internationals' against touring teams years earlier).

I opposed John Inverarity at the Adelaide Oval once and it was like bowling to a brick wall. Old South Australia was playing Old Victoria and Les Favell opened up against Gary Cosier, went bang, bang, bang before top edging one straight to Don Chipp at mid-on. There was one solitary barracker on the hill in front of the Moreton Bay figs. 'You always get out like that Favell,' he yelled.

Steve Waugh once took 32 runs from one of my six-ball overs. It was like a tennis match: 646466. Nigel Murch was at short cover and started laughing about ball 4. 'Don't think I've ever seen anything like this before,' he said. All six balls were well flung, same paced leg breaks. The gulf between Test and club players is huge. Waugh actually did me a favour, forcing me to extend my repertoire. I needed a ball to defend myself with.

Having left the *Sunday Observer* early in 1988, cricket has been a glorious, challenging constant and I've played non-stop every summer, except one when I snapped my achilles.

I won the bowling average in the firsts at Port Melbourne and the year I won the Ryder Medal in the thirds at Frankston Peninsula, I took two five-fors against Footscray and followed with another against South Melbourne: 15 wickets in three innings. That day, Geoff Joshua, who umpired at the highest levels, awarded me the pivotal three votes and I was to tie for first with Geelong's Justin Miller, who was as fast as anyone I ever faced, even Mick Lewis in the nets one Media Day at the MCG. At award's night at the Hilton, the MC Darren James from 3AW asked me if I happened to be working on another book. 'Yep,' I told a sold-out crowd. 'The Rat, the Johnny Platten Story. Don't miss it. Compelling reading. It's out soon…'

I had 13 or 14 years as captain-coach of the Frankston thirds. Never once was I asked to play in the seconds, but it was rewarding speeding the advancement of some terrific kids who were to play 100s of first XI games between them. Among them were Scotty Walker, Jimmy Miller, Darren Groves, Tiger Nankervis, Craig Entwistle, Cam Atkins, Steve Stubbings, Clay Riddle, Coo Cowen jnr, Jason Mathers, Leigh Lowry and Jarred Moore, who played League footy with Sydney. On the morning Jarred was drafted, coach Paul Roos called me over and said, 'We've got one of your boys.'

Eight of my lads were in the Grand Final XII, including Jarred, when the firsts played off against St Kilda one year at the Albert. We lost but it was still a proud moment to see these motivated young men – 'my boys' – competing and excelling at the highest possible club standard. Matthew Mott was our inspirational captain and worth three players in the top-order. As a teenager he and his mate Andrew Symonds had shared a 466-run stand for Gold Coast in 1992. Motty was a Queensland country boy originally from far-north Ayr. Everyone improved under his example. We also had a great coach in Keith Jansz, who allowed the kids to blossom naturally, their way. Later, Keith and I hooked up again at Over 60s level. Motty coached New South Wales, Glamorgan, the Australian women's team and is now UK based looking after England's white ball teams.

Early on in my time in the thirds, emerging fast bowler Brett Harrop played a comeback game or two after injury. We were at Fitzroy-Doncaster and I started him into a stiff breeze, initially using big Griff, his senior, downwind. Brett bowled at half ratpower for three or four overs before I asked him if he wanted to have a few from the top end. 'Sure,' he said. I was at gully and after the first two high-speed deliveries flashed past the nose of the unfortunate striker, I burst out laughing. 'Brett,' I called, 'I promise never to bowl you into the wind again!' He played for Victoria. His brother Dean was also a most promising leg-spinner.

On a wet wicket at Como Park late in our first season, I scored a 100 in the first 40 overs, having promoted myself to No.3. It was a wet wicket and I played shots, trying to set the tone for the others, unused to the conditions. In the club's annual report captain-coach Shaun Graf said:

> 'Ken Piesse did a fine job as captain of the third XI. His enthusiasm, temperament and will to win certainly shone out not only with his team but his own individual efforts. Who could forget – he wouldn't let us anyway – his superb maiden ton for the club against Prahran.'

Young Coo Cowen got a seven-for one day against North Melbourne, the last from a nick to me, scooped up at slip. It was their No.11. I threw the ball in the air with a jubilant 'Yeahhh' and we walked off. I did feel a little bit guilty, but we all wanted to end it. They were 100 runs or more behind. Coo came over and asked, 'did you catch that Master?' 'No,' I said. 'Have you ever got seven-for before?'

'No,' he said. 'Have a look in the book. You have now.'

We played once or twice on the main oval, named after Adrian Butler, Alan McGilvray's son-in-law. Griff was coming downwind as always. There was an early nick and it flew low and wide and somehow stuck in my outstretched left-hand. It was a fluke. Turning to my second slipsman, Craig Entwistle, I said: 'Better than sex, Wiss. Better than sex.' He looked at me as if I was from outer space. On the Monday morning I was talking cricket on Sport 927 with Michael Christian and Angela Pippos and she happened to ask me about how I'd gone at the weekend. 'Glad you asked, Ange,' I said, before relating the catch and the conversation. She burst out in incontrollable laughter. As did Chrisso. It was fantastic radio. For the next few Mondays, she'd ask: 'Any more slips catches, Ken?'

We never once made the finals in my time. We went close the year we defeated Melbourne University after I'd appealed against their opener Lachie Allardice for handling the ball. I'd often position myself at mid-off so I could mentor the young bowlers and this day he kept stroking the ball to me, not at any pace and calling, 'Wait, wait, WAITING' really loudly, hoping I'd fluff one and allow him a bonus run or two. He had this inpertinant grin. The cocky ones had always riled me. Soon afterwards a return from Heada (Jason Mathers) was a little wide of the mark and instead of swaying out of the way and allowing our keeper Grant Gains to take the ball, Allardice caught it in his left hand. Instinctively I appealed. The umpire looked at me and said: 'Are you appealing Ken?'

'Yes,' I said. 'Then he's out' and raised his finger.

The University boys went troppo, the next man in walking straight to me at mid-off saying exactly what he thought. The Students had a weekly newsletter and my picture was on the frontcover with a heading: 'PUBLIC ENEMY No.1'. When Allardice went to pick the ball up in the nets at training the following week, everyone started appealing. I took three or four wickets that day, with their middle-order players running at me and trying to smash me into the Jubilee Park swimming pool. There was no handshaking after the game. Normally you'd do an umpires' report, but their captain just took off.

In another match, against Essendon, their opener had all these Steve Smith-like idiosyncrasies and was rarely ready when our bowlers were at the top of their mark. Our over rate was suffering and I reminded the umpires that this fella was wasting time. He got to 50 and as he was acknowledging his mates in the Pavilion, I walked past and told him he shouldn't be proud. He'd batted like a prick. He got to 100 and acknowledged me first, before his teammates. He was promoted to the seconds, made another big score and by the month's end was playing ones.

INJURIES AND DEPTH were always a complication for us post-Christmas and as a feeder team to the firsts and seconds, our mantra was always to reward performance. Seeing the best kids advance was reward enough, even if our season invariably ended early in March. Some of the kids were stars in the making. In a one-dayer against Melbourne University at Parkville, I shared a late innings stand with Miller, who later was to win a Ryder Medal at Prahran. Even as a 16-year-old he was a glorious strokemaker and made 50 that day; my contribution: 10. The Uni lads were typically mouthy, one from gully calling me a 'mattin' cricketer' after I'd lifted an early ball over the top of mid-on as we looked to increase our run rate. I stopped play and walked to the fella and told him I'd covered Test cricket for two decades, written a host of books and if he didn't shut up he'd get whacked with the bat. Uni loved to bully younger teams.

Bryce McGain should have been our first Test player but he stagnated too long in the seconds, joined Prahran, within a year or two was playing for Victoria and in 2009, had one Test for Australia. Bryce would organise our golf days, including the riotous Sunday when we had a nude tee-off just behind the church on the 12th at Flinders Golf Club. We'd planned an entire nude hole, but to general disappointment Fuhrer Graf ruled against it on the day.

Bryce's advancement was extraordinary and was triggered by his afternoon sessions in the nets at Loxton Oval opposing Dave Hussey and Jon Moss, two of Prahran's champion interstaters. He was invited to be a practice bowler for Victoria and was soon its specialist spinner.

One night I swapped myself into the first XI net and started bowling at Billy Goggin, our star import from Brisbane. He'd batted in the first four for Queensland. One leg-break gripped and he all but nicked it. 'Yeesss,' I said, genuinely excited. Bryce was in the next net: 'Did you get him Master?' 'Nah, just beat the outside edge.'

One year the Kenyan international Kennedy Otieno Obuya had a half season with us. He was an excellent player and exceedingly polite. One time I was pointing something out to him and in crisp Kenyan, he replied: 'Yes Master'. The boys just broke up.

Dave Archer was captain of our fourths and came in one night and said he'd just created a new club record, having bowled 37 overs on end. Chris Bull was our third's leg spinner and having bowled the last eight overs on Day 1, I started him off again on Day 2, determined that he'd get to 37. He bowled the whole day, 40 in a row – or 48 if you count the previous Saturday. His figures were also a record: three for 177!

At Jubilee Park, I was responsible at the end of sessions for the cooldown lap with stops for hovers, sit-ups and stretches. I joked one night that when it was warm enough we should all dispose of our kit and do it nude. The young blokes never needed an excuse to parade around in the raw. One Christmas breakup it was a ferociously hot and one said to me, 'Tonight, Master?'

'All right tonight it is,' and within seconds, 20 maybe 25 fellas threw off their kit and embarked totally starkers on the cooldown. Motty and Shawn Flegler just stood in amazement, keeping their gear on. We stopped as normal for our hovers and got two thirds of the way around the railway wing when one of the board members, our club photographer Brian Nankervis, Tiger's Dad, ran at us and said: 'Stop… stop. You've gotta go back.' Upstairs in the viewing lounge, Bill Foley, Dennis Prendergast and the board had invited the parents of the WJ Dowling Under 16 kids to the club to show them around and have some Christmas drinks. All the committee had their backs to the viewing area, trying to hide our nakedness.

Tiger was taking strike in the firsts at Fitzroy-Doncaster one day and Darren Berry, the 'keeper, said, 'Hang on a minute Dave, Brian's not in position yet.'

In a tense one-dayer at North Melbourne one day, I was batting well out of my crease when struck on the pads by Rex Bennett, a much-travelled paceman who had played plenty of first XI cricket. I'd made 20-odd and was determined to be there at the close but was given out. We won the game and on a high, I told the umpire he'd only been guessing and he booked me for dissent – my one and only report in a lifetime of sport. He was a tenderfoot and wasn't to last at District level. He just wanted to make a name for himself. Peter Binns at Cricket Victoria reckoned I was sure to get two matches, so I rang around and collected a host of character references from other umpires and also one from my mate, the legendary football coach Allan Jeans. 'I don't want to miss a game Yab,' I said. Jeans thought it hilarious. 'Misbehaving – and you in the meedya too,' he said. He duly penned a reference, one of six which were handed by my advocate president Bill, to tribunal chairman, Judge Tom Wodak.

The Judge ruled that my behaviour in questioning a decision was poor and ill-advised. As captain I needed to set a better example. 'Normally,' he said, 'there would be an automatic two-match suspension, but I have in front of me all these character references written by some very eminent people and taking that into consideration, your sentence will be suspended until the end of the year. Please don't appear in front of me again.'

I'D ONLY JUST turned 16 and was still at Beaumaris High when I spent an inaugural season with the Prahran fourths and averaged 7.33 – and I was their opening bat. No wonder I was relegated to 12th man for the semi. My one-and-only higher-level game that summer was as an 11th hour fill-in for the seconds against Hawthorn-East Melbourne at Glenferrie Oval, where I was out first or second ball and didn't bowl.

My main task was having to fetch the straight 6s off the railway tracks at long-on from the bowling of our off-spinner Ian Zimmer. There must have been five or six this particular afternoon – and Zim could bowl. But that straight boundary was so incredibly short. One night at Loxton Oval I faced an over in the nets from our first XI fast bowler Patrick Smith. And lived... but only just. I was totally out of my depth. Duncan Sharpe was our playing-coach and he had some brilliant battles in the nets with our mature-age leg spinner Ian McFeeters from East Malvern. The only player who could dance at the bowlers like Duncan was my teenage mate from Highett, Whatmore, who was also to play Tests.

My fourth XI captain was Ian Crawford, a club icon loved by all. Once he took a '10-for' against star-studded Melbourne at Como Park which I was able to include in the paper's Monday morning District cricket notes. Years later, in the first week of December, during my initial season with Frankston subbies, Crawford rang saying Prahran had a vacancy in its first XI for a wrist spinner. The kid they had played in the first month was a left-arm wristie and too erratic. Would I like to come back and play? I was flattered. It would have been the highpoint for me as a late-blooming cricketer. But I told 'Oysters' that my first XI teammate, Brian Keogh, would be a better long-term proposition. He was just 18 – half my age – ambitious and more athletic. Susan and I had four children at the time, with a fifth soon to come. I was working freelance and didn't think it was fair on her with the extra time required for travel and practice. I'd switched from Port Melbourne to Frankston just months earlier to reduce my travel time. I'd never bowled better and had perfected a slider after the mauling from Steve Waugh at Royal Ascot. I knew I could have been competitive. Beeks played two games at Prahran, didn't take a wicket and returning to us after Christmas, won the bowling average. What could have been eh!

15

IN SIGLEY'S SHOES

'In between the tapings, I asked Rich what his wife Daphne had given him in the lead-up to his birthday. "A new No.1 wood," Benaud said, "and I can truthfully say I am hitting them out of sight."'

Years ago, on Melbourne's 3AW, famed broadcaster Ernie Sigley interviewed rock-and-roller John Fogarty. Ernie loved music and Creedence Clearwater and it showed. It was a fabulous 15 minutes of radio, right up there with the best of Michael Parkinson. Soon afterwards at Docklands – it was a Footscray 'home' game – Ernie and I sat at the dinner table and talked music: Elvis in Hawaii, Creedence and the Beatles. I told Ernie how much I loved his Fogarty interview. It was rolled gold and had flowed so magically. He thanked me warmly. He knew Fogarty's story backwards and simply listened and responded at the right time to his answers. It was inspiring radio and a lesson for any interviewers on the rise.

Sigley knew his interview subjects intimately and those he didn't, he and his producers would research exhaustively. It always made a difference. He was so natural in his delivery. I loved appearing on *Ernie in the Afternoon*.

Knowing when and when not to talk are unbreakable bastions for the best. The conversations flow naturally and can lead down unexpected, rewarding avenues. Once, while in the MCG Test umpire's room with the lovable David Shepherd, we were talking about the green, green grass of home and he broke out into a Welsh rugby song. All of us joined in – and I recorded it all. It made for fantastic radio played and replayed by morning hosts Michael Christian and Micky McGuane.

I've always mixed my writings and love of feel-good anecdotes with radio and TV and, for the last decade, entertaining thousands on the big cruise ships. I was World of Sport's cricket presenter for a time, spent years contributing features to Fox and have worked on radio with 3MP, Sport 927 and RSN since the mid '80s. We won four Cricket Victoria Major Media awards with my features for Fox and *Inside Cricket*. Two more 'MM's' followed for my features in *Pavilion*, the magazine of the Australian Cricket Society.

On his 75th birthday in 2005, Richie Benaud graced our top-of-town studios for both a radio and a TV interview promoting his latest book *My Spin On Cricket*. In between the tapings, I asked Rich what his wife Daphne had given him in the lead-up to his birthday. 'A new No.1 wood,' Benaud said, 'and I can truthfully say I am hitting them out of sight.' Richie always had time for the young ones and remained a dynamic media performer well into his 70s.

I'd introduced a nostalgia feature into *Cricketer* magazine, interviewing former Test players with significant stories to tell from old Bodyliner Leo O'Brien through to Bradman Invincibles Doug Ring, Neil Harvey and Sam

Loxton. I'd visit O'Brien regularly on my way back home from Prahran to the Mornington Peninsula. He lived in bayside Mordialloc and even into his 70s would play a mid-week game or two with the MCC's golden oldies, the XXIXers. Invariably when I dropped in, he'd be out the back in his footy shorts and singlet, listening to the races. He'd played two Tests in the infamous 1932-33 series and as Australia's 12th man in Adelaide, was the inadvertent informant when news leaked of Bill Woodfull's angry dismissal of the MCC's tour manager PF 'Plum' Warner from the dressing rooms in mid-Test. 'I don't want to see you Mr Warner,' Woodfull began. 'There are two teams out there; one is trying to play cricket and the other is not. The matter is in your hands, Mr Warner, and I have nothing further to say to you. Good afternoon.' Warner left in tears.

O'Brien rejoined his teammates in the viewing area. 'Woody is in a bad way,' he said, before relating word-for-word his conversation with England's 'Mr Cricket'. Woodfull's comments were shared with a pressman and remain among the most famous Ashes quotes of them all.

I was in my third season as the magazine's editor. Our circulation was strong and knowing the great Bill Ponsford was about to turn 80, I asked Leo, one of his oldest mates, if Ponny would care to be interviewed. He was the only Australian to twice amass scores of 400-plus. He'd made 100s in each of his first two Tests and a double century in his last. If the boy wonder Bradman hadn't emerged, he'd would be feted as the ultimate run-making Colossus. He'd averaged 136 in one Sheffield Shield season and 152 the next. 'Do you think you could put in a good word for me Leo?' I asked, 'and see if Ponny would talk to me.'

'Ken,' he said, 'you've got no chance. I ring Bill once a week and can barely get a few words out of him. I don't reckon he would have done any sort of interview for 20 years.' I'd followed up with a phone call to Bill's son, Geoff, who thanked me for my interest, but his Dad was very private.

He was back in the care of his family and didn't follow the cricket much anymore. 'He wouldn't have done an interview in 25 years,' he said. 'But Ken I'll let him know that you called. Thank you again.' A week or so later, Geoff rang back. 'Dad will see you after-all Ken,' he said. 'Can you come on Monday after work?' Somehow my interview with an icon had been revived.

Having spent much of the weekend researching and re-reading Jack Fingleton's essay, The Champion who was Colour-blind, an ode to Ponny from his masterly *Masters of Cricket* – one of my old favourites from the Parkdale library days – I typed out my notes and formulated half a dozen questions. Partnered by a news photographer from *The Age*, John Hart, out we went to Glen Waverley. It was a cold winter's night and Mr Ponsford was rugged up in a large white polo jumper and grey woollen slacks. 'What would you like to know Ken?' he asked. To my dismay, within the first minutes, Mr Ponsford uttered just a 'yes' and a 'no' to all six of my typed questions. There were no detailed explanations, just one-word answers. Looking around the lounge-room, desperately trying to buy some time, I said: 'Mr Ponsford, you have been one of Australia's finest cricketers and sportsmen, but there's nothing here to show it... where's all your memorabilia and collectibles... your stumps and blazers?' There was a pause. 'Arr, stumps,' he finally said. 'I use them as tomato stakes. And the blazers... they've been keeping the dogs warm for years.' I burst out laughing; as did Geoff and old Bill. It broke the ice and my interview stretched into a second hour and made five pages of the October 1979 edition of the magazine.

As a 15-year-old in short pants, Ponny had been playing for the first time at St Kilda's Junction Oval against a representative finger spinner from Fitzroy named William Cannon. 'I couldn't hit it off the square,' he said, 'but he couldn't get me out.'

We talked of his phenomenal run feats and the season in which he'd made 1000 runs in just five hits before January 1, including the second quadruple century and highest score (437) of his remarkable career. 'Mr Ponsford,' I asked. 'You were Australia's outstanding runmaker of the 1920s, not Don Bradman. Why didn't you try and chase him?'

'I knew it was always hopeless to chase Bradman,' he said. 'He was ruthless… he had a second shot at me. The records were there to break.'

He baulked at only one question: Bodyline. 'I'm sorry you brought Bodyline up,' he said. 'It wasn't the game. It wasn't very pleasant with six and seven chaps around your body (close-in on the legside). You had to take it, get smacked, or get caught. Bradman tried to back cut them. I used to take the knocks.'

He played in only three of the Tests, his 85 amidst all the chaos in Adelaide an incredibly brave effort. Having toured England one last time with the 1934 Australians, he played only Saturday afternoon cricket, working Monday to Friday as a clerk in the MCC's membership department. He won the club's first XI batting average in five of the next seven years and still played socially after the War. Our interview remains one of my most memorable and I'm still close with all the Ponsford family, including Bill's granddaughter Megan, herself an author. The Melbourne Cricket Club named its Western Stand in old Bill's honour and when it was rebuilt, kept the name. At the re-launch, Billy Ponsford jnr approached and said, 'Ken, great to catch up. It doesn't seem like 20 years since you did that great interview with our Dad. He loved it. We all did… but Ken, you were so lucky to get it.'

'Yes I know, Billy,' I said. 'What happened?'

'It was your mate Leo, Leo O'Brien. He rang Dad every day for a week until he said "yes". ' Bless you Leo.

16

SCOOP OF A LIFETIME

'Grand Final day is the culmination of everyone's season and to have a role in reporting the joy of those who had been on the ground never loses its appeal.'

Premierships are for everyone. It was Grand Final day 1993. Kevin Sheedy's Essendon had just won the flag and there was immediate pandemonium in the rooms. It wasn't a boilover, but it was close. The Bombers were raw, but ready and saved their best match to last. Centreman Michael Long was unstoppable with his wizardry out of the centre and was a runaway winner of the Norm Smith. A young James Hird showed class way beyond his years. He was one of 12 under 25 years of age. I'd been given the Essendon rooms to cover and quickly spoke to four or five of the winners, including Paul Salmon and Tim Watson, then an elder statesman in his comeback year.

Salmon was surrounded by family: wife Jo, his two brothers Mark and Grant and proud parents Alan and Elizabeth. Minutes earlier Jo had been standing on her seat next to Gary O'Donnell's wife, Lisa. They were jumping up and down and hugging each other like excited schoolgirls at a George Michael concert. Metres away, the whole Watson clan, including Tim's wife Susie and their two eldest Billie and Jobe were also embracing. In the commotion, Tim had forgotten his promise to hoist eight-year-old Jobe onto his shoulders for the premiership lap of honor. 'He looked at me and looked at the premiership cup and went with the cup,' Jobe was to say.[69]

The Big Fish, impossible to miss at 208cm (6ft 10in) had been terrific all day – and all season. Tim was quieter by his own stellar standards, but he'd been instrumental a week earlier in helping the Bombers qualify for another playoff after one of the goals of the season at a crucial time in the preliminary final against the Crows. The Dons had come from seven goals behind, with Watson active in the late charge.

At the siren, all the journalists had been led around the boundary to the rooms. The crowd, especially the Essendon fans, were manic. They had pinched a premiership against the odds. I recognised an old field umpire from Beaumaris days. He'd given me six 15-yard penalties in a row, taking me from a half-back flank into the opposition's goalsquare because I dared question his decision... again and again. He was smiling and gave me the thumb's up.

Afterwards, as I raced out of the rooms onto the MCG to hurry back to the press box, Scot Palmer rang and asked how I'd gone. 'I've got three stories, maybe four,' I said.

'Great. We've got an early deadline. I'll put you straight onto a copytaker.'

---

[69] On SEN Radio, September 2019.

'Scotty,' I said. 'I need 10 minutes to unravel the quotes.'

'No time. Here's Susan...'

I delivered as required, speed reading my notes and dictating the stories as I walked.

All my stories were used, one leading page 3 of our lift out. The party continued at the Hilton and I duly filed a 10pm report. Grand Final day is the culmination of everyone's season and to have a role in reporting the joy of those who had been on the ground never loses its appeal. I covered more than 30 Grand Finals, including the two draws. Re-reading what I had dictated the previous day, I was pleased. The stories flowed with lots of colour and quotes.

Just a few years earlier, when Collingwood broke its premiership drought against Sheedy's Dons, Darren Millane was the hero, having played the entire final series with a broken thumb. Scotty and I arranged for him to share the story of his emotional September campaign in depth in the following weekend's *Sunday Press*. I duly went to his house in Noble Park around 10am on the Tuesday and he waltzed in soon afterwards, dressed only in footy shorts, a premiership boater and odd shoes. We had a hilarious two hours. As a kid, he'd been snubbed by Hawthorn but was a folk hero at Collingwood. He'd always been a mischief maker, one pre season bringing some lifelike foam bricks with him to one of Leigh Matthews' summer sessions. Paired with Tony Shaw, he was laughing and grinning and lifting the bricks like marshmallows. Suddenly he stopped and threw one straight at Shaw. 'Geezes Pants, what are you doing?' said Shaw, before realising the bricks were imitations.

In the 2008 Grand Final, which Hawthorn stole from Geelong, Stuart Dew was an unlikely hero, being decisive in the third quarter charge which denied the Cats back-to-back premierships. They had been beaten only once all year. Normally the barrel-chested Dew played in defence but this day was in the centre bombing the ball long to the electric Cyril Rioli.

Hawthorn had no right to still be in the match, so dominant was Geelong early. Three or four of us including AAP's Paul Gough, a Hawk for the day, were in the overflow area on the southern grandstand wing. I ran into my Beaumaris buddy Coo Cowen at half-time and I said: 'It doesn't look good mate.' 'But have a look at the scoreboard,' he said. 'There's only a few points in it.'

The Hawks kicked 10 of the last 15 goals after half-time to stun the Cats and steal the flag. I had the winner's rooms and marched in and bee-lined straight into Dew. 'With all respect Stewie,' I said. 'Weren't you meant to be at half-back? What were you doing forward of the centre?'

'I'd done my groin and was trying to get myself up forward,' he said. 'The ball just kept landing on my head. It was a fluke.' Again, golden, exciting quotes, capturing the moment.

SUSAN AND I WERE celebrating her birthday at The Rocks, one of our favourite restaurants in Mornington. It was a warm night and many were also seated outside, including a wide-shouldered, mid-20s gentleman in a bright blue XXL Hawaiian shirt. With his ultra-short crew cut and square jaw, he was immediately recogniseable. 'Is that Jacko (Mark Jackson) over there?' asked Susan.

'Yep,' I said. 'I reckon it is. I nodded to him – and him to me. Later, as we were waiting for the bill, I approached him and said g'day. 'Ken Piesse,' he said. 'I was trying to think if you were on my hit list.'

Jacko could be a firebrand and had more clubs than most, but he had a good heart. In his autobiography *Dumb Like a Fox*, released in 1986, he wrote of me:

> Ken Piesse (Sunday Observer): 'Burnt me a couple of times. When I've met him he's seemed like a fair bloke but he mightn't be a big wrap because I've worked for an opposition paper in the Sunday Press.'

Jacko had a love-hate relationship with so many journalists... and his fellow players. He was a larger-than-life character, impossible to miss in any crowd. Tony Jewell had sacked him halfway through a season at St Kilda as he wanted to rule the forward line his way rather than involve others like the goalsneak rover Silvio Foschini. 'Piss off, piss off,' he kept saying in that shrill voice of his. He wanted to be totally one-on-one with his full-back and not have anyone else in his vicinity.

His best media ally was Jon Anderson who wrote his book. Jonny had been a long-time mate of mine, too and I said so to Jacko at The Rocks. That immediately cleared the air and Susan and I ended up going up to Ringwood to see him one day. In his loungeroom was a huge larger-than-life portrait of himself.

Jacko had a quick fuse, especially if umpires didn't grant him the free kicks he believed he deserved. Once Glenn James ignored a shoulder-high tackle and called, 'Play on.' Jacko erupted saying he'd come and burn down his house. 'You can't,' said James. 'It's made of corrugated iron.'

Even Jacko had to smile at that.

MY BIGGEST EVER footy story in the *Sunday Herald Sun*, also came during a Grand Final week, in 2006. It was the front page of every News Limited Sunday paper in Australia. Years earlier I'd met big Darren Jolly at Melbourne's summer training at Trevor Barker Oval in Sandringham. Trevor had coached two premierships there in three years and ran the King Club in nearby Tulip Street. Darren was a big, gangly teenager newly recruited from Ballarat. He was on an exercise bike working out while the Demons trained. I introduced myself and I said: 'Darren, before you finish your career you are going to do thousands of miles on that bike. Big guys like you need all the leg work you can get.'

Jim Stynes was Melbourne's No.1 ruckman and Darren was to blossom at Sydney and then Collingwood, playing in premierships with both clubs. He thrived on the responsibility of being No.1 ruck and early into his time with the Swans, we did a feature story, talking about his bush beginnings, his love of the game and his goals and ambitions. It ran all editions.

Sydney won the 2005 premiership and were targeting another, having beaten Fremantle in the preliminary final on the Friday night at Sydney's Olympic Stadium.

I was in Sin City finishing my latest Cricket Summer Guide magazine and went to the match seeking a different angle to the dailies. The rooms were jampacked and all the daily journalists crammed into a small side room to capture the immediate quotes from Sydney's coach Paul Roos and its captain Barry Hall. I hung back and the media manager Steve Brassel, one of the best operators of all, asked if I'd like to talk to a player instead. 'Yes please. I'm filing for Sunday,' I said.

'What about big Jol? He was pretty good again tonight.'

'Sure,' I said. 'Love talking to the country boys.'

I shook Darren's hand warmly and congratulated him on being into another premiership play-off. 'You're going to need about 50 extra tickets this week. I reckon half of Ballarat will be wanting to come.'

'Yep,' he said. 'I do... but I'm not sure about Deanne...'

'Oh. Is everything ok?'

'Oh yes,' he said. 'It's just that she's due on Saturday. It's our first.'

'Wow. Next Saturday? Grand Final day?'

'Yep.'

'Wow. What are you going to do?'

'I'm going to be at the birth of our baby.'

'Have you told Roosy?'

'Nah, not yet. I was waiting to see what happened tonight.'

By then, Susan and I had five children with Bec's arrival, in 1993. 'I'm pretty expert in these sorts of things,' I said. 'Is she really showing the bubba way out front?'

'Sure is.'

'Arr, in that case it's sure to be a boy. They like hanging on. You'll be able to play Saturday and she can have the baby Sunday.'

I shook his hand and wished him all the best before looking back over my shoulder. No one was near us. It was an exclusive, the scoop of a lifetime.

It was well after 11pm. I dared not use my mobile phone just in case someone was listening. Instead, I went to an old red phone box – they still existed back then – and called my sports editor, Scotty's successor Glenn McFarlane. 'Mac,' I said. 'I think we've got the big one.'

I duly filed the story the next morning and a photographer took Darren and Deanne's picture. The heading on our frontpage story was: 'I'll put Baby before Grand Final.'

Little Scarlett, a girl, was induced on the following Friday night – and Darren got to play in the Grand Final, after-all. They lost but he was still a winner that weekend. So were we. Big-time.

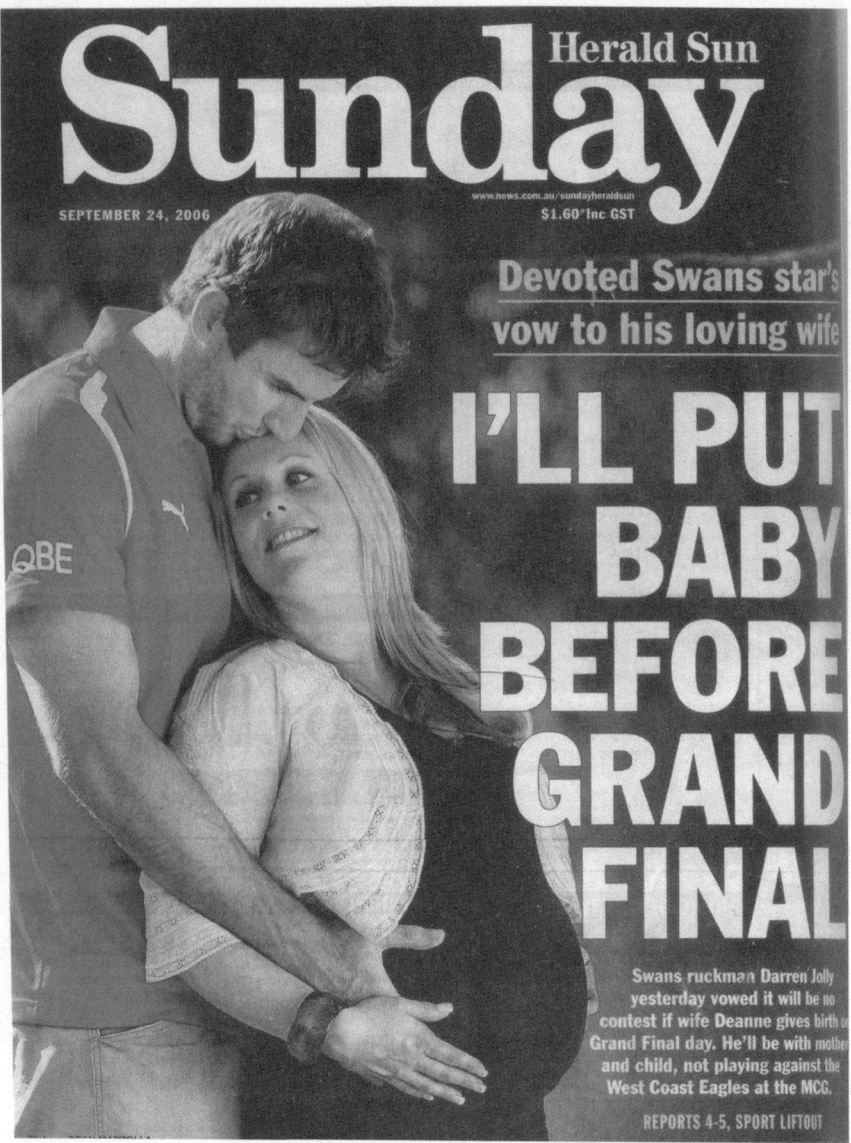

My biggest ever footy scoop made the front page of Melbourne's *Sunday Herald Sun* during Grand Final week 2006.

17

GHOSTING THE STARS

'Before sending him to the big House, Judge Greaves called Jenner a parasite and a pathological gambler who had offended again and again...'

When Paul Salmon first joined Hawthorn, famed coach John Kennedy snr thought he was coming purely for his superannuation. Five years later, aged 36, he was named in Hawthorn's Team of the Century[70] alongside some of football's most celebrated: Dunstall, Brereton, Knights, Scott, Matthews and Tuck. Few imports of any era were as dynamic or had more impact. He'd been a rucking understudy to Simon Madden at Essendon before his powerhouse years at Hawthorn where a champion became an icon. I organised a two-book deal for him with Bob Sessions at Penguin and on the release of the first, his autobiography *The Big Fish*, he inscribed my copy with a:

---

70 Salmon was the only player from another Victorian-based club to be selected in Hawthorn's Team of the Century.

> *'Master, without your enthusiasm, support and great faith, this would never have been possible. Thanks mate… for everything!'*

We'd see each other weekly for his column. No one changed offices more often. He was determined to be a force in business, too. From Kew to Queens Road and Victoria Parade, we'd meet, talk footy and family and chat about Hawthorn's next opponents. The Hawks were set to play an in-form North Melbourne, on its way to the Centenary Year premiership. Corey McKernan had been monstering opposition ruckmen all year at the centre bounces, jumping into them early and belting the ball forward and running on to be an additional marking target beside the King, Wayne Carey. He'd rucked for Victoria earlier in the year, was dangerous on the break and in stunning, career-best form.

'If they stopped the Brownlow now Fish,' I said, 'McKernan would win it hands down. I don't know what you can do, mate… but somehow, you have to come up with a strategy, something different to combat him. Otherwise, you'll just become his latest step ladder.'

We did a segment for his book, maybe the one where he first met the love of his life Jo, a bouncy brunette who worked at the gymnasium Paul had just bought in the eastern suburbs. One of Paul's responsibilities at the gym was rosters and he made sure that Jo was on every shift with him. Now they have three wonderful kids, happily none as tall as Paul – though Lachie got close. It's expensive buying super-big furniture!

Come matchday, Paul and McKernan faced off, 20 yards apart, at the opening bounce. This was going to be a joust for the ages. Run-ups were allowed then and McKernan's rivalled Michael Holding's. He was intent on establishing an immediate superiority, jump as high as he could into Paul before sprinting forward. It was a perfect centre bounce, high and straight – may this institution long be maintained. McKernan made his trademark early leap, straight at Paul and at the last instant, Paul baulked and instead of being able to use his body as extra leverage, McKernan jumped into thin air and fell flat on his face. Paul took the ball one-out and punted it forward. It was the first of his 22 centre clearances, which must be some kind of record, especially for a ruckman. Soon afterwards at a boundary throw-in, they again faced off before McKernan sprinted for North's goal square. Rather than following him, Paul raced towards his own goals, hoping *he* could be an extra marking target. McKernan stopped, did a '180' and belted after Paul to pick him up. 'I knew I had him then and there,' said Salmon. At 34, he wasn't an athletic match for McKernan yet was able to use his footy smarts and frame and dominate. He went within three votes of the Brownlow Medal that year and was to maintain his momentum across all five seasons. Few have played a stronger first 100 games – and 'Kanga' Kennedy, the legend's legend, congratulated him warmly at the club's Team of the Century celebrations. With so many departed stars, Salmon had helped give Hawthorn renewed mettle when many were expecting the club to slide.

Paul's autobiography is one of almost a dozen football and cricket titles I have ghosted, alongside books written on behalf of Jason Dunstall, Dermott Brereton, Tony Lockett, Tony Liberatore, Johnny Platten, Robert DiPierdomenico and cricketers Max Walker, Terry Jenner and Brad Hodge.

Plugger's memoir was published by Pan Macmillan. I was photostating two copies of the deluxe manuscript, one for Tony and the other for his manager Robert Hession. 'What are you doing?' said Hession. 'Tony's not going to read his book.' Only one line was changed in the entire 50,000-word manuscript. Instead of Tony's last book read being 'Chopper Read rides again' we made it 'The Greg Norman Story'. 'Much more family orientated,' said Hesh.

I'd visit Tony at his Devon Meadows farm and we'd spend an hour polishing and embellishing the script. One time there was no answer when I knocked on his front door, so I went around the back and down to his men's shed, home to his greyhounds. He had 13 or 14, all in work. 'Sorry,' he said. 'I lost track of the time. Geezes, where's Tiger?'

Luckily for me, Tiger, his security dog, was in his lock-up. Growling menacingly as we walked past, he had a head only a mother would love. 'It's your lucky day,' said Tony. 'If he'd been loose, he would have gorn ya.'

He introduced me to each of the greyhounds, all incredibly gentle dogs. Each of them had a pet name. He was so animated and loving towards them all. 'This is Jimmy,' he said. 'He's just about my best. Certainly the smartest.'

That back shed of Tony's was his haven, where he could be anonymous, away from the pressures of being League football's biggest name. He had implicit faith in his dogs; not so humans.

During one of his suspensions, I visited on a Saturday and three or four of us had a few beers with sausages in bread and a heap of mustard. 'If only Huddo could see me now!' he joked. Peter Hudson was one of those closest to him at St Kilda, a guide and key mentor in keeping him focussed. Every now and again Tony liked to be himself, have six beers, maybe more, and party with those he trusted.

Trevor Barker launched the book at St Kilda's Social Club at Moorabbin, telling stories of Tony's first reluctant years in the Big Smoke. 'He was shy as,' Barker said. 'Still is. Back then we trained only on Tuesdays and Thursdays and he was forever hightailing it back home (to Ballarat). I'd bring him to the King Club and he'd sit behind the counter, eyes down, hardly saying a word. One of our regulars, a married lady, started to bring in some extra cooking for him, casseroles mainly and always in these same-sized plastic containers. Tony would always thank her sincerely. One day I had to put my car into Straitway Motors up on

IN MY LIBRARY: As Mark Twain once said, 'Find a job you enjoy doing and you'll never have to work a day in your life.'

SPORTS-MAD: At 26 Deauville St. Beaumaris with Mum, Annie, Geoff, Jim (front) and Jinx.

FIRST RUCK (Right): I always played in the ruck, at Beaumaris state (Dalgetty Rd), Bowie high and with the Sharks. We figured in three Grand Finals in my 100-plus games and we won them all, including one in 1972 at Moorabbin, home of St Kilda FC.

Seven of our lads later played in the VFA: captain Ken Ansell, big Jake, Ross Ellwood, Spider Kennedy, Marty Lyons, Micky Mac and Kenny Robbo. Marty also played League football, as did his son Jarryd.

ST. KILDA F.C.

UNDER 17 — **1972**

LIGHTNING PREMIERSHIP

JUNIOR CLUBS
Won by BEAUMARIS F.C.

K. ANSELL capt.   P. CORNFORD
D. CONNELL   P. CRAVEN
P. CUMING   R. ELLWOOD
M. HALL   T. HOPE
S. JACOBSEN   S. KENNEDY
I. LETCHER
M. LYONS
P. MARSH
P. McLEOD
M. McNICHOLAS
K. PEISSE
C. POWELL
K. ROBINSON
C. SCOTT
M. WARR

ASS. COACH
A. SHELDRAKE

MANAGER
J. SPOTSWOOD

COACH
E. KING

JUNIOR CRICKET: We won the Under 14s Federal District grannie against Mentone at Cheltenham. I carried my bat for 65. At 21 I captained the first XI alongside coach Kevin Graves, the fastest bowler in bayside cricket. Above: One of the boys in our second matting team Graham Brown nicknamed me 'Mantis' because of my long arms, taking catches they reckoned no one else could reach. Back row, from left: me, Graham, Billy Quaife snr, Kevin Maguire, Phil Goldsworthy, Tony Noel, Ken Stephen. Front: my best teenage mates Col Gooch and Coo Cowen, Dave Golden and Graham Standish.

WORKING FOR A LIVING: (Right): With David Gower, Bobby Simpson and Greg Chappell. (Far right): In Bowie blue and gold, having a kick at Como Park with Sheeds and Mike Sheahan. Our news editor at *The Age* Geoff Barker is scouting.

SOME FAVOURITE MOMENTS: Piggybacking big Mick Nolan in Adelaide, golfing at fabulous Royal Melbourne and on the morning of an MCG Test with everyone's favourite umpire, David Shepherd.

LATE '80s (Right): With Paul Reiffel at Lord's, with little Jessie at Eastcote, playing in the Twenty20 final for Port Melbourne against Jaffa Cosier's Saints (JB Walker is in the background) and interviewing champion Hawk Gary Buckenara after the 1986 preliminary final at 'Arctic Park'.

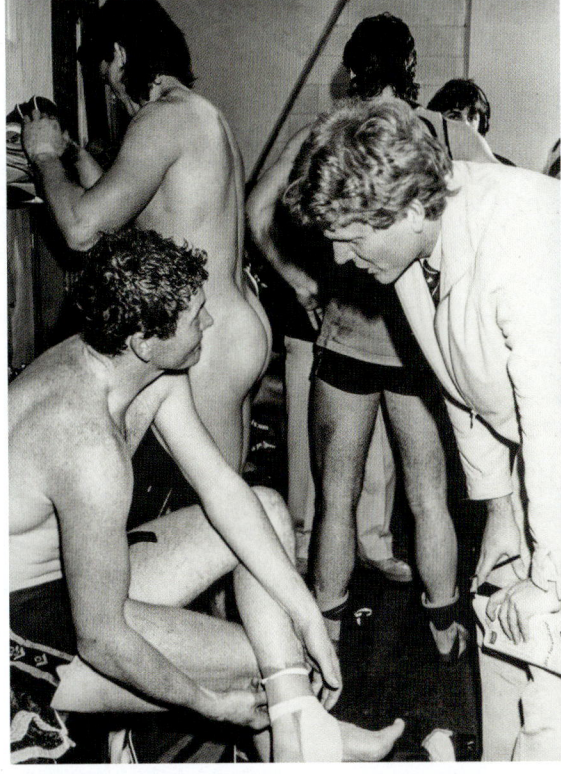

AN UNEXPECTED AWARD: (Top left): With Cricket Victoria's Jack Edwards and Geelong's Justin Miller after we tied for the Ryder Medal for the third XI in 1996-97. (Top right): Bowling at the 'G in the Prime Minister's XI match. Bob Hawke doesn't seem too keen to get up my end. (Above): With Trevor Barker and Tony Lockett at the launch of *Plugger*.

MY SECOND HAT-TRICK: (Top): I dismissed Gippsland Over 60s trio Fred Debono, Rob Bachetti (No.8) and Barrie Nunn with consecutive deliveries at Elsternwick No.2 one Sunday. The keeper is Marino Bovo. (Above): Port Melbourne premiers, one of the greatest thrills of all. We are mates for life: Back row, left to right: Gary Phillips, Peter Vesty (scorer), Lew Coyle. Me, Stretch, Beva, Sheck, Luigi. Front: Nuff, Bunk, Arms, Bobby Allen, Fab, Crock, Dusch and Teddy (12th man).

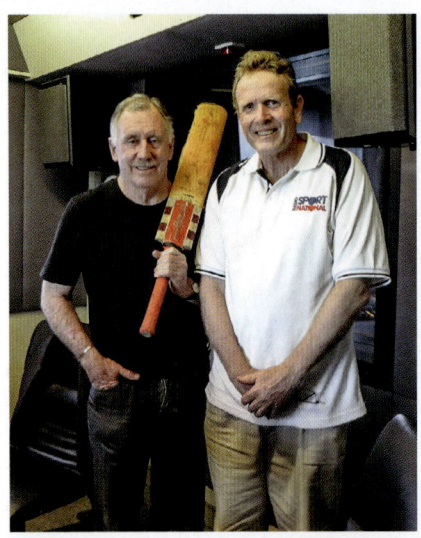

HIGH SOCIETY: With Ian Chappell, rising sta[r] Sophie Molineux and Sir Geoffrey Boycott. Below left: Susan and I at Newlands in 2018 when I had one of my best years of cricket a[t] club and Australian Cricket Society level.

A SPECIAL FAMILY PHOTO: James and I are outnumbered by all the girls, from left: Ever-mischievous Tori, Jess, Bec, Min, Susan and Alzina. James should have been holding the guitar. He can play… I can't. Top: At Somers with Bec and Jack.

CO-HOSTS: Susan and I hosted 10 overseas tours. They were all memorable, particularly the Windies (1999) and South Africa (2018). We had the Monday off after the 'sandpaper Test' in Newlands and ventured south west to the Cape of Good Hope.
Our tour group, from left: Allan Clarke, Graham Lockwood, Susan, Graham Brown, Nan Entink, Wayne Ross, Pam Bishop, Kathy Clarkson, Gail Ring, Cooky (at back), Rhonda Ross, Mary-Lou Beames, Mike Rose, Roger Williams, David Beames and me. Drew and Johnny C were AWOL.

CANBERRA WINNERS: Was proud to be a part of Victoria's third XI which won the Over 60s title in Canberra in 2017-18. We defeated Ewen Chatfield's New Zealand in the final.
Back row, left to right: Ian Dinsdale, John Porter, Gordon Cowling, John Wilson, Peter Ridgwell, me, Peter Neville. Front: Dave Leach, Ian Rowlands, Noel Sharpe, Ian Gibson (captain) and Steve Siggers.

ON TOUR: Fun in Cardiff 2009; the gear we arranged to assist Vanuatu cricket; with Susan in Bali; and with grandson No.1 Orion back home on the Peninsula.

2024 OVER 60s STATE CHAMPIONS: Pictured at Windridge Oval, Rochester, our Australian Cricket Society lads won three of our four games, including the final against Sunbury-Macedon Ranges. Our team, back row, left to right: Peter Robinson, Paul Morrey (captain), Jeff 'Junior' Scotland, Will Johnston, Jude Rose. Middle: Andrew Chisholm, Mark Dunstan, Neil Smith, David Long. Front: Peter Glenton, Keith Jansz, Tim Corney, John Flynn and me.

MEMORABLE MOUNTIES: My 6-19 day for the third XI against Baden Powell at Wooralla Drive in 2022. We won 99 to 97 in the closest match of my career: Back row, left to right: Joe, me, Hollywood, Foxy, Coina, Prez (Wayne Hicks). Front: Breeny, Frank, Skipper Phil and Bernie Cooper. Bergs left early. Coina took my wicket No.5 a backward square leg having told me, 30 seconds earlier: 'The ball isn't going to come here.'

COMPETING: (Top): Working on my flatter leggie on the Pacific Adventure. (Bottom): With Mocca Dunstan after winning the qualifying final against Geelong at Windridge Reserve, Rochester in 2024. Mocc almost tonked one into the Murray that day.

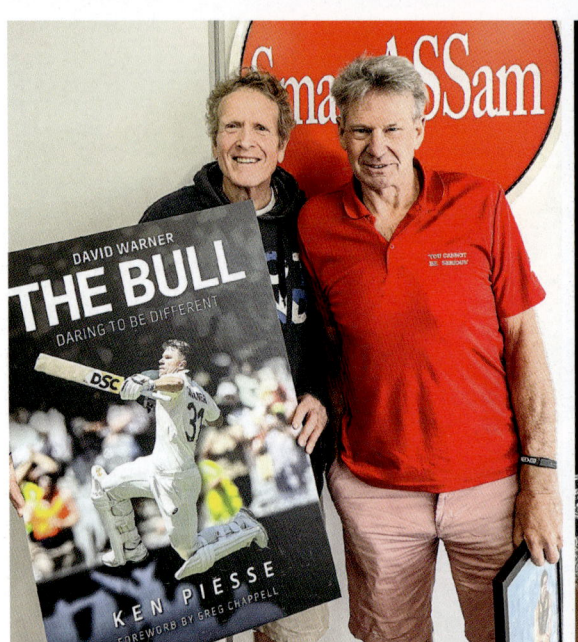

ONE OF THE GREAT DAYS (Above): With Mum on her 100th, the best innings of all.
(Top): With Sam Newman after our controversial 'x' rated late 2023 podcast and on the Pacific Explorer with Susan. Happily, she says she will stay with me while we are still cruising…

the highway for a service and Tony was driving me around. We stopped off to pick up his boots and I got out of the car, next to his garage. There was this unbelievable stench coming from inside. "What's that Plugger?" I asked.

'He opened the roller door and there were all these food containers, all the casseroles, neatly stacked up, all uneaten. He hated casseroles but hadn't wanted to disappoint the lady.'

During one of our tapings for Tony Liberatore's book, his boy Tom, then six and now a Bulldog's champion, was playing corridor footy with a balloon, complete with the full commentary, Rex Hunt-style. 'Big Scotty Wynd goes up. What a game he's having,' Tom called. 'He knocks it to Romero, onto little Libba, on his own again and down the throat of Grant it goes... YESSS! Another shot at goal for the boy from Daylesford... the Doggies are on fire today.'

'Tom, Tom,' said Libba. 'Can you tone it down a bit. We're talking here.'

'Sure Dad,' he said. 'It's almost orange time.'

YEARS AGO, one of Melbourne's finest journalists Alan Trengove was commissioned to write Keith Stackpole's autobiography. He was very pleased with the first 30 or 40 pages, before realising that *he* was telling the story and not Stacky. He threw the originals in the bin and went back to his tapes.

One of my first football books, *Blues, Blinders & Ballbursters* was published by Pan Macs in 1991. It featured direct contributions from the biggest names in the game: Brereton, Salmon, Gary Pert, Kevin Sheedy, Garry Lyon, Gerard Healy and Stephen Kernahan, the star Blueboy. I rang Steve to check he'd received it and he said, 'Mate. It's very nice, but it's just not me.' I started all over again.

Pan Macs asked me to do several more books, including *Hooked on Cricket*, with Max Walker and *Hooked on Football*, with Brereton. One of the sub-editors rang one day and said, 'Wow, they are completely different.' That was a nice compliment. I'd been doing my job.

I was on my way home from cricket up north one Saturday night and stopped in at Johnny Platten's mansion on a hill in Donvale. He'd left school at 15, various teachers admonishing him for being 'easily distracted', 'lacking dedication', 'immature' and 'making no effort.' He was a footballer first and foremost and according to Allan Jeans who wrote the foreword to his book *The Rat*, 'pound for pound, he's as good as anyone I have coached.'[71] That night the whole Platten family were sitting around the table for dinner, their Saturday night speciality: fish fingers with tomato sauce. 'We put tomato sauce on everything,' said John. 'The more the better.' That night at home I told Jessie, then 11 and a great Platten fan, that her hero lathered tomato sauce on everything. The ice-cream tub was on the table and she helped herself and was just about to douse it in sauce when James stopped her. 'Think Dad was joking, Jessica,' he said.

JASON Dunstall's first night at Glenferrie Oval coincided with Hawthorn's annual summertime time trial. Four laps as fast as you can. After the first 400, he was 100 metres behind and was almost lapped by the end. He was unprepared and overweight. Hawthorn selector Normie Goss said: 'Who put up their hand for that bloke? The fat little fella at the back?' 'You're looking at him,' said coach Allan Jeans.

Dunstall was immediately dubbed 'Freddie Flintstone'. Later it became 'Bung' for his penny-bunger physique. Jeans had him running up ramps

---

71   *The Rat, a football braveheart*, John Platten with Ken Piesse (HarperCollins, Sydney, 1997)

at Sandringham Yacht Club, helping to fast track his fitness. Six times he was to kick 100 goals or more in a season. In 2024 he became the AFL's 32nd official Legend.

We co-authored a book, *The Goal King*, the rags to riches story of a young Queensland kid with all this puppyfat who was to become Hawthorn's most prolific goalkicker. Often, I'd trail down to Glenferrie Oval on a Wednesday night for some extra taping time and Dunstall would be there with his mate, club runner George Stone, doing repeat sessions of chin-ups and weight work. Stone would drill head-high flat punts from close range and Dunstall would mark effortlessly, always meeting the ball with outstretched hands. They'd finish with some goalkicking practice outside, Dunstall booming torpedo punts from 60 metres. I'd have to walk 20 metres towards him and scuttle low-trajectory punt kicks just to get the ball back to him. 'If you work hard enough, you improve,' was his motto. A fortnight after being held goal-less by Carlton's Bruce Doull, he kicked six against his hero in the 1986 Grand Final. 'That really kicked things off,' he said.

Very late one night on an end-of-season trip to Los Angeles, Dunstall and three of his premiership teammates had spent most of their cash and rather than paying the taxi fare, tried to do a runner. Producing a rifle, similar to one used by Chuck Connors in *Rifleman*, the driver hopped out of his car and yelled: 'FREEZE… or I'll shoot'. Jeans was called and hurried down to find the four miscreants sitting in a gutter with the taxi driver, still furious, guarding them. 'Sir,' said Jeans. 'I'll pay whatever you want. See those two fellas on the end, you can do what you like with them. But see the fat fella in the middle. That's my full forward. Please sir… don't shoot him.'

I WAS AT ARDEN Street, North Melbourne, in 1988, when a tall and tanned 16-year-old Wayne Carey walked into the office. Recruiter Greg

Miller had plucked him straight from school in Adelaide. To fill-in some time, Carey began to help me with some match-by-match details for a coming edition of *North News*, a job I'd inherited from Greg Hobbs. Denis Pagan, then coaching the Under 19s, came in and introduced himself. 'Pleased to meet you son,' he said. 'See you at training tonight. We're at Kensington.' Carey looked at him and smiled. 'Thanks Denis,' he said. 'I'm here to play ones.'

In the mid-'90s, I wrote Carey's column for *North News* and *Football Australia* and he was on the front cover of another book, *Football Skills and Secrets*. The Sydney-based publisher of 'Skills' had never heard of him. I assured him he was football's next superstar – and he was, warts and all.

His premature departure from Arden Street was tragic. He'd had a brief affair with Kelly Stevens, wife of one of his best mates, his vice-captain Anthony Stevens. It created enormous angst and still does now. It cost him Shinboner of the Century status.

Carey had been North's youngest-ever captain at 21. Everything revolved around him, on and off the field, 24/7. He'd decide where everyone was going for coffee, lunch or drinks. Having played Friday nights, he'd lead a group of six or seven to Sydney for weekends on the suds. They'd have 30 beers each, sometimes more. And do it all over again the next day before flying back for Monday morning training, Wayne sucking mints to mask his intake. He admits now that he was an alcoholic even then.

He wanted to be loyal to his lovely wife Sally but there were too many temptations. Like Warnie, he was in high demand. To squeals of delight, he once appeared in a club fashion fundraiser, on a catwalk dressed in just a pair of tight leather trousers. My pal Ken Rainsbury, our North News photographer, covered the event. They were page 1 pictures and I rang Wayne for his approval. 'Do you mind if you don't?' he asked. 'Sally won't like it.'

He drove down to Mount Eliza one day for a column and we sat in the back garden in our gazebo having a drink and some of Susan's banana bread. He was always delightful company and like Tony Lockett, totally loyal to his mates. He hated missing games and willed himself to get out onto the ground even if he was only half-fit. Often he'd war with the umpires over free kicks. Once in Sydney he invited an umpire out the back after the game. He wanted to punch him.

At his best and most focussed, he was unstoppable. When it was tight, coach Pagan would only have to eye-ball Wayne at a three-quarter time break; he knew the game was in his hands and invariably he'd lift.

Another of the game's modern day champions Tim Watson was moved onto him one day and Wayne made mincemeat of him. 'He was too big, too athletic and too good,' said Watson. Wayne's best was unmatchable, peerless, ahead of them all: Whitten, Skilton, Matthews, Ablett, Cripps, Danger... everyone.

Wayne and I met in Adelaide one day for a coffee and I outlined the five-figure sum a Melbourne publisher was prepared to pay for his autobiography. It was attractive money but Wayne was also on a mega-wage, the highest of any footballer at the time. Our window table was facing out into the street. It was a warm day and the pretty girls in summer dresses a constant distraction.

Once out of his football routine, his life became incredibly complicated. He couldn't go even a month without being involved in a headlining incident. He needed a full-time minder. There were too many excesses: girls, booze, drugs. A friend of mine, Charlie Happell, ended up writing his book for a rival publisher. It was the most honest and confronting life story I've ever read. Wayne and his family had run away from a violent drunk of a father when he was 13 before Miller discovered him by accident. He was blown away by Wayne's remarkable drive, athleticism and skill. Like Andre Agassi's autobiography *Open*, it was impossible to put down – and explained so much about why the ultimate footy star's life so imploded. I was closer to Wayne than any journalist, but Charlie did a brilliant job.

ANOTHER WHOSE life went pear-shaped after their career finished was Australia's Test cricketer No. 248, Terry Jenner. He was sentenced to six and a half years imprisonment after repeated embezzlements. Before sending him to the big House, Judge Greaves called Jenner a parasite and a pathological gambler who had offended again and again. He was to serve three years non-parole and no restitution. In jail, prison officers watched as he changed. 'You'll find out 'oo your fooking friends are now Jenner,' said one.[72]

Before going to court, Jenner wrote a confession to his employer saying he'd frittered $5000 in two hours at the Adelaide casino. He was an addict and didn't know how to stop. Deep down, he knew he had to go to prison.

Years later, I wrote his book *TJ Over the Top, Cricket, Prison & Warnie*, which went into multi editions. It was an emotional, roller-coasting journey of extremes. His marriage had broken up and access to his daughter was limited. Few of his mates visited. He was scum and believed it.

I spent a week with him in Glenelg. The first night, around midnight he broke down weeping. Years on, he was still ashamed. His partner Anne said: 'Terry, tell Ken exactly the way you told me. Don't leave anything out.'

---

72   *TJ Over the Top*, Terry Jenner with Ken Piesse (Information Australia, Melbourne, 1999)

The three 'jail' chapters we penned, 'Welcome to Hell', 'The Bongolong Hilton' and 'Paying the Price' were powerful and heartfelt, the most emotive in my lifetime of writing and publishing.

Once during recreation time, TJ was chatting with a fellow prisoner. 'Do you miss your wife?' he was asked. 'Yes,' said TJ. 'I hope it'll work itself out.'

'Gosh,' he said. 'I miss mine. And I know I'll never see her again.' He started blubbing like a baby. Turned out he had stabbed her with a kitchen knife and virtually cut off her head. It was all over the papers that week.

The prison system is designed to break your spirit, Jenner said. 'The tension was unbelievable. You had to learn to survive with people you had nothing in common with.' There were some hard cases at Yatala, including the rogue cop Colin Creed, one of Australia's most notorious criminals. One day Jenner walked into a gymnasium with him and afterwards a fellow prisoner tapped him on the shoulder, saying Creed was the worst kind, a low-life and he should distance himself from him at all times. 'Aren't we all equal here,' he said.

'Some of us are more equal than others.'

Jenner worked as a short-order cook, expert in creamy mashed potato, using lashings of butter. The 'lifers', the murderers and really mean ones demanded that their food be cooked exactly the way they wanted it – or there would be retribution.

TJ was a walk-up start as captain of the prison cricket team. 'No cricket team had a better record than our XI,' TJ told me. 'We had a murderer, a drug pusher, two embezzlers, a couple of bank robbers and a few who had tried to diddle social security.' When the bus arrived for a game at Waikerie one day, a member of the opposition asked Jenner if his team had a scorer.

'Yes Mum's here. She's got the afternoon tea too,' said Jenner before telling the fellow he'd score. 'What?' he said. 'You're in for embezzlement...'

'Mate,' said TJ. 'I can add up. I just forgot to bank it.'

He made one friend in prison, Frank, a fellow embezzler and they vowed when they were free to see Andrew Lloyd Webber's classic *Phantom of the Opera* in Melbourne. They went on the very day Frank's parole expired. Jenner so loved Phantom that he saw it seven times.

TJ was on parole when he first met Warnie, just returned from a youth tour of the West Indies. He had bleached white hair and an earring. They shook hands and Warnie looked him right in the eye. TJ liked that. 'Show us what you've got son?' he said as they walked down to the Adelaide No.2.

Without any warm-up, Warne delivered the most perfect leg-break Jenner had ever seen. It veered, hummed and spun big. 'Geezes fucking Christ,' Jenner said aloud. 'What have we got here? Tossing the ball back to Warne, he said: 'Must have hit a stone son. Try another.'

The next one turned even further. Jenner became his coach and 708 Test wickets later, Warnie is regarded as the Bradman of bowling, the Messiah, the greatest of them all.

Shane wrote the introduction to our book. He rated TJ as the best leg-spin coach who'd ever lived – 'with daylight second.'

'His involvement with me and with the others at the Cricket Academy was important in his own rehabilitation,' Warne wrote.

TJ and I had watched most of the opening Test from his Glenelg loungeroom, while we taped his memoirs. So comfortable were his leather recliners that it was easy to doze off. On the final morning, the Windies collapsed for an ignominious 51 in 20 overs and neither of us saw even one wicket 'live'. It was their lowest Test score and Brian Lara, the West Indian captain, was pilloried by the local press, inter-island jealousies rampant once again. Lara's double-century in the second, however, was lauded by the same pressmen and suddenly the series was all square at 1-1.

On publication day, I told Terry how proud I was of the book. I couldn't have written it any better. It was a quality hardback with a lovely dustjacket which soon went into reprint. In his inscription on my author's copy, he wrote:

> *'Dear Ken*
>
> *'I am pleased our book is the best of them all. Thank you for understanding me and my needs.*
>
> *'Kind regards,*
>
> *'TJ'*

TJ died young, at 66. He lived hard, still gambled, but only on the gee-gees. He shunned casinos but bought Lotto tickets. One of his columns for a suburban paper was funded by his local liquor shop. He liked being paid in spirits.

Once I was having trouble getting a leg-break past even our ageing practice captain at Frankston Peninsula and wrote to Terry for some advice. I was in my late-50s, but still keen to compete. Maybe I didn't have enough momentum at the crease? Maybe I wasn't spinning it hard enough? Could it be my follow through?'

Within 24 hours, TJ replied. 'Master,' he said, 'have you thought about retiring?'

18
NUGGET

'Oh Ken,' he said. 'I'm so glad you're here. Don Bradman ruined my life.'

My buddy Daryl Timms had just joined Truth as its sports editor. It was the start of the new Test summer, in Brisbane and Daryl rang me in the 'Gabba pressbox, looking for his star columnist, the iconic Keith Miller. 'Nah, Dazz, (he's) not here,' I said. 'But I'll go and look out the back.'

'Hurry, we're right on edition time and he hasn't filed yet.'

My phone rang again minutes later. 'Any luck?'

'Nah.'

'Geezes… I've got five minutes. There's a huge hole on the back page for his copy…'

'Do you want me to be Keith Miller?'

'Can you?'

'Sure.'

Timmsy put on a headset and in his best copytaker voice said: 'Daryl here. Go ahead please… and can you be hard-hitting and colourful?'

I dictated 300 lively Miller-like words, calling the touring Pakistanis a pack of clubbies and misfits and – borrowing a line from Geoff Boycott – said how Keith's dear departed grandmother could have played most of their bowlers with a stick of celery. Keith also asked why his favourite strokemaker Kim Hughes had been dropped to No.5 behind an out-of-form Allan Border and said the Australians couldn't afford to be complacent as they were about to run into a West Indian maelstrom. 'That's a big word for Keith,' said Daryl, laughing. 'He'll like that.'

Daryl and 'Keith' made the deadline, just and the next day, 'Nugget' rang, thanking me for bailing him out. 'That's the first time I've ever missed a deadline,' he said. 'The copy read well Ken. Nice and lively. Thanks again.'

Weeks earlier Keith had suggested that 'the young South Australian' Jeff Crowe could be in line for a Test promotion having made another Sheffield Shield century. I rang Daryl and said that Crowe was actually NZ-born and ineligible. 'Whoops,' he said.

Nugget and I had been mates for years. He had the enviable gift of remembering everyone's name and with Sir Donald Bradman preferring a more anonymous life, Nugget became the new face of the game, via TV, radio and his extravagant columns. After one Perth Test, we shared a taxi back to St Kilda and Keith's lady friend, Marie. 'You take it on from here Ken,' he said. 'Where are you going? Mt Eliza? No worries. I'll sign for it now.'

With his good looks and charisma, Nugget was the Errol Flynn of cricket with mates at every turn, from jockeys and strappers through to the Queen's younger sister, Princess Margaret. On his annual trips to Lord's, Miller would often take 45 minutes making his way from the Grace Gates around to John Paul Getty's private box. So many wanted to shake his hand and say hello. His columns were invariably provocative and if he was ever challenged by an aggrieved player, he'd say: 'You don't take any notice of that rubbish, do you?'

We'd have a cuppa or something stronger once a month at his house in Mornington, just off Main Street. He used a frame to get around his house. He'd fought cancer, arthritis and a stroke. Father Time has no heroes. One morning he rang, all excited. Michael Parkinson had been on the Andrew Denton show, *Enough Rope*.

'Were you watching the ABC last night Ken?' he began. 'Oh g'day Nug. No, I wasn't. Who was on?'

'My mate, Parky. He was being interviewed by Andrew Denton. And guess what Ken… out of all the actors, actresses and the most important and influential people of the world, guess who he said was his all-time hero?'

'I've got no idea Nug.'

'Mee,' he said. 'Mee, little ol' Nugget'.

He was in his early 80s and then in a wheelchair, but he was so animated, almost childlike.

Next time I saw him, maybe a week later, he was in tears. 'Oh Ken,' he said. 'I'm so glad you're here. Don Bradman ruined my life.'

'Hang on a minute Nug, I'll turn on my recorder… this could be good,' I joked.

'You know what I mean. I should have been captain and would have been but for Bradman.'

'Of course, Nug,' I said. 'You were the best player and the best leader – just like Warnie – but you weren't actually on the Don's Christmas card list were you? Remember that bouncer which almost cleaned him up in Sydney?'

'It just missed his ear didn't it?' he said.

'The Don was about to be knighted…'

'Hmm, yes,' Nugget said, nodding and half-smiling.

The pair's politics had never aligned. Miller loved and respected Bradman the cricketer but felt he was too intense and too obsessed about winning. For Miller, cricket was a leisure. For Bradman, it was a war.

In 1954-55, the conservative Ian Johnson was appointed Australia's new Test captain ahead of Miller and all these years later, Nugget was still hurting at being denied the ultimate honour. He reckoned Johnson was Bradman's golden child, a 'yes-man'.

Fellow-Invincible Sam Loxton had been fielding at mid-off that autumn-time Saturday in 1949 when Miller unleashed back-to-back bouncers at the Don. Sammy was horrified:[73]

> *'The Don hadn't picked up a bat in six months, maybe longer. He'd been talked into playing as it was an end-of-season testimonial for two of his old teammates (Bert Oldfield and Alan Kippax). Here he was back at the Sydney Cricket Ground where it all started. It was a Saturday, almost noon and 40,000 in. Everyone wanted him to make one last century.*
>
> *'Nugget was bowling and walked up to me and said: "The crowd's pretty quiet Sammy. I might try and wake 'em up a bit".*

---

73 *Cricketer* magazine, 1980-81

'Miller pranced in and pitched short. The Don rocked back onto his back foot and struck the ball with the speed of sound through mid-wicket. If a dog had got in the way he would have killed it. If the fence hadn't stopped it, it would have gone all the way to George Street. It was the most gorgeous shot... one I'll never ever forget.'

Even Miller stopped and applauded. At 40, the Don was still extraordinarily good. Miller walked back past Loxton again, this time going back a little further. 'Sammy, I think I'll give him another,' he said.

'No, no, no, Nug, you can't do that.' He knew Miller's faster bouncer could be lethal.

But it was too late. The anti-authoritarian Miller was already bounding in, this time with extra intensity. He pitched short again but it was two yards quicker than the first, close to 90mph (145km/h) and just as Bradman was raising his bat to repeat his pull shot, the ball flashed past his face.

The Don turned white and by now the crowd on the Hill were all their feet, booing Miller.

A week or two later Bradman was among the selection panel which omitted the charismatic, maverick allrounder from Australia's touring team to South Africa.[74]

Their friendship always teetered, Miller joining Bill O'Reilly and Jack Fingleton among those who regularly and fiercely questioned Bradman's selections and Board policies in newspapers and in a series of Miller's own books, co-written by another anti-Bradman man Dick Whitington in the '50s.

---

[74] Miller was to be reinstated on the eve of the first Test after Bill Johnston injured his knee in a car accident.

At Miller's funeral, John Bradman, Sir Donald's son, said the pair had enjoyed 'amicable relations'. But that wasn't even half right. It was more like a feud.

The Don had asked Miller to bowl quicker at one of his old Services' mates Bill Edrich during the 1948 tour. He bowled slower. 'The last thing Bill needed was to be flattened by a cricket ball,' he said. 'He'd had a serious war.' [75]

IN 1997, Miller's story was featured in *Wildmen of Cricket* which I co-authored with Brian Hansen, one of Miller's long-time media mates. Nugget rang, delighted about his entry. 'You even had the name of my sportsmaster at Elsternwick state (Mr RJ Gainey) in there,' he said. 'I'd forgotten his name.'

After his Ashes debut in 1946 – when he took nine wickets and made 79 – Nugget wrote to his old mentor[76], thanking him for his time and patience a decade and a half earlier. Mr Gainey had insisted that he would be a success. He had talent and he believed he would use it.

> 'Dear Mr Gainey,
>
> 'Perhaps I will be a stranger to you, but I am Keith Miller, the boy you encouraged at cricket at Elsternwick state school all those years ago.
>
> 'I always said that if I should one day represent Australia in cricket, I would write to you. That explains this letter. It was always in my mind that I would try and to do justice to the faith you once had in me… and that I'd prove your judgment true.

---

75 *Sporting Profiles, 60 Heroes of Sport*, Michael Parkinson (Pavilion Books Limited, London, 1995)
76 *Wildmen of Cricket*, Ken Piesse and Brian Hansen (Brian Hansen Publications, Moorabbin, Victoria, 1997)

'Thank you again.

'Yours sincerely,

'Keith Miller'

I told Nugget how his mate Hansen had written his chapter and wanted to know if he'd join us at the Emerald in South Melbourne to wet the baby's head. 'Arr,' said Nugget, 'A book launch. Who's coming?'

'A few of your old mates. Johnno (Ian Johnson) for one.'

'Count me out,' he said.

They'd almost come to blows in Bridgetown one evening in '55, after Johnson had denied Miller the new ball. 'Things got nasty,' Colin McDonald told me years later. 'Miller said he couldn't captain a tiddlywinks team. Johnson suggested they meet outside. Even though all the players had the highest possible regard for Miller, we all knew he was in the wrong. We immediately put a stop to the silly nonsense and the journalists covering the tour missed a bonanza.'[77]

One Saturday night on the 1956 tour, Johnson was in a dinner suit, ready to take the train to London. 'Gee you're' all dolled up,' said one of the young players. 'Where are you off to?'

'Dinner at No 10 Downing Street... with the Prime Minister.'

At the other end of the dressing room, his vice-captain Miller was also in bow tie. 'You going out too Nug?' asked one of the younger ones.

'Yes,' he said. 'Buckingham Palace. Princess Margaret awaits!'

When word about Nugget's latest fling drifted back to Sydney and his American-born wife Peg, she said: 'That's Keith for you. He has always had a way with the girls.'

---

77 *Taking Strike, the Colin McDonald Story, collector's edition*, Colin McDonald (cricketbooks.com.au, Mt Eliza, Melbourne, 2015)

19

DERMIE

'Gee the soup smells good Jean,' I said. 'Ken,' she said, laughing. 'That's for the dog…'

It was a tight, low-scoring game at Waverley and Hawthorn's coach Allan Jeans was at his stormiest. Calling for his runner George Stone, he said: 'Go and tell that blond ponce if he doesn't get a kick soon, he's coming straight off.'

Stone immediately ran towards Dermott Brereton. Seeing him approaching, Brereton hissed: 'If you wanna live, don't come near me.' He didn't have to be reminded that he wasn't having his best day. Stone kept running, straight past Brereton and delivered the message to Russell Morris, the other blond, also at half forward.

'What did he say? What did the Kid say?' asked Jeans.

'Not a word Yab. Not a word.'

With 10 premierships in his CV, five day and five night, few footballers are as decorated, or as loyal as Dermott. We play cricket against each other and one year when I turned an easy three into a hard run two, Dermie stopped the game and said, 'Fellas, with all respect Piessey… throw to Kenny's end.'

Dermie was a star on the field, volatile, menacing and good. He mowed through packs, warred with umpires and kicked amazing, athletic goals. Not all his decisions were good ones, but every team admired and wanted him when he was at his best.

We'd been mates since his teenage days at the VFL. Few are as engaging or as natural. His 21st at the Frankston Yacht Club was hilarious. His Dad, Dermott snr wore a bright pink singlet and Dermott a lime green one.

In *Inside Football* one day, I railed against the Coodabeen's songster Greg Champion calling Dermott a 'hood' as not everyone would know that Greg was joking. When a yobbo had a go at Dermie after a reserves match one day at Princes Park, I said the fella had got his just desserts.

Dermott and I wrote two books together. I'd 'ghost' his column in *Inside Football* and we'd often play nine holes of golf with his Dad on match eve, as part of his warm-up for Saturday.

On one cold winter's night, Susan and I were heading for our holiday house at Somers and stopped off on the way. The most aromatic sensations were coming from the kitchen. Dermott's Mum was cooking vegetable soup, croutons and all. 'Gee the soup smells good Jean,' I said.

'Ken,' she said, laughing. 'That's for the dog.' Jean was gentle, incredibly caring and spoke with an entrancing lilting Irish accent.

One night at Frankston CC, Dermott and I both had on dark sunglasses with flickering party lights. My kids were in the room and four-year-old Jessie grabbed Dermie around the calf, thinking he was me. 'Wrong one,' he laughed, picking her up like she was a snowflake.

Jessie loves dogs, the bigger the better and 'KD', Dermott's St. Bernard, towered over her. He was the gentlest of souls and had been named after Dermie's Frankston near-neighbour and Hawthorn teammate Kelvin David Moore: Dermie reckoned both were super slow. Dermott snr took the front seat out of the family's car so he could walk KD at Frankston beach.

All his footy mates still call Dermott 'the Kid'. Daryl Timms had asked to interview him after his five goals on his senior debut in a final. Coach Jeans declared him off limits, saying, 'The Kid is just a kid.'

Dermie drove me across to Cranbourne one day in his red Ferrari. It was a tight fit but it was fun. Jeans had always wanted him to ditch the fast car and buy an old reliable Holden with room to move. 'It'll be better for your back lad,' he said. Years earlier, Dermie and his young mates had been pinching golf balls and one golfer had whacked Dermott across the lower back with a four iron as he looked to escape over a fence.

Jeans worried about his star's off-field image. Could his headlining forward consider being less lairy and more conservative? 'What happens Dermie,' he asked, 'if you need to go and ask a bank manager for a home loan?'

'Yab,' said Dermott. 'I won't need to go and see a bank manager.'

Rarely would Dermott touch any of his footy monies – a substantial six figure sum from the mid '80s. Instead he'd rely on his earnings week-to-week from his panel beating business in South Melbourne.

He'd been a crack footballer, a champion in any Hall of Fame setting, only for injury to slow him down in his final years.

From his mid-20s, he had an eye on TV and Ernie Sigley became a friend and mentor. Dermott would sit on the side, off camera, watching and learning from one of Melbourne's very best interviewers and show business personalities. Now he's the consummate media professional. And a friend for life.

20
LEARNING TO LISTEN

'Asked about his Bradmanesque average, big Bill smiled broadly and said, "You know Ken. I did bat at No.4 for Beeac High."'

I love the story of WH Moule, the Victorian County Court judge, who was semi-snoozing through a case about a Ballarat man accused of a petty crime. He was innocent, but his memory for detail was poor. During a break, rising young barrister Robert Menzies asked about the man's interests: roses, chooks, maybe sport? 'Oh yes,' said the man. 'I played against Ivo Bligh's (English) team in 1882…'

Menzies stepped back into the court room and within minutes shared the story of the great cricket match, Twenty of Ballarat v All-England. The elderly Judge suddenly bubbled with excitement and delight. Leaning forward in his grand chair, he asked the defendant, 'Did you play? Were you a batsman or a bowler? Did you make any?' The gent was soon acquitted. Menzies knew his Judge. Bill Moule had played in the very first Test match in England.

Every sportsman has a story. And if you happen to have played cricket or football, no matter the level, I'll ask when and where. Graham Perkin had always championed the most inquisitive. One day I visited the gynaecologist George Thoms at his home in the west. Like Judge Moule, he'd also played a single Test for Australia, opening up with his Melbourne University and state partner Colin McDonald. His cricketing mates reckoned that George had the best job in the world and called him 'Dr Gyno'. George was in mid-story when suddenly he stopped. 'You're a very good listener Ken,' he said.

'I'm just loving your stories George. Please do keep going…'

The opportunity to engage so many Test cricketers – past, present and future – in Australia and beyond for feature stories and comment in my cricket magazines every year since 1978 has been a blessing. From Bill Ponsford and Bill O'Reilly to Keith Miller, Greg Chappell and Steve Waugh, I've been fortunate to have met and befriended some of cricket's most celebrated. Greg and I share the same early August birthday and regularly correspond. He agreed to contribute the foreword to *The Bull*, my 2023 biography of David Warner, before seeing even one word of the manuscript. Greg had been one of the few mentors Warner respected and embraced during his exasperating early years of non-selections when most regarded him purely as a white-ball slogger. Greg had always backed him. 'I lost count of the phone calls I made to "Tabbsy" (Brian Taber, NSW's selection chairman), pleading with him to pick him,' Greg said. 'I thought he could be outstanding across all three formats – and he was. He's not everyone's cup of tea of course; he's a buzzer, he's in your face; but he's also an outstanding talent.'

Chappell had been a virtuoso as a batsman and slip fielder. Most eastern States viewers missed seeing him reach his century on debut in Perth in 1970 as the ABC switched to its normal 7pm Sunday night news bulletin in Melbourne and Sydney.

Ian Chappell became an even finer player with Greg's emergence. He wanted to keep up with his younger brother. Ironically, Greg's finest tour, in the autumn of 1979 when he made three 100s in a row for the World Series Australians in the Caribbean, is not part of his official record. He made more than 600 runs across five Supertests at an average of almost 70 against the likes of Holding, Roberts, Croft and Garner. Like Neil Harvey in 1950, Bradman in 1930 and Ponsford in 1927, he was at his absolute zenith. He never expected to fail.

Once, in some cross-correspondence, Greg referred to me as a 'cricket nuffie'.

'Is that a South Australian term, Greg?' I asked.

'No offence meant, Ken,' he immediately replied.

I was privileged to witness so many of Greg's finest moments – as well as his worst: Black Sunday in Melbourne when he ordered his younger brother Trevor to finish a match with an underarm. Like Steven Smith in Cape Town in 2018, Greg that day was unfit to be Australia's captain.

Watching from the viewing area, the Australian Cricket Board's Bob Parish answered the nearby phone. It was Sir Donald Bradman, watching from his lounge room in Adelaide. He was beside himself. Sam Loxton walked down the stairs to the Australian rooms in tears. 'Helluva way to win a cricket match fellas,' he said.

SPORTSMEN LOVE TO TALK and there are few important ones I have missed over the years. Even Parky wasn't able to get close to Sir

Donald Bradman, but I did. I have almost a dozen letters from the Don, including one where he answered staccato style my query about Clarrie Grimmett's controversial exclusion from the 1938 Ashes tour. 'In regards to Grimmett,' Bradman wrote, 'he was finished. Yours sincerely, Don Bradman.' Years earlier the Don had edited my manuscript for a school-age biography, entitled *Famous Australians: Donald Bradman*. I still treasure his notes and hand-written suggestions. His son John attended the launch of my centenary book in his father's honour.

Having given a lifetime to the game, the Don retreated from public gaze and refused most interviews. On Friday mornings, however, he'd drive to the Adelaide Oval to sign a stack of books, photographs and memorabilia, all neatly arranged in chief executive Barry Gibbs' anteroom.

Greg Chappell was coaching South Australia's Sheffield Shield team and would regularly wave and say hello to the Don. As a young, emerging batsman in Adelaide, Chappell had been advised by Bradman to change his batting grip and his offside play had immediately flourished. Chappell had enormous respect and admiration for the Don.

'Generally, we both went our separate ways,' Chappell said, 'but this day I sensed he was wanting to chat, so I stopped and asked him some questions, from the secrets of his preparation through to World Series Cricket and why he had been so rigid in his opposition. "When sport becomes a business Greg," he said, "it loses something."' The Don hated the integrity of the game being eroded. Bradman wasn't everybody's favourite off the field, but few have the full package. Look at Warnie, Boycott and Cronje in cricket and Ablett snr. and Carey in AFL.

Most of the Don's 1948 immortals were champions on and off the field. Among the warmest was Colac country boy Bill Johnston. The War had delayed his entry into the international arena. 'Big Bill', gangly and double-jointed, considered himself a finger spinner, first and foremost, but cricket's telegraph is powerful. One practice night at Old Scotch, now the site of the Rod Laver Arena, a hop, step and jump across Brunton Avenue to the MCG, he'd taken a longer run and whizzed a bouncer straight past the nose of 50-year-old Jack Ryder, known to everyone as 'The King'. No-one was as influential in Victorian cricket circles. He'd been Bradman's first Test captain and remained among his closest contacts. Bradman was chatting to Johnston soon after the War and asked him about *that* ball, years earlier to Ryder. 'Oh, I was just mucking around,' said Johnston. 'Just letting off a bit of steam. I like (bowling) spinners the best.'

Bradman told Johnston Australia had a surfeit of slow bowlers but lacked pacemen, especially quality left-armers. An Ashes tour approached. He could be part of it – bowling fast.

Paired with Ray Lindwall and Keith Miller, Johnston was to form the most potent Ashes new ball trio of all, taking 27 wickets as Australia won four of the five 1948 Tests, the team undefeated all summer. On his next English visit, the 1953 Coronation Year tour, Johnston was thrilled to average 100-plus – an extraordinary effort for a No.11. His tour aggregate was 102 runs for once out. He batted 17 times with 16 not outs. Asked about his Bradmanesque average, big Bill smiled broadly and said, 'You know Ken, I did bat at No.4 for Beeac High.'

That '53 Coronation Year tour was the happiest of all, Keith Miller's all time favourite, the friendships unwavering and the fun unlimited. It was still the era of ship travel and Miller reckoned every night was like New Year's Eve.

Another of the Invincibles was Sam Loxton, a fabulous character who I'd known since I was 16 in my first year at his club Prahran. His Dad, Sam snr, had an electrical shop in nearby High Street, directly across the road from the Bush Inn (now Hawksburn Hotel). Young Sam debuted in the thirds as a 12-year-old and even then was better than most of the men. He was the club's first Test player and juggled the duties of being chairman of selectors with his role as Australian selector. Five or six of us would gather as he demonstrated a cover drive. His bat would always finish over his left shoulder like his hero, Don Bradman. Dav Whatmore was easily the best of us and at 17 already a superb player with rare balance. He was good enough to play in the first XI immediately, alongside our captain, the dashing international Duncan Sharpe. But Sam wanted him to excel in the thirds and kept him there until the final weeks of the summer, building his confidence for the challenges ahead. Dav became Prahran's most prolific batsman, a 100-game Victorian player and represented Australia in seven Tests during the years of Kerry Packer's World Series. In 1996 he coached the mighty minnows Sri Lanka to the World Cup and is still coaching at elite teenage level now.

Sam had been the last player chosen on the '48 tour. It was the highpoint of his wonderful and varied life, which included three marriages and two decades as the Liberal Government's Chief Whip. Sir Henry Bolte, Victoria's premier for 17 years, was his long-time boss. Sam called him 'Curly'… Sir Henry had little hair. On their initial meeting, Bolte told Loxton he'd just be making up the numbers as the next election was only weeks away. 'Sir,' said Sam. 'I don't go into anything to run second.'[78]

I introduced Sam to our third XI lads at tea-time one day at Frankston and he went overtime, still chatting as the umpires and the two not out batsmen patiently waited for us to reappear.

In 1948, the man Sam was competing against, Queenslander Len Johnson, took six Test wickets on the very day the touring side was

---

78   *Invincible, the Life & Times of Sam Loxton* (cricketbooks.com.au, Mt Eliza, Melbourne, 2020)

announced, but it was too late. The final XVII had been decided the previous night and was released immediately the Test finished. Sam was the superior batsman and fielder but Johnson the finer bowler. He, too, was destined to play just the one Test.

Another of my old buddies was Bill Brown in Brisbane. He penned a foreword for my book *The Waugh Zone* and we were forever chatting. The day after one golden morning of reminiscing, I rang Bill to thank him for his time and congratulate his wife Barbara on the quality of her freshly cut cucumber sandwiches. 'Ken Piesse,' exclaimed Bill. 'I know you. Do I owe you money!'

THERE ARE FEW like me who eat, breath and sleep cricket 24 hours a day – and that's according to Ricky Ponting in a foreword to another of my books *Favourite Cricket Yarns*. Ricky was not only an illustrious batsman, right up there with Neil Harvey, Greg Chappell and Steve Smith, he's the game's leading commentator, invariably an over or two ahead of the game.

As a 16-year-old, he'd first attended the Australian Cricket Academy in Adelaide. Head coach Rod Marsh had never seen such an accomplished teen. Rod's party trick during Week 1 was to have all the new scholars kit up, helmets and all and in turn, face bouncers from the bowling machines turned up to speeds of 90mph and more (upwards of 150kmh). No one matched Ponting's signature pull shot. He simply smashed the ball into the side netting.

Ricky has been patron of the Australian Cricket Society for more than a decade. We backed his charity the Ponting Foundation, caring for families of kids with cancer. In 2013, we hosted the Melbourne launch of his book *Close of Play* and as a backdrop had extended film of his very first Test innings, against the Sri Lankans in bouncy Perth, when he made 96 before unluckily being given out lbw when hit on his hip. Immediately recognising the moment, he looked away from the screen in disgust. 'I don't need to watch that again,' he said. 'No way that was out.'

Ponting is among cricket's most passionate and caring ambassadors. Steve Waugh is another. No-one was prouder or hungrier to wear the baggy green. His 199 at Bridgetown in 1999 is etched in my memory, especially considering he played and missed 19 times at Curtly Ambrose and Courtney Walsh on a Kensington greentop in his first hour or two at the crease. He almost ran out to bat that day, so keen was he to influence the match after early wickets. Colleague Malcolm Knox and I were among just three writers to quiz him immediately afterwards in the rooms. 'Steve, with all respect,' I started, 'you must have played and missed a dozen times early...'

'I counted 19,' he said, smiling.

Whenever we meet, the 32 runs he took from one of my overs of extravagantly flung leggies at Royal Ascot in 1987 is invariably soon tabled. Paul Jackson was bowling at the other end and said the ball came back all disfigured with tram tickets on it.

My leggies, however, did once claim David Hookes caught on the far fence at the Melbourne Cricket Ground. But, in Hooksey's defence, the old Southern Grandstand had been flattened and I was bowling with the wind directly behind me. His towering grandstand-high hit was heading into the worker's smoko shed before it dropped like a nine-iron into the hands of my outrider, Cricket Australia's David Richards, at long-on. 'Hookes, caught Richards, bowled Piesse. What a moment. Well done Master,' he later wrote on the title page of his autobiography *'Hookesy.'*

Had he been hitting *with* the wind, it would have ended in the second tier – like one of Greg Matthews' off-breaks smashed back over his head by Victoria's Simon O'Donnell. A coloured seat and plaque remind fans every matchday of the massive hit. 'Mo' refused to look, simply looking down the wicket to O'Donnell and saying: 'It's big, isn't it!'

The wicket of my life: David Hookes, caught David Richards from my bowling in the mid-'80s. But he had already hit me for two earlier 6s! His signed book is one of my dearest possessions.

21

ORGANISED CHAOS

'I shared the vision of Jones' remarkable innings on World of Sport that late-September Sunday. Channel 7's Gordon Bennett had given me an opportunity to head the cricket segment...'

1987 was a very good year for Australian cricket – and me. Allan Border won the World Cup with a young, emerging team, the first steppingstones towards the unofficial world Test championship, clinched in the West Indies in 1995. Susan and I toured England for the first time with the Crusaders, our 24-match itinerary including matches at dreamy Arundel Castle, Fenners and Oxford.

I'd become editor of *Personal Success* magazine, the publisher lived close to us in Mt Eliza. While in London and beyond, I interviewed many ex-patriate Aussies who were succeeding overseas. Among them was vivacious fashion designer Dale, Lady Tryon, an ex-Melburnian nicknamed 'Kanga' by her friend then-Prince Charles, businessman and philanthropist Basil Sellers and even the Formula 1 racing car driver Gary Brabham at Brands Hatch. The front page of our October edition proclaimed: 'Aussie Assault. How seven Australians took on the Brits and won.'

It was an unforgettable trip, the wildflowers and the little villages with their colourful upstairs window boxes a delight. In the first match at Eastcote, a crazy little ground with the curator's cottage at backward square leg, I took a four-for – my only wickets as it turned out for the entire tour. The pitches were slow, allowing me little of the slide or bounce I enjoy back in Melbourne. Anything short or offline was fodder. As our team's frontline legspinner, I still was on my 'L' plates. At Royal Ascot, Steve Waugh teed off, scoring 90-odd from about 45 balls. Dave Gilbert and Brad McNamara also played that day. Steve's hands were so quick. Having smashed me everywhere, he calmly marked his guard ready to do it all over again.

We had a strong, seasoned squad with a few younger and more athletic ones like Australian-to-be Paul Reiffel, Paul Jackson, Michael Dimattina and Brian 'Freddie' McFadyen, later a stellar coach across multi-levels. Test legend Rod Marsh also made a one-off appearance, a thrill for all of us. We took a team photograph at Lord's in our brand new stripey English-style jackets. For most, it was our first time at the holy of holies – an unforgettable, almost-cathartic time. There was an aura and a unique atmosphere at the game's revered headquarters, a little like Augusta for golfers and Cardiff Stadium, the rugby capital of Wales.

At Amersham, batting at No.10, I shared a 30-run stand with Jacko to help bring us home. We laughed later. He didn't realise that I could play. Earlier in the game, a pretty blonde lass had come in at No.4 – and struck her first ball straight back at me with genuine ferocity. Everyone retreated to their normal fielding spots. On a high after our narrow win,

I approached her at the after-match, saying she was a very fine player and should look to develop her talent. Our wicketkeeper Mark Foster overheard the conversation. 'You idiot Piessey. That's Jan Brittin. She opens for England!'

In the lead-up to the tour, we played a dozen games against the private schools including a memorable tussle with Mentone Grammar at the Keysborough Playing Fields. In at No.4 for Mentone was a tubby kid by the name of Warne, Shane Warne. His hair was white blond and he had a heap of zinc cream on his nose. He made 38 with some adventurous offside flails, through and over point. Mentone's opening bat, a tall lad, Raj Krishnan crashed a succession of impeccable drives through the covers and was soon 80 and then 90. Rarely had we opposed such an assured schoolboy. Our captain for the day, the old Melbourne footballer Neil Crompton was called away early and I stood in for him. Going around the wicket to big Raj, I cramped him for room and bowled him around his legs. There was a hush of disappointment as the main scoreboard had '99' against his name. But the scorers recounted and he became one of the few lads to score an even 100 against us. We won the match but not before the Warne kid took several wickets with big-spinning leg-breaks, including me stumped by Jimmy Whitla, son of one of my ex-Beaumaris teammates Alan Whitla. The ball fizzed out of his hand, veered, dropped and spun – far too good for me. I was stranded in mid-pitch. There was a jubilant 'Howzzaaatttt' and no need to look at the square leg umpire. Later, at the after-match, we heard that Shane was also a talented footballer and was intending to try out for St Kilda. His hero was the charismatic Hawk Dermott Brereton. He liked his swagger, profile and coloured boots.

Mixing and playing with so many of the Crusaders' elite from Max Walker and David Hookes to Rodney Hogg and Gary Cosier had fueled my desire to play regularly again on Saturdays. Coze would often come to Friday night practice at Dingley. He had a giant of a bat and would slam anything overpitched straight back at you so hard you almost needed a helmet. Swan Richards invited all the visiting internationals for a game or two and the venues were top notch, including the MCG where I played under Ian Chappell's captaincy and the Adelaide Oval, where Bob Blewett, Greg's Dad, bowled me first ball.

We toured to Canberra one long weekend, everyone crammed into a 15-seat minivan. Our wicketkeeper from Port Melbourne Ken Spicer was driving and we were pulled up halfway up the main drag. 'Sir' asked the Constable. 'Have you had a drink in the last 24 hours?'

'Sir,' said Spice. 'I haven't had a drink in the last 24 years.'

THE FORTUNES of the Australian cricket team in the mid '80s revolved squarely around Border. No one was more formidable or placed a higher price on his wicket. He was horrified to lose to New Zealand, both at home and away and in 1986, having said, 'I've almost had enough of this bunch' he was dubbed 'Captain Grumpy', a nickname still used today. NZ fielded two immortals, allrounder Richard Hadlee and champion No.4 Martin Crowe. It was no shame to lose to a Kiwi XI which included those two. In Brisbane, where the Gabba dog races were still a Thursday night institution, Crowe made an imperious 188 and Hadlee took nine for 52 and six for 71. Border soared to his left like a soccer goalie to take a stunning, one-handed slips catch, ending a century knock from the Kiwi leftie John Reid. AB's bulldog determination, impeccable technique and tenacity forced play into a fifth day, his 152 not out, still not enough, however, for Australia to avert an innings defeat. Watching the gifted Crowe shadow-batting before his net was always an education. He was so upright, so assured, so certain. Hadlee wasn't as fast as some, but he bowled a quintessential stump-to-stump line, almost touching the umpire as he glided to the crease. His ability to seam the bowl both ways on even the flattest decks even had opponents nodding their heads in appreciation. When the Kiwis toured again two years later, noted No.11 Mike Whitney played out a maiden over against Hadlee in Melbourne to force a draw. He regards those dramatic five minutes as fondly as almost any in his lifetime in the game.

Bobby Simpson's appointment as Australia's coach added the professional dimension the team had lacked for years. In one Test match in Adelaide, Bill Lawry and I were polishing Lawry's column when I pointed downstairs to Australia's team manager Bob Merriman, in dress shirt and tie, hitting short catches in-between innings to a group of three or four. 'Phanto, have a look at that,' I said. Merriman had been a very fine club cricketer and was a sterling administrator. But he was being asked to wear too many hats. It took years for those around him to agree to fund extra team assistance positions – jobs now taken for granted.

At Simpson's suggestion, Dean Jones took a lighter bat (2lb 3oz) into the Test series in India in 1986-87 and scored an epic double-century first off at Madras. He displayed remarkable courage despite heat dehydration. Repeatedly throwing up in mid-pitch he said to Border in mid-innings that he simply couldn't continue. 'Get off then you bloody weak Victorian,' AB snapped. 'Get me a Queenslander. Get me Greg Ritchie.' [79] Jones batted on.

Madras weather in September is hot, hotter and hotter again. Jones looked gaunt, almost ghostly as he trudged off, having endured the toughest eight-and-a-half hours of his life. Simpson said he'd never witnessed a braver effort in any sport, at any time.

In-between overs, Jones had tried to relieve his physical agony by

---
[79] *Border's Battlers*, Michael Sexton (Affirm Press, Melbourne, 2019).

imagining he was back in Melbourne sipping cold beers with his buddy Ray Bright on a Sunday afternoon. Blacking out in the rooms afterwards, he was put on a drip and taken by ambulance to hospital. He'd lost seven kilograms in a day and a half. Next to him in the emergency ward was an Indian man who'd been in a car accident and was in a bad way. Jones was immediately ushered in first. 'What about that guy?' he said. 'You're Dean Jones,' said the star-struck attendant. 'The other fella can wait.'

On match-eve Border had called Jones to his room. He was straight to the point, telling Jones he was going to be Australia's new No.3 for 'the next couple of years'.

'Do you want it?' Border asked.

'I've been waiting two years for it.'

Jones left the room feeling 10 feet tall. 'I thought I was invincible. I thought AB put a red cape on my back and an "S" on my chest. I felt like superman.' [80]

I shared the vision of Jones' remarkable innings on World of Sport that late-September Sunday. Channel 7's Gordon Bennett had given me an opportunity to head the cricket segment, following the retirement of Doug Ring. I'd been supplying cricket features for the 6pm news as well as presenting Seven's late-night sports bulletins most nights around 10.30pm. Seven sent a few of us to a speech coach where we learnt to read advertisements, emphasise important words and pause regularly to add dramatic effect. I shudder when I hear some of the current presenters on radio and TV talking about 'twennie twennie' cricket. How can they possibly keep a job?

Sandy Roberts was a long-time host of World of Sport, the consummate professional, smiling, genial and unflustered. 'Uncle'

---

80   *Border's Battlers*.

Doug Elliot was in charge of the advertisements. From Patra orange juice to Bertocchi ham, his spruiking was expert, exuberant and authoritative. One time he dropped his strides as Sandy was reading a live add from a large sheet of butcher's paper. It was hilarious. Sandy didn't miss a beat. Almost everything was done on the spot. On my first report, instead of looking down the immediate camera lens, the one with the red light directly in front of me, I looked at Sandy as I spoke – but soon learned to relax. I was mixing with some media legends from Lou, Jack and Bob through to the big boss Ron Casey, Sam Newman and Neil 'Coconut' Roberts.

One morning, at the start of a springtime show, I watched in awe as Bill Collins introduced the winning jockey Gary Stewart from the epic two-horse showdown between the two Kiwi gallopers Bonecrusher and Our Waverley Star, still among the finest Cox Plates of them all. Bill was calmly smoking a cigarette as the countdown to 11am began: '10-9-8-7-6-5-4… you're on.'

Tossing the half-smoked ciggie over his shoulder, Bill did the smoothest, most lyrical introduction, saying what a privilege it had been to be at Moonee Valley to witness the Race of the Century. His call over the last furlong was incredible:

> 'Bonecrusher, Our Waverley Star, stride for stride! Nothing in it! Our Waverley Star the rail. Bonecrusher the outside… and Bonecrusher races into equine immortality!'

Rarely has there been a more stirring race-call. Bill was media royalty and the spring carnival his favourite weeks of the year. But his intro without even one note in front of him was something else again. I was off camera about three yards away from his right shoulder and couldn't believe the ease of his delivery. The words just flowed effortlessly, with incredible punch. It had taken him a lifetime to get that good. Like Ernie

Sigley's brilliant interview with Creedence Clearwater's John Fogarty, it remains an indelible, pivotal moment in my own media education.

Lou Richards was the engine room and the life of the show. From baiting Captain Blood (Jack Dyer) or handing out the goodies to the coaches and occasionally even getting Yabbie Jeans to smile, he did everything with an infectious mischievousness. Often after a segment, he'd come over and ask, 'How was I?'

'Lou,' I'd say. 'You're Lou Richards. You're always magnificent.'

Peter McKenna knew I played cricket at Port Melbourne and would be always be asking how I'd gone. He'd coached the Burras not too many years before. Dyer was walking past one day as Jack O'Toole's familiar voice-over to the woodchopping segment was starting: 'Axemen ready. One-two-three... Arr, old Jack,' he said. 'Haven't see him for ages. Must go down to the Green Room and have a jar with him.' No-one had told him that O'Toole had died two years earlier.

Rodney Hogg was just back from the rebel tour of South Africa where he and others been beaten up by my hero Graeme Pollock, still a superstar at 41. Hoggie had agreed to come in but was late and I was panicking, big-time. It wasn't until I'd already started the segment that he slipped into the seat beside me and I said, 'And we just happen to have one of the stars of the tour here, Fred and Dulcie's little boy, rebel fast bowler Rodney Hogg. Welcome Malcolm (his middle name).' It wasn't Bill Collins, but it was still okay. Everyone was grinning afterwards. We'd made it by the hair of our chinny-chin-chins. But that was World of Sport. Organised chaos.

CRICKET ALWAYS FINDS a way to surprise. It's one of its enduring qualities. In the New Year of '87, when the advance-aged Peter Taylor was included in the Sydney Test having played only once all Sheffield Shield summer, he was dubbed 'Peter Who'. Even the one-eyed Sydney press asking if the wrong Taylor, Peter, had been chosen, instead of emerging opening bat Mark. Taylor responded with a man-of-the-match performance, taking eight wickets and making 53 runs in Australia's only win of the Ashes summer.

Opening bat Geoff Marsh, fast bowlers Merv Hughes and Bruce Reid and allrounder Steve Waugh had been introduced the previous summer as part of Australia's rebuild. David Boon was also new on the scene. All were to play significant roles in Australia's renaissance.

Twelve months earlier, Hughes had taken one for 123 in an inglorious beginning against the Indians in Adelaide, prompting Ian Chappell to say that the problem with Merv Hughes 'is that he thinks he's a fast bowler'. Merv carried the clipping in his wallet for years. In taking 200 wickets he was to join a pantheon of Australian fast bowling greats.

Waugh became the most-capped Aussie of all, an outstanding batsman and captain and in his early days, a medium pacer with attitude who once bowled three bouncers in a row at Viv Richards. Eight of Waugh's Test 100s came before his 30th birthday and 24 afterwards. He was incredibly enduring. He'd always said age was only a number. One day I walked with him across to the nets in Melbourne. 'Do you know,' I said, 'that Jack Hobbs made 100 100s after turning 30.' Steve liked that.

Years later, in his last Ashes summer he was under siege for his place and 100s of Melburnians turned up for practice on Test-eve to support him. Waugh and Justin Langer walked into neighbouring nets and there was a standing ovation. Looking across to Waugh, JL grinned and said: 'Was that for you or me, mate?'

22

SMOKIN' JOE

'He so mastered Graham Gooch, England's champion opener that Gooch left a message on his answering machine: "I'm out at the moment, probably lbw Alderman. Please leave a message."'

Rodney Hogg was renowned for pinging batsmen with his skidding bouncer. His direct strikes hospitalised dozens, at club, state and Test level. He was brooding, menacing and different. To hype himself up before a Test or a one-dayer, he'd take himself off to a little anteroom – he called it his 'war room' – and start slapping his own face, harder and harder again until his cheeks were red raw. No one was as afflicted by white line fever. Once in a Melbourne club match he extended his follow through and stood beside the striker, St Kilda's Andrew Lynch and said: 'This fella is not only playing for his wicket, he's playing for his friggin' life.'

In a Test match at the MCG, he struck the iconic West Indian Viv Richards directly on his jaw. He waited for him to crumple, in slow motion, like in the old westerns. But King Viv just stood defiantly staring straight back down the wicket, chewing his gum. Hogg's next ball landed 20 rows back over the fence at fine leg.

Of all cricket's outstanding overseas batsmen of the last half-century, Richards has no peer. Sobers, Kohli, Pollock, Lara, Tendulkar and Barry Richards were all incredible players, but Smokin' Joe was better. The best No.3 since Bradman, he struck the ball with awesome timing and power, playing with flair, spirit and unparalleled hand-eye co-ordination. Few could contain him. And in the field, he was as electric as Bland, Randall and Symonds, his three run outs in the inaugural World Cup final at Lord's in 1975 pivotal in the West Indies' famous win. He was also a champion for his people and at Test match time in Antigua would amble around the food booths in his hometown St John's chatting and laughing with stallholders. So loved was Viv that when he married Miriam, his childhood sweetheart in 1981, the ceremony was given as much attention as a royal wedding. Among the attendees was Antigua's Prime Minister and national hero Vere Bird. Viv was too nervous to make a speech.

During the '99 Australian tour of the Caribbean, I was privileged to meet West Indian post-war great Everton Weekes, then 74 and still working for local Bridgetown radio. He was a kind, gentle man and like Tiger O'Reilly, full of stories from the past. Even he conceded that Viv was the finest of all. I had Bridget Lawrence's West Indian cricketers book with me, a who's who of the Caribbean's best. Sir Everton signed and so did Viv. 'Yeah maan, I'll sign,' he said. He was affable and generous with his time.

Few of his era boasted his record of 35 international 100s. None matched his exhilarating strike-rate. One of his Test 100s came from 56 balls, clean hitting unmatched in the history of Tests. An ODI century in Melbourne in the first week of summer in 1979 was out of this world. It was an idyllic Melbourne Sunday and after spending most of the morning at the *Sporting Globe*, I slipped down to the MCG as Viv helped himself to 153 not out, an Australian-high against the might of Lillee, Thomson and Hogg. No one in the world could have batted better. He played with phenomenal power and majesty. So hard had he struck the ball, he often did not have to run, even on the expansive MCG.

The practice nets in Melbourne were on the ground back then, in the forward pocket where Jezza had broken Collingwood hearts on VFL Grand Final day in 1970. The West Indian fast bowlers would all walk to their mark backwards, vigilantly watching Richards or Gordon Greenidge, just in case they unleashed a head-high straight drive. A few of us were camped close to where Michael Holding began his extended run-up. 'Don't take your eye off them,' he said. 'One could be coming our way.' Mikey liked to chat and was always keen to glean any inside mail on that day's race meeting.

The West Indian teams of the '80s were star-studded, as formidable as any Test team of my time. If the Australians happened to get lucky and take four or five early ones, wicketkeeper Jeff Dujon would invariably lead a revival from No.7. The best teams always find a way. The Windies also possessed a never-ending arsenal of quality fast bowlers. There was no need for a specialist spinner, like Gibbs, Ramadhin or Valentine from earlier eras. After seeing his team humiliated downunder in the mid-'70s, captain Clive Lloyd changed the dynamic of Test cricket, selecting a fourth specialist fast bowler and deliberately bowling fewer overs in a day to lessen their fatigue. His speedsters included Roberts, Holding, Marshall, Garner, Croft, Daniel, a young Courtney Walsh and the Jamaican express Patrick Patterson. Soon afterwards, Ian Bishop and

Curtly Ambrose arrived, big Curtly just about the best of them all.

For years at teatime in the Test matches in Adelaide visiting teams would line-up and meet Australia's ultimate celebrity, Sir Donald Bradman. Patterson had muscles on his muscles and he couldn't believe how short the Don was. 'Hey maan,' he said. 'You only a little guy. Ida knocked your block off.'

'Weelll,' said the Don in that little squeaky voice of his. 'You'd need to improve Patrick. You couldn't even get Merv Hughes out today.' *(which was true: Merv made 72 not out on a road of a wicket).*

'Ok maan. How much you average against me, Patrick Patterson, the fastest bowler in the world?'

'Oh, maybe 55 or 56.'

'Only 56!'

'Weelll,' said the Don. 'I am 80 you know.'

THE MOTIVATION for the harder edge to West Indian cricket, triggered by his team's potent array of strike bowlers, had been a direct result of the 1975-76 summer, 'the hardest and meanest' [81] of any during King Viv's celebrated international career:

> 'It changed my whole idea of Test cricket. Until then I had believed, however naively, that Test cricket was the ultimate sport of gentlemen. The Australians smashed that view wide open. It came as a total surprise to me to come up against a team that contained so many openly aggressive people. It was a kind of nastiness I had never encountered previously. Not

---

81 *Hitting across the line, an autobiography*, Viv Richards (Macmillan Australia, Sydney, 1991)

just in cricket, but in life in general. The force of their hostility was nothing short of frightening.' [82]

Richards rated the bowling from Lillee and Thomson as 'violent' and said racial abuse was rife, with several Aussies calling the Windies 'black bastards'. Unfortunately, abusive language was a part of cricket at most levels, poor behavior escaping censure. There were no stump microphones back then. 'The Australians humiliated and ridiculed us,' Richards said. 'We took so much stick. In every conceivable way, we were utterly savaged.' [83]

Australia won 5-1, with record attendances reveling in the carnage. From 1980 until 1995, however, the Windies didn't lose even one series and were folk heroes in Australia with their wide smiles and exuberant, dynamic skillsets. In 1984, they won 11 Tests on end, King Viv treating Melbourne to a dazzling double century, the first by a West Indian downunder.

In the 1988 Christmas Test where the Australians were thrashed by almost 300 runs, Allan Border said batting surely could not have been any harder in the summer of Bodyline. Melbourne's two-paced, uneven wicket had reminded of the dangerous pitches of the early '80s. Australia's dressing room was like a casualty ward. Dean Jones was nursing badly bruised ribs, Graeme Wood several broken fingers and Ian Healy's groin was black and blue from repeated direct hits. In the match of his life, Patterson took nine wickets for just 88 runs. There was no respite for the Aussies. The West Indian first and second change bowlers were as menacing as the openers. The pressure was unrelenting. Test cricket was the toughest of schools. To survive, you had to be brave and incredibly good.

---

82 *Hitting across the line.*
83 *Hitting across the line.*

APPROACHING THE 1989 Ashes tour, Border had won just one of his first eight series as captain. He was dour and unimaginative but there was never any question of him being replaced. A *Cricketer* magazine special I edited a few years later was entitled *Simply The Best, the Allan Border Story*. He was sporting royalty, with few batting peers in the world.

The first time he toured England as Australia's captain in 1985 he described himself as 'a nice guy who had come last'. The team won at Lord's but were uncompetitive most everywhere else. Armed with a far stronger squad in '89, the Australians lost only three of their 37 fixtures, winning the Tests 4-0. Leading into the first Test at Headingley, the Aussies were massive 11/4 outsiders before they started with 7-601 declared. Suddenly, after years of anguish, everything Border touched was turning to gold. The weather was fine and the team performed brilliantly, first-time tourists Mark Taylor, Steve Waugh and Dean Jones dominant. So supreme were the Aussies that the margin could easily have been 6-0 but for rain at Birmingham and The Oval.

Returning rebel Terry Alderman was Australia's bowling star, taking 41 wickets in six Tests – 19 lbw! He so mastered Graham Gooch, England's champion opener that Gooch left a message on his answering machine: 'I'm out at the moment, probably lbw Alderman. Please leave a message.'

Border demanded a high-edge of competitiveness which left little room for on-field friendships, England's captain David Gower calling Border and his team 'unsociable and unpleasant'.[84] 'He was mean to the opposition, the press and indeed some of his own players,' Gower said. 'He sledged pretty fiercely too. It was hyper unfriendly.'

No wives were allowed on tour until late in the campaign. Even then, they weren't allowed to stay in the same hotel as their husbands.

---

84   *Simply the Best, the Allan Border Story*, Ken Piesse (Syme Magazines, Melbourne, 1993)

The whole squad were guests of honor at North Melbourne's Grand Final Breakfast in 1989 before parading in open-topped cars around the MCG leading into the epic Grand Final play-off between Hawthorn and Geelong, the game in which Gary Ablett snr kicked nine and still played on a losing side. I was seated next to the team's leg-spinner Trevor Hohns, later a Test selector. He and the others were astonished at the warm and generous receptions they received. They hadn't realised the joy their performances in England had generated. They were feted as heroes everywhere they went. Everyone loves a winner.

The victorious '89 Australians received a standing ovation as they paraded in open-topped cars as a prelude to the '89 MCG Grand Final, the toughest in decades. Pictured from left are Terry Alderman, Steve Waugh and local hero Merv Hughes.

Cricketer magazine

23

A LEG BREAK FROM HEAVEN

'He bowled two or three of the most perfect leg-breaks to me. They dipped, hummed and scuttled sideways at pace, reddening my hands. Ever since the juniors at East Sandringham, he'd always had the leg-break from heaven...'

The Victorian cricket team was at Bat & Ball in Dudley Street, West Melbourne for pre-season nets. Shane Warne was in comeback mode after shoulder surgery. It was reassuring to once again see his familiar short approach, his energy at the crease and humming leg-break. It seemed as good as ever. Coach David Hookes approached. 'Shane,' he asked, 'how long does it take for everything to feel like it's back in sync? How many days? How many sessions?'

'About 20, maybe 21 balls,' said Shane, smiling broadly. He was a once-in-a-lifetime genius, captivating, charismatic and ferociously competitive.

His surge to stardom via a sports scholarship at Mentone Grammar and Brighton's second XI had been stunning. A rock star in creams, his appeal transcended sport. He revived a lost art and inspired millions globally to love cricket. He told Michel Parkinson once he wasn't the sharpest tool in the shed and would continue to make mistakes. We readily forgave his flaws and follies and years after his retirement, all smiled at his high-rolling ways and hung on his every word from commentary boxes worldwide. He was always so perceptive and passionate – and along with Keith Miller the best captain Australia never had.

His pals ranged across every spectrum, from sport to rock and roll. He and Coldplay's Chris Martin had met in a London lift. They stared at each other. Martin spoke first: 'Are you…?' and Warnie countered: 'And are you…?' Soon they were firm friends, Warnie even playing harmonica on stage one night with Martin's band, Coldplay.

From first carting beds to pay for his fags and fast food to owning some of the biggest and most desirable Brighton mansions, he was 'The King', cricket's consummate bowler and showman. He did everything at pace: dieting, drinking, smoking, the gym, golf and roulette. It was part of his charm and addictive personality. Warnie's life was a scriptwriter's dream, full of extraordinary highs and eccentricities. For a time he was even engaged to a leading English actress. Few had as firm a handshake, wide smile or zest for life.

At his very first club session at St Kilda, coach Shaun Graf asked the club's practice captain Noel Harbourd what the kid with the long blond hair said he did. 'He told me he was a batsman who also bowled a bit,' said Harbourd. 'Not sure about his batting,' said Graf, 'but he sure can bowl.' No one could forecast that the precocious 17-year-old was to become Australia's most magnetic and admired sportsman since Miller and, according to Ricky Ponting, 'the best cricketer who has probably ever been'.[85]

Thanks to his longtime coach Terry Jenner he also became a master strategist, delighting in setting up hundreds of batsmen for an "lb" or a stumping. The New Zealander Andrew Jones once struck him for a soaring six over cow corner. As Steve Dunne was raising both his arms to the scorers, Jones smirked down the wicket at Warne. Walking back past the umpire, Warne said: 'He thinks he has got me'. He followed with three perfectly pitched leg breaks, two at normal pace and the third a little quicker, Jones defending each of them. Just one ball remained in the over. 'Watch this one,' he said to Dunne as he walked past him to the top of his mark. It was his deadly flipper, his lbw ball. Jones misread it as a longhop, went for another pull and was caught plumb in front. Dunne had his finger up almost before the Australian appeal. No one could 'work' the umpires like Warnie. When Warne was good, Jenner once said, he was very good and when he was bad, he was still very good.

When first shown the flipper – the faster, flatter ball squeezed out of the front of the hand – Warne couldn't initially control it. 'The square leg umpire would have been in danger, so wide did Warnie bowl it,' said Jack Potter, his first coach at the Australian Cricket Academy in Adelaide. 'Yet within days, having practised incessantly with a tennis ball down a corridor, he'd mastered it. He called me over: "Jack, Jack… I can do it". And he could. He had this extraordinary gift to run with a new skill and perfect it quickly.'

The flipper became his signature, confounding elite batsmen everywhere. It was cricket's most lethal delivery, deadlier than Lillee's outswinger, Wasim Akram's dipping yorker or McGrath's leg cutter. And

---

85 *Dynamic Duos, cricket's finest pairs and partnerships*, Ken Piesse (Five Mile Press, Melbourne, 2012)

no one had bowled it better, not Clarrie Grimmett, Cec Pepper, Bruce Dooland or even Richie Benaud.

I shared Richie's contact details, helping a young Warnie connect with the great man. At an airport lounge he showed him his version of the flipper and within weeks, Warnie was bowling it, perfectly. One of Richie's proudest moments was witnessing the Warne flipper which castled champion West Indian Richie Richardson and triggered Australia's win in Melbourne's 1992 Christmas Test. He was caught on the crease and it was through him before he could defend it. Richie reckoned Shane was so good he could spin the ball on ice.

Richie Richardson's dismissal, which won a hometown Test, was the precursor to the 'Ball of the Century', the delicious leg break which spun drunkenly to hit Mike Gatting's off stump in the opening 1993 Ashes Test at Old Trafford. It was Warne's first ball in a Test in England. Gatt's bewildered shake of the head began 15 years of bullying of every English XI Warne opposed. No one competed as hard, were as driven or so excelled in the big moments. 'There was no batsman alive Shane didn't think he couldn't dismiss,' said his long-time wicketkeeping buddy Ian Healy,[86] renowned for saying most overs: 'Bowling Shane.' Ironically, one of his first open-age captains at Brighton, Mike Tamblyn had suggested he concentrate more on his batting.

More words have been written about Warnie in newspapers, magazines and on-line than any cricketer, even the Don. Tens of thousands were mine. Among my first were in December 1990. Freshly expelled from the Australian Cricket Academy for 'mooning' some hostesses around a Darwin hotel pool, Warnie had driven back to Melbourne and was immediately chosen to make his state second XI debut for a mid-week friendly at the Albert Ground in Melbourne. Umpire Darrel Holt had

---

86 *Dynamic Duos*.

officiated at a club game and at a chance meeting with state selector Jim Higgs in Jolimont suggested Higgs should go to St Kilda's next practice as 'this kid is already better than you'.

Victoria's second XI was opposing a West Australian XI which included Justin Langer, Damien Martyn and Stuart MacGill, all destined for Test cricket. It was a sleepy Wednesday and only a few spectators were in, most from nearby inner-city offices. Lunch was called and instead of walking off with his teammates, Warne readily agreed to my request to be photographed, close-up, from the bowling crease by Peter Charles, our *Sunday Press* snapper.

He bowled two or three of the most perfect leg-breaks to me. They dipped, hummed and scuttled sideways at pace, reddening my hands. Ever since the juniors at East Sandringham, he'd always had the leg-break from heaven.

Within weeks he was playing for Victoria and just over a year later, for Australia.

As his legend grew, the demands on his time multiplied. In 1996, Victorian cricket celebrating its centenary with a Gala Dinner and 89-year-old Leo O'Brien, Victoria's oldest living player and one of the last survivors from the Bodyline series, asked to be introduced. 'Yes, sure,' said Warnie, 'where is he sitting?' He spent the next 15 minutes with Leo. It made Mo's night. He wrote Warnie a letter of thanks which I dropped around to him at Half Moon Bay.

The grief felt on Shane's early death, aged just 52, on that early-autumn weekend in 2022 was universal. Tens of thousands attended his MCG farewell. We were united in tears. Like the deaths of JFK and John Lennon, we all could remember exactly where we were on hearing the news. Shane's heart had stopped. He'd had a warning in Melbourne shortly before flying overseas. Melbourne's *Herald Sun* stopped its presses at 1.30am and changed its front page, a rare event, before conveying the news to 85,000 in its city precinct.

That Saturday at Mt. Eliza – and at thousands of cricket clubs throughout Australia – we all wore black armbands. The atmosphere was eerie. I told the young ones in our team how extraordinarily gifted Shane was – and how relentlessly he'd worked to perfect his skills. Asked once how many hours he'd taken to fine-tune his game, he said, '10,000… minimum'. That's a monumental amount of practice.

Millions worldwide still can't believe he has gone. His shocked parents said they would never come to terms with their son's premature passing. His daughter Summer said she wished she could have hugged her father tighter in 'what I didn't know were my final moments with you'. Son Jackson said he wished it was just a horrible nightmare and that his Dad would again roll through the front door, armed with pizzas saying, 'who's hungry?'

During his halcyon playing days and fairytale ride in the '90s and early '00s, I wrote three Warnie books and he contributed forewords to two of mine. We also worked on some wrist spinning tips for kids and feature stories for *Cricketer, Australasian Post* and assorted general interest magazines.

His most fabled on-field triumphs came in England in 2005. England won one of the greatest Ashes series of the modern era, yet Warne took 40 wickets – at a time when his off-field misadventures cost him his marriage. Wife Simone arrived at Heathrow to the latest sex scandal, a total set-up by unscrupulous British tabloids and within days returned to Australia. There'd be no more chances. Australia's coach John Buchanan marveled at Warne's ability to remain focused, amid the headlines and his personal turmoil.

When he came on to bowl at Birmingham, England's 'party' Test, large sections of the crowd in the Hollies Stand started chirping: 'Where's your Missus gone… far far away.' In his last overseas Ashes, Warne was determined to excel. 'Whatever was happening in my personal life, when I crossed the line I told myself: "I'm not going to stuff this up. I'm not going to let people down." If anything, I was extra driven,' he said.

When his Foundation was exposed – *The Age's* Nick McKenzie discovered that it had massive administrative costs and had been donating less than 30 per cent of proceeds to its chosen charities – he pledged the fund's last $300,000 to assist the family of Bayside teenager, Will Murray, who had become a quadriplegic after diving into shallow water off a pier at Half Moon Bay, directly opposite the Warne family's house in Black Rock. The Foundation distributed more than $4 million, much of it raised by Warne himself. In 2020 his baggy green was sold for $1 million to assist the east coast bushfire victims.

Warnie's life was one roller-coasting drama, full of twists, turns, texts, mistakes, pretty girls, set-ups and yo-yo diets. He led a high-octane Peter Pan-type lifestyle. From driving a Ferrari, professional poker in Las Vegas, a hole-in-one at Augusta through to his coaching, mentoring and being a Dad, his influence was multi-tiered. He was truly larger-than-life, a man for the people, loved and idolised everywhere. Don Bradman may always be cricket's No.1 batsman, but Shane Warne is its ultimate bowler… and celebrity.

He added more glamour, mystery and prestige for wrist spinners worldwide. Bars emptied at the announcement: 'And coming into the attack from the southern end: Shane Warne.' Now the Great Southern Grandstand is named in his honor.

How privileged were we to see him at work at his favorite backyard, the MCG and major cricket grounds around the world. Always the grand master, he brought an unequalled theatre to the game. He truly was a one-off.

24

TUBBY'S TIME

'Ambrose exploded: 'Man I'll knock you out here and now. I don't care if I have no career left...'

May 19, 1994: Moree airport, north-west NSW. Mark Taylor was sitting in his best suit at the airport lounge waiting for the 8am plane to the Big Smoke. A farmer approached, in check shirt and overalls. Looking intently at Taylor, he said: 'You're Mark Taylor, aren't you?'

'Yes sir. That's correct.'

'Sydney-bound?'

'Yes sir.'

'Allan Border retired last week, didn't he? You're vice-captain. I reckon you're off to Sydney because you're the next captain.'

'If you can work all that out,' said Taylor, 'you've got a four-hour exclusive, because no one else in Australia is going to find out until midday.' [87]

---

[87] *The Taylor Years, Australian Cricket 1994-99*, Ken Piesse (Viking, Melbourne, 1999)

Taylor, 28, had been staying at the 800-acre farm belonging to his friend and Northern Districts teammate Peter Taylor waiting for confirmation that the job was his. He must have looked quite a sight sitting up in his mate's old truck complete with its dirty steel seats, bumping the 35 kilometres into the town's airport.

Australia's 39th Test captain was duly anointed and after his media conference and appearances on *The Midday Show* and *A Current Affair*, he took the night plane back to Moree for a celebratory dinner organised by the Taylors at a local restaurant. The owners had prepared a huge, complimentary seafood platter. They were thrilled to be hosting Australia's new captain.

At his presser, Taylor spoke honestly of his goals and ambitions. After some wild times in South Africa where Shane Warne and Merv Hughes had been fined and disciplined, Taylor said no one would ever again have a reason to reproach his team for poor on-field behaviour. The players were grateful for their opportunity to be ambassadors, home and away and would be humble going forward, win, lose or draw. Twelve Tests and two major tours in seven months beckoned. Taylor wanted to defeat Pakistan for the first time for 35 years on the sub-continent and defend the Ashes before taking on the world champion West Indians in the Caribbean. 'We want some revenge, for AB,' he said.

The Australians were just back from South Africa and Border had angrily stepped down just days earlier, claiming officials had harassed and hurried him into making public his retirement. Taylor, 28, had been his deputy for 24 of the previous 26 Tests. He'd led New South Wales with flair and flourish. Just weeks earlier in Stellenbosch, he'd counselled an angry Warne, saying Warnie had badly overstepped with his salty send-off of South Africa's Andrew Hudson at the Bullring in Johannesburg and was not acting like the Shane Warne he knew or the Shane Warne the players loved and respected. The Hudson incident was ugly, unsavoury, and unpalatable. The Victorian admitted he'd succumbed to all of the early hype, pressure and taunts and was genuinely sorry. 'I hope I don't get hung for it for the rest of my life because I stuffed up once,' he said.[88]

Steve Waugh said he couldn't remember a more hostile reception for an Australian touring team, anywhere, any time. 'There is a percentage of people who are there for the sole purpose of abusing us whenever they see fit,' he said.[89]

True to his word, team behaviour improving immediately under Taylor. Only a missed stumping at Karachi by vice-captain Ian Healy cost the Australians the series in Pakistan. The English were blown away in the Ashes and finally, the Windies vanquished in the Caribbean.

Glenn McGrath and Steve Waugh were most influential in the autumn-time unseating of the long-time world champions. Having bowled at second change in the first two Tests, McGrath was offered choice of ends and took a Test-best six for 47 on a wet deck at Port-of-Spain, including Brian Lara, the world's No.1 player, to an off-cutter which jagged and caught an edge. 'It was the moment for me when I realised I could compete against anyone in the world,' McGrath said.

Waugh's sheer courage and commitment all tour was remarkable. He was struck 10 times during his innings of 63 not out and 21 at Queen's Park Oval. West Indian captain Richie Richardson had to pull an enraged Curtly Ambrose away after Waugh had sworn at him. Ambrose said out loud: 'Man, I deserve a little more respect than this.' He extended his follow through and told Waugh never to cuss him again. When Waugh said he could say what he liked, when he liked, Ambrose exploded: 'Man I'll knock you out here and now. I don't care if I have no career left.' [90]

---

88 *The Complete Shane Warne*, Ken Piesse (Viking, Melbourne, 2000)
89 *South African Tour Diary*, Steve Waugh (HarperCollins, Sydney, 1994)
90 *Time to Talk*, Curtly Ambrose with Richard Sydenham (Aurum Press, London, 2015)

A week later, Waugh's epic double century in the deciding Test at Sabina Park against Ambrose, Walsh and the two Benjamin's clinched the series. Few were more dedicated, or prouder to wear the baggy green. A jubilant Border was among the insiders to celebrate with the team.

Waugh was irresistible in the mid-'90s, topping Australia's batting averages in four series out of five. He and Ambrose were to kiss and make-up, Waugh even contributing a foreword years later to Ambrose's autobiography:

> 'I loved the challenge of batting against him, for it provided a benchmark for me to where I was at. He was the best I faced. To succeed against Curtly Ambrose you had graduated as a Test batsman… his presence for many was overwhelming, with his towering height, deathly stare and imposing body language, leaving many batsmen unsure of his motives.'[91]

'That tour was the Steve Waugh show,' said Healy. 'He dominated it from start to finish. He was the rock which held the team together.' Waugh stopped the good balls, swayed out of the way of the short ones and smacked the bad ones. His hands were unbelievably quick. At indoor practice in the mid-'80s, Dean Jones was talking to us about 'this Sydney kid' who hit the ball past point at the speed of sound. 'He's got a brother who's meant to be amazing too,' he said.

Steve Waugh had leadership aspirations from a young age and was a natural mentor to the young ones – even advancing Ricky Ponting some extra tour allowance after he'd over-indulged at the racetrack in the opening weeks.[92]

'Steve was nowhere near as talented as Mark in terms of timing and reflexes,' said England's Robin Smith, 'yet he averaged 10 runs more in

---

91 *Time to Talk.*
92 *The Taylor Years.*

Tests... with the right mental approach and work ethic you can achieve far more than those with more natural talent.' [93]

MARK TAYLOR's promotion was inspired. He was to win 26 and draw 11 of his 50 Tests leading with common sense and team-first philosophies. We wrote a coaching column together for *Australian Cricket* magazine. He was always eloquent, helpful and generous with his time. Late in his career he suffered a form lapse, before a remarkable late revival. In Pakistan in 1998 he made a career-defining 334 not out, his popularity so soaring that in 1999 he was accorded Australian of the Year status, the Australia Day Council saying:

> 'Cricket fans or not, we admire his strength and the reflection in his character of the best of what is Australian.'

Taylor had been subjected to a forensic trial-by-media in the first six months of 1997. For all his positivity, he was in a horrible form slump and never before had he felt so vulnerable. Approaching the first Test in Edgbaston, he hadn't made a Test 50 in 20 innings. He'd stood down from the ODI team for the second time in two months. 'No other Australian cricketer has survived as lengthy a period of failure,' said Malcolm Knox.

Having made just seven in the first innings of the opening Test at rowdy Edgbaston, he was preparing to drop himself, in favour of Michael Slater, five years his junior. 'I could see the effect my run of low scores was having on the team,' he said. 'I knew I had one more bat (to atone). How do you captain a squad in England when you're not playing?' [94]

The Australians trailed in mid match by 360, before Taylor averted the embarrassment of an innings defeat with a plucky 129 in six-and-half

---

[93] *The Judge*, Robin Smith (Yellow Jersey Press, London, 2019)
[94] *Inside Story*, Gideon Haigh and David Frith (News Custom Publishing, Melbourne, 2007)

hours. It opened fresh avenues which saw his career revive remarkably, his stability and access to the world's most dynamic duo Warne and McGrath leading the Australian team to stellar highs not enjoyed since the Bradman era. After the horrors of the mid-'80s, his XIs had rare depth and drive. Unlike Border who was known to uncouthly stick his fingers in the air towards certain journalists he didn't respect, Taylor totally embraced every aspect of his leadership and befriended the writers. He also worked at his batting skills with renewed vigour. In the winter of 1998, approaching the springtime tour of Pakistan, he and McGrath subjected themselves to a vigorous 16-week fitness campaign under Sydney fitness trainer Kevin Chevell, lifting weights, cycling, rowing and running. Everything was done at an exhausting intensity. Every session, four and five days a week, Chevell would have the pair's hearts thumping at 90-95 per cent capacity. 'We always worked flat out, looking to challenge every single fibre and not just physically but mentally as well,' Chevell said. 'Having got through something like that, the player automatically has fresh belief in himself. And that's the difference between the players who succeed and the ones who just exist.'[95]

Taylor told Chevell that the 1998-99 season would be his last and he wanted to be at his most vibrant and once again be a pivotal on-field contributor as he was in his maiden seasons. Within 10 weeks, Taylor had shed 6kg of body fat. After 16, he'd lost 10kg and gained 2-3kg of muscle tissue. His mates still called him 'Tubby', but his chest was flat and firm and his suits no longer fitted. In the nets he was sharper, quicker and more balanced, as if he was 10 years younger. In the second Test in Pakistan, at Peshawar, he made 334 not out and 92 – the first Australian to score more than 400 runs in a Test.[96]

Dropped twice before passing 25, Taylor batted for two days and had

---

95 *Body, Mind, Life*, Kevin Chevell (Information Australia, Melbourne, 1998)
96 Only one other, England's Graham Gooch had made 400 runs in a Test.

the opportunity to reach Brian Lara's world record of 375 – but preferred not to. By declaring Australia's innings closed on the third morning, he equalled Don Bradman's highest Test score of 334. He wanted the Test win, caring little of personal accolades. Back home, we embraced his unselfish ways. He was a shining light, a sports ambassador with rare substance and strength.

EVEN THE GREATS fade, some more gracefully than others. In Cape Town in 1994, Allan Border was having trouble hitting the ball off the square. At a break, Ian Healy playfully pretended to dip his bat into an ice-bucket. 'Better we cool this baby down,' he said. 'It's running too hot.' AB, ever combative, saw red. 'Listen mate. I'm batting my bloody arse off out there... why don't you go and play with your schoolboy mates?'[97] It was to be Border's Test farewell, but he continued into his 40th year the following summer, assisting Queensland to its first-ever Sheffield Shield title. His TV commitments in the Caribbean coincided with the team's victory tour of major Queensland bush centres from Cairns to Longreach. The victorious Bulls carried a cardboard cut-out of AB and teammates would raise it each time he was introduced. 'AB always got the biggest cheer, even though he wasn't there,' said Healy.[98]

A decade or so earlier, in 1981-82, Greg Chappell made five ducks across 22 days in seven Test and ODI innings. The best since Bradman had momentarily forgotten to watch the ball. Greg reckons he was batting well but was simply getting out. He soon returned to something like his best and two summers later left Test cricket with an imperious 182 in Sydney, passing Don Bradman's famous run aggregate of 6996. In taking three slips catches, he also broke Colin Cowdrey's world record for the most catches in Tests by a non-wicketkeeper. On the final day he

---

97 *The Ian Healy Story*, Ian Healy with Robert Craddock (Swan Publishing, Perth, 1996)
98 *The Ian Healy Story*.

alternated from second slip to third and back again, anticipating where the nick would fly.

The ability of champions to fight back from adversity always inspires. McGrath had missed 10 months through injury in 1997-98 before refining his goals and bounding past Dennis Lillee's long-time record mark of 355 Test wickets. As a long, lean teenager barely getting a bowl even in local cricket at Narromine, he'd been discovered by chance, playing in a bush match against a Sydney invitational XI which included Doug Walters, the famed ex-international. Walters rang Steve Rixon, who organised an immediate trial for McGrath at Sutherland. A place at the Cricket Academy also opened, McGrath becoming the first to play for Australia direct from Academy ranks where one of his tutors was Lillee, a long-time hero.

McGrath thrived on work and playing regularly without a break and soon was to be rated alongside Pakistan's Wasim Akram and Shoaib Akhtar among the world's elite pacemen. His eight for 38 against England at Lord's in 1997 was a fabulous moment. At the other end, my old Crusader's teammate Paul Reiffel took two and still proudly talks of the day how he and McGrath bowled England out for 77 at cricket's headquarters…

McGrath's remarkable partnership with Warne saw them amass 1001 Test wickets side-by-side in 104 Tests. They were pivotal in Australia winning 16 Test wins in a row from 1999-2001.[99] Six times they grossed 15 wickets or more in a match, a Test-best 18 coming against the Old Enemy at The Oval in 2001. For a decade-and-a-half the Aussies were the undisputed champions of the world. Thanks to their two most eminent bowlers, the Australians won Test matches of which they had little right.

McGrath was extraordinarily frugal, hating to concede even singles.

---

99   Australia also won 16 Tests in a row from 2005 to 2008.

Behind his easy-going country boy smile was a coiled tiger who clinically bailed up batsmen with unerring accuracy, seam and bounce before delivering withering knockout blows. 'Glenn was two bowlers in one,' Steve Waugh once said. 'He could keep it tight when you wanted him to, and he could also be aggressive and take wickets.'[100]

He dominated England's renowned opener Mike Atherton, who averaged just 14 against him, compared with Atherton's career average of almost 40.

MARK WAUGH was also a champion – and easier on the eye than twin brother Steve with his classic, unhurried style. Springbok great Barry Richards once told me if he knew Steve Waugh was going to make a 100, he'd play golf as usual and drift down to the cricket later. But if Mark was to make a 100, he'd cancel everything and be there from the first ball. Steve's back foot whips through cover point were his signature. Mark would score classically in the 'V' with majestic drives down the ground. He used bats which were two inches longer than most. His century on debut in Adelaide against England in 1990-91 was an artistic masterpiece. He was 25 years of age – Steve had first played at 20. As Mark was taking guard, short-leg Robin Smith offered some encouragement: 'Time to release the hand break, Champ,' he said. He stroked his first ball from Phil 'Daffy' DeFreitas wide of mid-on for three and finished with 138. Ninety-five came in the most exhilarating session of the summer. He'd never batted better and wondered what all the fuss was about Test cricket. 'It got harder after that,' he said.

Like the best of Stan McCabe in the '30s, three of Mark's centuries are considered all-time classics. At Sabina Park in 1995, he and Steve

---

100   *Dynamic Duos, cricket's finest pairs and partnerships,* Ken Piesse (Five Mile Press, Melbourne, 2012)

shared a stand of 231, Mark making 126 after Australia was 3-73. In a gripping finish at Port Elizabeth in 1997, his free flowing 116 enabled the Aussies to chase down 271. And for the first time in his career, in Adelaide in 1997-98, he batted through an entire day's play for 115 not out as Australia forced a controversial draw, the South Africans claiming Waugh had hit his wicket at 105 after a short delivery from Shaun Pollock numbed his elbow. While Waugh had hit his stumps with his bat, the contact was inadvertent and he was deemed under Rule 35 not to have been playing a shot, but the tourists were incensed. Cricket had yet another monumental controversy.

Shane Warne and Glenn McGrath lightened the burden of captaincy for Steve Waugh. Together, they averaged 10 wickets a Test, the all-star Aussies dominating world cricket for a decade and a half.

25

AMBUSHED

'Warne left the meeting feeling totally betrayed and contemplating immediate retirement. He sulked through the entire Test week, his relationship with Waugh forever fractured...'

Susan and I were flying into Bridgetown, the Caribbean's exalted cricketing Citadel in 1999. It was a full plane and we were among the last off. Having identified our bags, including a large cricket kit on wheels, we were about to join a queue which was already almost 100 yards long. 'You with the cricket sar?' boomed a security officer. 'Sure am,' I said. In an instant a side gate was opened and we were ushered through, totally bypassing customs. Welcome to the West Indies!

We'd arrived for the last two Tests in Barbados and Antigua. Terry Jenner was also in the Caribbean. He'd come armed with a special shiraz to share with his star pupil, Shane Warne, still in comeback mode after shoulder surgery. Warnie had tired of Stuart MacGill cornering the spinning limelight. He was jealous of his success. He wanted to be *the* man all over again, but TJ was concerned he'd returned too soon.

With the series deadlocked at 1-1, thanks to a classic Brian Lara double-century in Jamaica, we all felt blessed to be there. There was hardly a spare bed in all Bridgetown, our tour group being split into two, our hotels 100 yards from each other close to a bay with the most dazzling and warm aqua blue waters. It was our first-time co-hosting[101] and we were just as excited as our group as we watched locals expertly carving up pineapples with razor-sharp machetes and others shinning up coconut trees and offering us drinks, before reverting to their hammocks and easy chairs. We witnessed limbo dancing for the first time with the bar being lowered again and again. Finally, it was doused in flames and was no more than six inches off the ground. Miraculously the girls still got under it. Within days we were walking to their Calypso beat, no rushing, no deadlines. Everyone was so relaxed, friendly and laidback. With the big cricket in town, it was party time. We took a car around the island, past Barbados's famed surf beaches and marvelled at the tiny corner blocks, many with grass pitches all rolled and ready to use, a tethered goat invariably nearby grazing. We even attended our first jungle disco. It was like a wild Mosh party and we all danced into the night, feeling like free-and-easy teenagers again with no responsibilities.[102]

During our Barbados week, Susan and I walked into a hotel for dinner and half the Australian cricket team happened to also be there, most huddled together under trees in the beer garden trying to be inconspicuous. At the front bar sitting on stools, impossible-to-miss, was Warnie and a young West Indian girl, her hair beautifully braided.

---

101 Susan and I were working with Kevin Dale and National Network Travel. Our subsequent eight overseas tours were hosted on behalf of Glenn and Gayle Hedley from Events Travel, long-time gold travel partners of the Australian Cricket Society.
102 My Mum was looking after our kids. One night she fell into the bath… to widespread laughter.

She was staring into his eyes. I nodded. He said, 'G'day Ken' and we kept walking. Inside the dining room, Susan asked: 'Was that Shane Warne?'

'Was it?' I said.

He'd always had eyes for pretty girls. One night at a function in the UK I co-hosted with his mate Darren Berry, Warnie sat down and cased the entire room. Susan was amazed at his cockiness. It was if he was a blond Elvis. But it was just his way. Women loved him and he loved women.

DESPITE THE mania for cricket in the Caribbean, quality practice wickets are a rarity and in most capitals the Australians organised centre wicket practise at local clubs. Ground bowlers would often be given equipment as a thank you. But this time they were each demanding $US50 cash a session and manager Steve Bernard was unimpressed. Seeing some younger ones in our tour group, 'Brute' was rapt when a few of us volunteered to be extra fielders. The wicket was lively and Greg Blewett, Australia's No.6, had his thumb badly bruised by a rising delivery from Jason Gillespie, giving Ricky Ponting his first Test of the tour. It was a full-on, urgent session. The West Indies were no easybeats. All the frontliners had long spells, except for Warnie who sent down no more than a dozen balls in a side net to coach Geoff Marsh. Normally, even on match eve, he'd bowl for 45 minutes to an hour, spinning and spruiking, beating his chest like Tarzan. He was a game-changer and knew it.

Late in the session, with the main Test bowlers resting and even Andy Bichel the lionheart taking a breather, Justin Langer was having a second hit against Col Miller and I was asked if I'd like to bowl alongside him. Starting with two or three leg-breaks which all landed, I used my slider and struck Langer on his pads, outside the line of off stump, but it was still a good one. 'Hang on,' said Warnie from point. 'That was ok.' Michael Slater was next and within three or four balls, he ran at me and struck the most perfect six down the ground over long-on. 'That's it for you Master,' said Funky Miller. 'That ball… she's not comin' back.' On match morning, within the opening half an hour, Lara introduced his slow bowler Neramiah Perry and to his third ball, Slater danced at him and struck it onto the roof of the George Challenor Stand. 'You've played him into form Piessey,' said Margaret Milne, one of our tour group.

There must have been almost 1000 Australians on holiday, enjoying the banter and the tiny makeshift family food stalls at the back of Kensington Oval which sold everything from hard liquor, beer and cigarettes to soft drinks and candy bars. In-between overs, the ground announcer asked in beautifully-rounded, very formal English: 'Would Miss Kylie Minogue please come to the back of the members' stand? Mr Jason Donovan is waiting.'

I spent some time in the commentary box with Donna Symmonds and the legendary Everton Weekes who were broadcasting all over the islands for Carib Cricket Plus. I was doing radio crosses to Melbourne and Kevin Bartlett's breakfast show. TJ and I also met up for a midday stubby: our mutual choice Banks in its distinctive deep green bottle. Warnie's fitness and state of mind were concerns. He'd taken 1-129 from 44 overs in the opening two Tests and had little of his old zest, rhythm or bravado.

Despite a rocky beginning – Steve Waugh was in at 3-36 – the Australians had started with almost 500 and the Windies were backpedalling from the opening over when Adrian Griffith (on 0) went for a quick run to mid-off only for Ponting to pounce from cover and brilliantly throw the stumps down at the bowler's end. Warne was on in the ninth over, but purely to allow Glenn McGrath and Jason Gillespie to change ends. McGrath was Lillee-like, bowling full and straight and with nine wickets for the match, increased his series haul to 24. He was fast becoming the champion's champion.

It was a magnificent, thrilling Test. Set more than 300 to win, batting fourth, the Windies were 3-85 on the penultimate night. The game was evenly poised, but the locals were sure they'd win. We were among the first arrivals in the grandstand and the local delicacies, the freshly fried fish-balls in high demand. The sellers would stay in the narrow aisles and in chain gang fashion, our monies and the food would be passed back and forth from patron to patron, all the way to us. 'We're goin' to beat ya maan. We're goin' to beat ya,' the vendors kept saying. Thanks to Lara's unbeaten 153, they did, by a wicket, a muffed catch by a half-fit Healy in the final overs costing Australia the Test. He was under increasing pressure for his place and had tweaked both calves, reducing his mobility and forcing team management to call for ODI wicketkeeper Adam Gilchrist to come early, on stand-by.

With Dizzy Gillespie off the ground for long periods, McGrath was stoic, bowling virtually unchanged from the members. All five of his second innings wickets came bowled or lb. Shortly after lunch, Lara ducked into a bouncer and exchanged words with the fired-up Australian. Having chested McGrath in mid-pitch – Lara was standing on his tippy-toes – he complained to umpire Eddie Nicholls about McGrath's aggression and language.

Warne had again been used at first change and overnight had none for 15 from 10 overs. But his changes were minimal. No flippers. No googlies. Just variations of his leg-break. Early on the third morning, an hour before the resumption, Jenner gave him some centre square tutelage, with coach Marsh intently watching from the bowler's end. Both coach TJ and pupil seemed ill at ease, Warnie's body language a dead giveaway. Spinners are meant to be in their element late in a Test match. But this wicket was hard and unscuffed and Warne struggling to compete. It was almost like he was back in India 12 months earlier opposing Navjot Sidhu, one of the few internationals to regularly collar him. With Lara in supreme command, Warne had six outriders protecting the boundaries. Rarely had he appeared so powerless. On 97, Lara beat the field with a classic off-drive against Warne, registering another 100, this one without even a half-chance. Bajans love their cricket and they rose as one, in acclamation. But none of the Australians on-field clapped Lara's milestone after his earlier disagreement with McGrath. Warne's first six overs for the day cost 33. When one Lara six soared high over square leg into the bleachers, sections of the crowd started chanting 'Warnie, Warnie… keep 'im on, keep 'im on.' Nothing beats being at the big cricket live. The Healy miss, high to his left with Lara on 145, saw the Windies defy the odds and the partying began afresh.

The press conference was packed, all the local writers wanting to fete Lara, a hero yet again. Tony Cozier had a smile from ear to ear. For many of us he'd been the face of West Indian cricket since World Series. 'Good game cricket,' he laughed as he rushed past. Clive Lloyd, the West Indian team manager said Lara's display was 'sheer genius'. 'You dream of watching an innings like that,' he said. 'It doesn't get any better than that. I will remember this for the rest of my life.'

Steve Waugh was at his most ambassadorial, saying it had been the best Test match he'd played in and the Windies deserved to lead the series.[103] Ominously, when asked about Warne's form, he said: 'No one has an automatic right to a place. We have to pick the best team to win a Test match (in Antigua).' I relayed Waugh's frank after-match comments back to Sport 927 in Melbourne. 'Surely they're not thinking of dropping Shane Warne,' said KB. 'He's the King.'

---

103   Waugh had had a magnificent match, scoring 199 and 11 and sharing a fifth wicket stand of 281 with Ricky Ponting, who despite searing heat, batted throughout in a sleeveless jumper.

One of the biggest sporting sensations of the decade loomed and on arrival in St John's, Warne, the team's vice-captain, walked into a selection ambush. Coach Geoff Marsh wasn't sure which way to go, but Waugh was adamant. Warne was out. And he had the big vote. Warne pleaded his case. He would lift. Hadn't he always lifted previously when it most counted? It was purely a form issue, Waugh said. MacGill was bowling better and his wrong-'un was troubling the West Indian left handers. His figures[104] were also clearly superior. MacGill was playing and so was Funky Miller. He could bowl fast and slow. Warne left the meeting feeling totally betrayed and contemplating immediate retirement. He sulked through the entire Test week, his relationship with Waugh forever fractured. They were never again close.[105] 'Disappointed is not a strong enough word,' Warne said of his expulsion. 'When the crunch came, Tugga didn't support me and I felt so totally let down by someone who I had supported big time and was also a good friend.'[106]

Waugh told us later that the attack needed freshening. 'Geoff (Marsh) and I both had a gut feeling that Stuart (MacGill) was the right man for this time,' he said. 'Shane did tell us that he was ready and fired up for a big one. But Stuart would probably say the same thing too.'[107]

Waugh also confirmed that Adam Dale was playing, with Gillespie still sore. There was only three days between Tests. Before seeking out Healy for an interview for the *Sunday Herald Sun* back home, I spoke with Gilchrist, who had just arrived. 'This is the fourth or fifth time I have been on standby,' he laughed. 'Heals would have to have a broken leg not to play.'

---

104 MacGill had taken seven wickets at 31 in the first three Tests; Warne two wickets at 134.
105 A decade later, in *Shane Warne's Century, my top 100 Test cricketers*, published in 2008, Warne rated Steve Waugh outside his best 25 players of his time. He had Mark Waugh at 9; Steve was 26th. As one of his closest pals used to tell me, 'Shane has an elephant's memory…'
106 *No Spin*, Shane Warne with Mark Nicholas (Penguin Random House Australia, Melbourne, 2018)
107 *The Complete Shane Warne*, Ken Piesse (Viking, Melbourne, 1999)

On arrival at St John's, Healy had bought a T-shirt advertising the 'St John's decider'. For one of the few times in his career, he felt vulnerable and wanted a souvenir just in case he'd played his last Test.

ANTIGUA IS HOME to some of the most alluring beaches in the world. Locals boast there is a different beach for all 365 days of the year. Our group was at the luxury resort village Jolly Harbour and had a couple of golf carts at our disposal. We joined Rick and Marg Milne at lunch one day. The local delicacy was dolphin. 'I'm not eating Flipper,' said Susan. And didn't. It was cruise ship Tuesday and a monster of a ship from Fort Lauderdale docked at dawn. It must have been 17 storeys high and looked totally out of place among the palm-lined beaches. We'd never seen so many pop-up stalls, all expertly arranged on both sides of the narrowest possible path, forcing cruise guests to walk at a snail's pace. When one stopped at the head of the line, everyone stopped. And browsed.

The Aussies trained for the first time in some quality nets at the local Club Med. In Barbados, we'd hosted Bernard and the Australian scorer Mike Walsh to dinner. Also in attendance was one of my Beaumaris pals, Andrew King, son of my old much-loved footy mentor Ted. He was tall and handsome with a highly manicured waxed moustache which curled up at the sides like Hercule Poirot. He was on his way to Haiti for a surfing holiday. Andy had been staying at the same hotel as us and wondered if I'd be over for the Tests. The Brute told us that net bowlers were again likely to be scarce at St John's. He was refusing to hand out cash. He asked me if any of our younger tourists could bowl at any sort of pace and I said, 'yes, Wayne Chisholm comes from Albury way. He's in his early 20s and plays Saturdays'.

'Bring him along,' he said. 'I'll tell Swampy (Marsh).'

I duly told our boy from Berrigan of his upcoming appointment in

Antigua. Come Test-eve, right on 10am, we were there – and so was Wayne, warmed up and ready to go. His first ball was as wide as Steve Harmison's that day at the 'Gabba. Marsh looked around at me, as if to say: 'Are you sure he's the best you've got.' His next was even wider. He was so nervous bowling to some of the Test players and was soon retired, his brief flirtation with stardom over just as it was starting. Damon Runyan would have been at his colourful best writing about Wayne's 15 minutes of fame. We thought he was a hero just for trying.

THE ANTIGUA RECREATION Ground, or the 'ARG' to locals, home to the fourth and deciding Test, is unique as the local prison is at cow corner and the prisoners have a clear view of the proceedings over the top of the small United Stand. We'd so loved our week in Bridgetown and this match was to be even livelier, on and off the field. From cowbells and cross-dressers to Chickie's disco, the matchday entertainment was lavish. In-between overs, Chickie would blast out an array of reggae favourites from Bob Marley to Desmond Dekker and the Aces. He even played a rendition of *Tie Me Kangaroo Down Sport*, pointing to all of us decked out in green and gold in the Andy Roberts Stand.

Each day at the gate, we'd be given a different coloured paper wristlet. Some of the more athletic locals climbed trees at the southern end and had some of the best seats in the house. We were in the front rows at fine leg. Rosemary, our youngest and most fun-loving tourist and a huge Glenn McGrath fan was in her element with her regular calls of, 'Oo, Arr, Glenn McGrath', as the big fella rested directly in front of us in-between overs. As in Bridgetown, the staple diet was chicken and rice. And rum – lots of it. A Langer run out when he was going for a third and two 6s from tailender Col Miller against big Curtly were early highlights, one of Funky's 6s bouncing into the prison wall. Attempting a third maximum against Test debutant Corey Collymore, Miller swung so hard he lost his bat and it almost sconed the umpire at square leg. A third dazzling century in a row from Lara made our 24 flying hours from Melbourne to the Caribbean all worthwhile. He smashed 100 from 82 balls – an extraordinary strike rate for the times – and when he was dismissed by McGrath, the scoreline was 3-136. One of 'Chip' Dale's overs cost 22. MacGill was also pummelled. In 40 minutes of mayhem after tea, Lara made 68 and David Joseph, eight, prompting an extra late afternoon show from Gravy, Antigua's famous entertainer. He saved his most vibrant costumes for the weekend, donning a cherry tutu on the Saturday and an orange bikini on the Sunday.

McGrath was the only one able to leash Lara. He conceded just six scoring shots (for 13 runs) off 21 balls. He had a mid-pitch altercation with Griffith, spitting in his direction and afterwards in the rooms Lara was apoplectic, screaming at the match referee to throw the book at the Australian. I was one of three, maybe four journalists in the room. Lara saw us and unleashed anyway. Never before had I heard such a rant. Wish I'd recorded it!

McGrath took six wickets for the match but was lucky to bowl as long as he did. After some ill luck in his seventh over, he kicked at an advertising hoarding in front of us, not realising it was made of concrete. He limped for the next 10 minutes and needed extra treatment from the Australian physiotherapist Errol Alcott. Later he was to be fined 30 per cent of his match fee for the Griffith incident. After the Australians had won convincingly, Waugh backed him unequivocally. 'I know Glenn and I know that there's no way known he'd spit at him…' Hmm… maybe he hadn't seen the replays.

The afternoon sun at St John's was warm and at the fall of almost every wicket, Bichel would sprint back and forth carrying towels and drinks. Warnie, the official 12th man, was supposed to do some of the hard yakka but preferred to play sulky schoolboy and remained unseen except at the tea-breaks when he and Matthew Elliott hit tennis balls back and forth in front of the rooms. He spent much of his time smoking in the toilet block at the back of the rooms, having already been caught once smoking in public, contravening his sponsorship contract with Nicorette. Was Waugh justified in dropping Warne? The new-look Australians won by 176 runs to square the series,[108] MacGill taking five wickets for the game and Miller three. Warne was back in Australia's XI four days later for an ODI.

With the successful defence of the Frank Worrell Trophy and many fresh arrivals for the soon-to-start one-dayers, the Australian team's party went all afternoon and long into the evening, Rosemary returning to our own farewell in Funky Miller's creams. She'd had a huge night. As did we. It remains our favourite tour of all.

Steve Waugh, Warnie and the Australians celebrate the series-equalling victory at the Rec Reserve in St John's, Antigua.

---

108   Australia scored 303 and 306 and the Windies 222 and 211.

26
DISCOVERING STEVE SMITH

'I immediately rang Rob Elliot, told him of Smith's extraordinary innings and recommended he sign him immediately – before someone else did.'

It was January 2008. I was at Haileybury College, half an hour south of Melbourne, when a baby-faced Steve Smith lit up a sleepy midweek afternoon with a brilliant century in a state second XI fixture. Commanding, inventive and pulsating, anything pitched straight was caressed with authority through mid-wicket and square leg, reminiscent of a young Greg Chappell. When the Victorians tried to bowl a restrictive fifth stump line, Smith unleashed several imperious cover drives.

The attack was fast and willing and included Peter Siddle and Darren Pattinson, who within months were both to play Test cricket, Pattinson for England. Even on a school pitch the gifted teenager was unstoppable.

LIVING THE DREAM

He made 162 in a game which also featured Beau Casson, Moises Henriques, David Warner, who batted at No.8 and a young Phil Hughes.

Smith had been the most rated teenager in Sydney grade cricket since making 90 on debut for Sutherland's first XI two years earlier. I'd never seen a more assured display from one so young. I immediately rang Rob Elliot, the big boss at leading local bat and ball manufacturer Kookaburra Sport, told him of Smith's extraordinary innings and recommended he sign him immediately – before someone else did. 'Super' had contracted Tasmanian prodigy Ricky Ponting as a 13-year-old. He loved unearthing young champions. Smith, 18, duly joined the Kookaburra stable and by 21, his precocious talents so captivated and tantalised sets of selectors Australia-wide that he was regularly representing Australia across all three formats: Tests, one-day internationals and Twenty20s.

He was to become Australia's Test captain and the greatest player of his generation. Like Warner, however, for all his dozens of Test and ODI centuries, Smith's inadvertent involvement in the volcanic sports scandal of the century forever blights his legacy. He lost key sponsors, a six-figure multi-book contract, the leadership and was given a 12-month suspension. No one has wanted to re-live 30 seconds of their life more than Smith. When told of Warner's monstrous plan, he should have rejected it totally. But he was exhausted and unfit to be captain. He didn't want to know about it. Soon afterwards, after the scheme's patsy, Cam Bancroft, was sprung on the Big Screen holding a small piece of sandpaper, Smith joined Bancroft and the umpires in a huddle. Returning to the slips cordon, he was clearly agitated and distracted. He knew there would be repercussions but had no idea they would be so extreme. That night he and Bancroft fronted the media and exacerbated an already volatile situation and enraged all of Australia with an explanation shown later to be totally untrue. Even the Prime Minister erupted. I was filing for sportshounds.com.au and our stories were punchy, relevant and right up there with the best of Peter Lalor in the Oz. Pete and I had worked at the *Sunday Observer* together. He was just a young buck then and he was to become an outstanding cricket writer.

Smith's apology to a nation was sincere and heartfelt. Not so Warner's. Had he possessed some of Shane Warne's flair and natural PR skills, we, the cricketing public, may have forgiven him – and even warmed to him. But he didn't. And we didn't. His explanations were lame and feeble. On Warner's Test retirement in 2024, ex-Australian Damien Martyn showcased the innermost thoughts of many with a simple hashtag tweet: 'Thank God it's all over.' No cricketer in history had been more divisive or as polarising. The Bull got caught up in his own world and lost focus.

In his autobiography, South Africa's Faf du Plessis said no other player 'roused the dog'[109] in him quite like Warner. 'The way he climbed into me at the Adelaide Oval (on his debut) in 2012 just strengthened my resolve when the team needed me most. But it just wasn't me,' he said. 'I was stunned that he got stuck into Jacques Kallis, one of the greatest players of all time. Warner had made his Test debut just a year earlier but that didn't stop him from sledging Kallis as if he was still a rookie. In all my years of playing against Australia, Warner sledged me the most.'

In a distinguished 262-match international career across three formats, du Plessis said the Australians 'unlocked the fighter in me – and Warner, in particular, did this just by breathing'. Opposing Australia was like being in a war zone. 'They were unrelenting and brutal. The only way to win against them was to match their aggression in order to neutralise their attempts at bullying you into submission.'

---

109 Ken Piesse, sportshounds.com.au, March 2023. Smith and Warner were to be banned for 12 months after Cape Town. Cameron Bancroft also had to serve a lengthy suspension: nine months.

In the ill-tempered series in South Africa in the autumn of 2018, relations between the teams soured from the opening Test in Durban which the Australians won thanks to some remarkable reverse swing bowling from Mitchell Starc. After AB de Villiers was run out in a misunderstanding with rookie Aiden Markram, the Australians taunted Markram mercilessly. 'They told him it was his fault,' du Plessis said. 'And he was going to cost South Africa the match and the series. Theunis de Bruyn was also a target. The Australians are bullish. They're at the top of their game when their abuse of opposition players seems to be working.' At the end of a session Warner and Quinton de Kock clashed as they were walking off. The South Africans claimed Warner had told de Kock he stank and was 'a friggin sook'.

'Quinny never says anything on the cricket field,' said du Plessis 'and although none of us knew what a sook was, even he couldn't take the sledging. He told us afterwards that he retaliated by saying something about Warner's wife's past. Warner exploded. His face and neck turned red and he looked like a man possessed by demons who chose a human body that was too big to contain them.'

In Durban the two dressing rooms are adjacent, accessible by a staircase. Walking up the stairs, the argument between Warner and de Kock escalated, threatening to get physical. Tim Paine had to restrain Warner and Smith stood in-between the two combatants. Du Plessis, with just a towel around him, shouted at Warner to keep his mouth shut. Kagiso Rabada joined in. The normal amiable Lungi Ngini was frozen. A gentle giant, he couldn't believe the heat between the pair. 'We all felt Warner's behaviour was contrary to the spirit of the game and if the umpires weren't going to do anything about it, we were going to make a lot of noise until it was addressed,' said du Plessis. Video tape was shown of the incident and Warner the provocateur was fined 75 per cent of his match fee and handed three demerit points, which put him one point away from a suspension. 'Australia wanted to bully us and we allowed them,' said du Plessis, captaining against Australia for the first time at home. 'We decided to fight fire with fire.'

Susan and I were on the spot for all the shenanigans. Normally our group would attend the first two Tests of the series, but a Cape Town-Johannesburg double to finish was alluring. The series was locked at 1-1 and we were able to see the farewells of some of South Africa's elite. Being on the spot led to a new edition of my book *Cricket's Greatest Scandals*. And, in 2023, I released a biography of Warner, *The Bull, daring to be different*, going into even more exact detail about Sandpapergate. It was no hagiography. I detailed all of Warner's indiscretions from his relentless sledging, his expulsion from the Centre of Excellence, his insanely stupid punch on Joe Root in Birmingham and his lead role in Cape Town. Later, after its release, I spoke to some key NSW grade tribunal members. They had some rip-roaring tales to tell. It was as if the enigmatic Warner was a cricketing Johnny Depp, a feisty, rollicking, swashbuckling pirate, oblivious of onfield etiquette and the game's unwritten rules.

Our series of launches ranged from land to the High Seas as we spent New Year's crossing the Tasman on P & O's Pacific Explorer. In Albury at St Patricks CC, home to one of Warner's most loyal supporters, 15-year-old Sam Williams, Sam's Mum Marita spoke glowingly of Warner's friendship and mentoring of her son. Sam, then nine, had written to Warner after Cape Town, saying the only mistake in life is not to learn from the mistakes you make. Sam had a wisdom way beyond his years. In gratitude, Warner invited him to his club, Randwick-Petersham, and gave him the best time. Marita Williams says Warner was no wild cannon. He was caring and would regularly ring her son no matter where he was in the world and ask how he was going. The tormenting little buzzard had a softer side. An updated version of *The Bull* promises to be even meatier.

27
HIGH SOCIETY

'"Ken," he wrote in explanation, "I am all meetinged out." I'd caught out a Prime Minister once but had never before sacked one...'

I was 15 when my Dad, Ken snr, first took me to the Charles Lux Pavilion in Prahran for an Australian Cricket Society quarterly meeting and paid $3.25 for my joining fee and student's subscription. An 1890 Wisden was being auctioned and he made sure he was the highest bidder. Years later, midway through my lifetime in cricket and football, I started editing the Society's flagship publication Pavilion and the Society's president Richard Elvins asked if I would be his successor. He felt my contact base and passion for the game could make the ACS more relevant and dynamic.[110]

Soon into my appointment, Richard rang very late one night. 'Ken,' he said, 'we're broke.'

---
110 I served as ACS president from 2006-2022. Previously Colin Barnes (1983-96) held the long service record.

The money reserves thought to be in the coffers had 'disappeared'. The only remaining monies were the proceeds from the sale of the cricket library belonging to an early philanthropist, Dean Chamberlin.

As part of our resurrection, over the next decade-and-a-half we were able to direct more than $30,000 to the Ponting Foundation, caring for the families of children with cancer, a charity particularly relevant for Susan and I as our daughter Tori was to die from cancer, aged 34. We're not meant to outlive our children.

Our vibrant new Society also saw the fast-tracking of dozens of young teenage cricketers with stars in their eyes to become better cricketers and people. And Susan and I led a host of overseas tours, triggering lifelong memories and friendships, a prelude to my sports entertainment role with P & O.

Richard's phone call was the genesis for our ACS Gold Partner corporate program, the appointment of a new, illustrious patron in Ricky Ponting and the beginning of our Academy and Literary Scholarship programs. All were my initiatives. John Howard had been our first patron but never showed – not even once. 'Ken,' he wrote in explanation, 'I am all meetinged out.' I'd caught out a Prime Minister once but had never before sacked one.

We ran a series of headline events, a Boxing Day Test function and launched the new football season each April featuring celebrities from Hawthorn playing icons Peter Hudson, Leigh Matthews and Dermott Brereton to Peter McKenna, Tommy Hafey and Ron Barassi. McKenna was one of the funniest. 'People say I come from Heidelberg West,' he began. 'We prefer to call it Toorak North.' Mal Brown heard that Barass was to address us and suggested he wasn't as sharp as he once was. I bought a tiny little bell with me to the event and told Ron I'd ring it every time he went off on a tangent. He gave me that famous Barassi stare and delivered the best 45 minutes of flowing footy nostalgia and anecdotes that most of us had ever heard. What an inspirational man.

Instead of what were once small lunches for a maximum of 20 around the chairman's table upstairs at the Kelvin Club, we ran major functions in big rooms, with high profile guests like Barass and Bradman Invincible Neil Harvey, an event which attracting almost 120, with tables stretching to every corner of the Kelvin. Australian captain Tim Paine appeared for us at the Junction Oval just days before flying out to lead the 2019 Ashes campaign. By enticing the biggest names in cricket and football to our functions, our audiences doubled and trebled.

With more than 350 members we have a fresh buoyancy. We meet, we tour, we play, we engage. It's a wonderful fraternity. And from having basically $10,000 in the bank – the proceeds of the sale of the Chamberlin library – at the time of writing we now have $30,000 at our disposal from which we have been funding our scholarship program, initially with our ambassador, my ex-Frankston clubmate Bryce McGain and in the following years with Keith Jansz, an expert coach and a Sri Lankan Over 60s international.

Susan and I hosted tours to the UK, New Zealand, South Africa and Zimbabwe, some of our friends coming with us five and six times. In the early Ashes tour years, 2009 and 2013, we also played several matches, most notably in Bath and in equally leafy Meopham in Kent, thanks to my school pal Drew Payne, now living back in Melbourne. I hosted Drew to the Saturday's play at the 2009 Lord's Test and he still talks about me ringing home on my iPad from the front row in the Mound Stand and asking to speak to Douglas, my chocolate labrador. On another of our tours, Drew was to meet the love of his life, Pam.

We all so loved being at the big cricket. Edgbaston 2005 was epic. On Day 1, as our group was walking in, Glenn McGrath was being stretchered past us. He'd stood on a ball and was out of the game. We took our seats and shared the stunning news of McGrath's injury with four well-dressed gents sitting directly behind us. We learnt later that they were lawyers. And very smart ones. Immediately pooling their available cash, one hastened to the betting tent out the back of the stand and casually asked the odds against McGrath not taking a wicket. He'd grabbed nine at Lord's. 'Oh mate,' he was told. 'You can have 15s. No, make it 20/1!'

The game was a thriller, thanks to the genius of Shane Warne. The louder the lads in the Hollies Stand booed and brayed, the better he bowled. It was my 50th birthday and Warnie the batsman almost brought us home, totally against the odds. That morning I visited the Ladbroke's boys and put 50 quid on the Aussies at 12/1. It was Sunday night in Melbourne and as the Aussie tailenders batted out of their skin, I did cross after cross with Andrew Kuuse back to the Sport 927 radio studios in Melbourne. 'Why is Andrew ringing so often?' Susan asked. 'Let him. He's bringing us good luck.'

With three to tie and four to win, Brett Lee pierced the infield and from our angle at fine leg, the ball seemed to be careering to the boundary ropes at point, only for a lone outrider, Simon Jones, to emerge from the shadows. It was just a single and Michael Kasprowicz, Australia's No.11, was out immediately afterwards.[111]

England had won by a whisker and I'd done my dough. My mate Dennis Coon was coming out to birthday dinner with us, but with the early finish, he'd found himself in Broad Street and the infamous Walkabout bar and was talking double-Dutch. A man is no camel.

---

111 Kasprowicz's caught behind dismissal would have been reversed via DRS today. Umpire Billy Bowden gave him caught off his glove, but his hand was off his bat at the time.

The 2019 Lord's and Headingley Tests were also remarkable, highlighted by the spitfire pace of Jofra Archer in London[112] and the incredible solo from England's now captain Ben Stokes in Leeds. This game ended in four days, allowing us to spend a blissfully warm Bank Holiday Monday in Scarborough after taking a fast train through the breathtaking Yorkshire Dales. That trip we'd started in Scotland, going as far north as Inverness in the Highlands and onto the west coast and the Harry Potter Hogwarts Express. Being a tourist is so much fun.

In 2018, our time in southern Africa included a stay at the century-old Victoria Falls Hotel and three days at the Lukimbi Safari Lodge at Kruger National Park, where we saw the Big Five and caught a rare glimpse of a cheetah, close-up. Outside the birth of our children and my Mum's 100th birthday, it was the best 72 hours of our lives, despite two of our tourists, David Beames and Cooky being chased down a dirt trail by an enraged female buffalo, unhappy at how close they had gone to her young calf which had strayed.

Just weeks earlier, in Cape Town, we'd witnessed the shambolic sandpaper affair which brought Australian cricket to its knees. I was filing for sportshounds.com.au and the editors back home were pressing me to include coach Darren Lehmann among the culprits. 'No,' I said. 'Please do not alter the copy. Lehmann is too good a cricket person. If he had known what was going on he would have stopped it, then and there.' *(It was my personal opinion at the time and still is)*

In the opening Test in Durban that turbulent autumn, David Warner had reverted to his heinous 'attack dog' ways and abused the younger South Africans, triggering the most tersely contested Test series since Bodyline. South Africa's cricket 'Godfather' Ali Bacher contacted Faf

---

112 Archer all but ko'ed Steve Smith, triggering Test cricket's first ever 'concussion substitute' – Marnus Labuschagne – who himself was also hit in the helmet, first ball. The BBC's Jonathan Agnew called it the most intimidating over ever in Ashes Tests.

du Plessis suggesting he walk off the ground in protest should the foul language and bullying continue. Another ex-captain Graeme Smith called Warner a fool. Australia's behaviour was the pits – no credit to captain Steve Smith, a hero months earlier in the preceding Ashes series, batting a record 34 hours and cementing his standing among the very best players to sport a baggy green. When AB de Villiers was run out after a mix-up, Nathan Lyon dropped the ball on his chest and raced off to celebrate with his teammates. Cricket Australia's chief executive James Sutherland was furious and rang Smith at the team's luxury hotel that night, saying it was the worst possible look for the game. Midway through his tirade, Smith interrupted: 'We'd just run out the best player in the world. He (Lyon) can do what he likes...'

Smith should never have been allowed to captain Australia again.

WE were in Trent Bridge at a huge barn of a banquet centre on the eve of the first Test in 2013. Almost 400 Australians were enjoying complimentary Peronis, mini pizzas and sausage rolls, all on the house, as we listened to the affable Lancastrian David Lloyd and other old Test stars debating the likely outcome of the Ashes. I told David of my biography in preparation of Cec Pepper, the volatile Australian who later became a county championship umpire. 'Yes, Cec umpired me as a 17 or 18-year-old,' Bumble said. 'He kept deliberately farting as I was bowling. He didn't think I could bowl a hoop downhill – and I couldn't.'

Initially our group had gathered at the back of the room before moving closer to the kitchen to partake in more of the freebees. Three of the Australian players were also present including the team's No.1 slow bowler Nathan Lyon. Immediately after the speeches, I bowled up to Nathan suggesting he should be back at the pub resting. 'Oh, they haven't picked the side yet,' he said diplomatically.

Actually, they had and wildcard Ashton Agar from Melbourne via Perth was to make his Test debut. His family had just landed at Heathrow. I reported back to Michael Christian and Angela Pippos at Sport 927, but minutes into our cross, the line dropped out before I could suggest a late change was likely – and that Australia would have a new spin specialist from left field – one who'd never played before. In 2017, Agar contributed the foreword to *Heroes of the Hour*:

> *'It was all so surreal. Only a fortnight earlier I'd been packing my bags in Bristol and looking forward to seeing everyone at home again (after the Australia A tour) when (selection chairman) John Inverarity called. He told me that I'd been selected to join the Ashes touring party, along with Steve Smith. It was unclear for how long I would stay in the beginning, but little did I know that things would change very quickly. It was a huge surprise.*
>
> *'Approaching Test match week, we'd had a warm-up game in Worcester.*[113] *I knew I was a chance to play at Trent Bridge as normally, especially for a spinner, they'd pick you in the final warm-up game before the Test so you could be in your best rhythm and have plenty of overs under your belt. I felt good. It was the best possible preparation.'*

Pre-game, Agar's captain Michael Clarke was asked by one of the umpires Kumar Dharmasena about Australia's teenage debutant. 'Not sure about his bowling,' Pup replied, 'but he can sure bat.' And, in a magical beginning, from No.11, Agar made 98 with a gnarly old bat, similar in looks to what Hookesy had used on debut in the Centenary Test in '77. He also took several key wickets. Had Stuart Broad walked

---

113   Agar, 19, bowled 50 overs across two innings on Test-eve at New Rd. Worcester, taking two for 79 and one for 86.

when he'd nicked one to slip, the Australians may well have won the game. Instead, they lost by 14 in a thriller. Two dozen of our ACS faithful were there to see it. We had the lucky seats that week.

CO-ORDINATING THE celebrities for our many Society events could be stressful, especially the day one player manager rang 48 hours before our annual dinner to say: 'Sorry, but Ricky can't come on Friday. His little boy is in hospital. Can you get someone else?' More recently, another guest, a high-profile Test player, was suddenly unavailable after being involved in a fist fight just days earlier. He was too embarrassed to show his shiner in public. His coach was ropable and as a favour to me, took his place.

In autumn 2022, Ashes hero Scott Boland was called to Brisbane for three days of extra training. He, too, wouldn't be able to fulfill his commitment. Happily, we were able to reschedule our dinner for exactly one week later, before Scott flew to Colombo for Australia's wintertime Test series in Sri Lanka. We played a highlight reel of Scott's remarkable onslaught during the 2021-22 Christmas Test, one member at the end of the night exclaiming: 'Play it again Scotty'. Scott appeared in dozens of photos with our award-winners and guests. He was so gracious and humble and it was a terrific night, despite one well-lubricated gent accidentally knocking over our merchandise table and spilling red wine over our books for sale.

At the very first of my 16 annual dinners, Australia's coach John Buchanan was guest-of-honour. The string section from Bec's school, Toorak College, played some beautiful pre-dinner mood music. John talked of his admiration for Shane Warne in being able to still perform so wonderfully well despite his private hell. Never before had he seen such a series of astonishing solos as Warnie was to produce in 2005, keeping the Ashes alive for the Australians until the very final afternoon at Kennington Oval. It was a rare and riveting insight from a cricket heavyweight.

Having the world-class David Hobson sing three songs in the prelude to Mike Hussey's address also made for a fantastic night. His version of the American folk song *Shenandoah* was breathtaking. So emotive, so powerful. David had also very kindly appeared at the Kelvin Club on Neil Harvey celebration day.

The High Tea launch at the much-loved Windsor Hotel (in 2008) of another of my books, *Our Don Bradman*, saw Sir Donald's son John appear, along with Arthur Morris and Kamahl. Our event was a sellout: 196 guests; the same number of runs Morris had made at The Oval in 1948. Four or five tables of corporates attended, including my Beaumaris buddy Ollie Powell and his mates from Mazda. It was a fabulous afternoon, ex-president Neville Turner welcoming guests with some piano solos before Kamahl sung *Ol Man River*, the Don's all-time favourite song. It remains my No.1 function among almost 140 ACS events I arranged.

Not all of our events were a success, however. One late January evening, in my early days, we had South Australian trio Matt Elliott, Mark Cosgrove and Lehmann address us at the 'G. Ten showed up. 'Where is everyone?' asked Boof. It was still a great, fun night. Just no one came.

SENDING A SHIP container full of cricket equipment, brand new sports shoes and books to Vanuatu one year gave us all great pleasure. The Islanders were ecstatic, with the gear being shared between many of their keenest male and female cricketers. Coach Shane Deitz invited me to train with their National team. Some had only thongs and board shorts, but they loved the game. And were good at it.

The Academy scholars have all been so grateful for their fast tracking. So far Australian XI allrounder Tess Flintoff is our biggest success story. She was first involved at Bryce McGain's Academy as a 13-year-old.

Interest in our playing XIs is ballooning and each autumn, we are a perennial force in the Echuca Over 60s state carnival, winning Division I honours in 2024 thanks to our 'Miracle at Cooma', where Peter Robinson and Andrew Chisholm starred after we were down and almost out at nine-for with still 25 needed and only three or four overs left. The mateship among us all is immense. We even have our own victory song, borrowed from the Carlton footy club:

> 'Bar-bar-bar-bar-bar,
>
> 'Bar-bar-bar-bar-bar,
>
> 'Bar-bar-bar-bar-bar,
>
> 'We are the ACS,
>
> 'The old dark ACS,
>
> 'We're the team that never lets you down,
>
> 'We're the only team from ACS town...'

The grandest of all my 140 Australian Cricket Society functions: the launch of my book, Our Don Bradman in 2008. Arthur Morris was guest of honour and Kamahl also attended, singing the Don's favourite *Ol' Man River*.

28

CROSSING DON BRADMAN

'For years Pepper lived in a menage-a-trois and had at least four boys with four different women, only one in wedlock...'

Gill Brewster was only half-joking. 'Ken,' she said, 'we'll have to blindfold you. No one knows where our warehouse is.' The Melbourne Cricket Club loved my idea of a book celebrating its first 125 years of Test cricket. Having access to little known photographs encouraged a vibrant sale and Gill promised me carte blanche to anything the club held – but only if I agreed to never, ever, divulge the off-site location.

So, somewhere north of the MCG, between Jolimont and Junee is this colossal treasure-trove in a century-old building in which one could spend a week and still not see everything. Gill drove me there herself and back to the club afterwards. 'It's good isn't it?' she said. 'Better than that Gill. It's phenomenal!' *Cricket's Colosseum* was published in 2003 in hardback by Hardie Grant, one of Melbourne's leading publishing houses. It featured some stunning imagery, the pictures all carefully copied at my request by the MCC's in-house photographer. They included:

- A Vicker's Gin sporting calendar from 1937 depicting, in colour, a recreation of Australia's first centurion Charles Bannerman leaving the MCG in 1877 to acclamation;
- The glide which took Victor Trumper to his one-and-only Test century in Melbourne in 1911;
- And a *Sunday Telegraph* newspaper banner of Don Bradman's full first-class season-by-season scores.

The originals would be worth hundreds. 'Colosseum' is high on my list among the most satisfying and attractive of almost 70 cricket books I have written, edited or published. To make publisher Sandy Grant's deadline, I cut short a season of Premier cricket, stopping at Christmas 2002 to work seven days a week to finish the manuscript. Bill Lawry provided a foreword saying how important cricket and the MCG had been to 'every fabric' of his life. 'Never have I felt more honoured, or as emotional,' he wrote, 'as when I joined the other living Australian Test captains at the MCG during the centenary Test celebrations… It remains my all-time favourite moment from 50 years in the game.'

My *Pictorial History of Australian Cricket* (Echo, 2016) was even more sumptuous, a coffee-table sized hardback with brilliant photography and an array of images of rare cigarette and trade cards, badges and Bodyline season postcards issued by the Melbourne *Herald* and loaned to me by one of Australia's greatest cricketing aficionados and collectors Gerard Conlan. I was in a moonboot on my visit and still remember negotiating Gerard's stairs! My favourite photo from the book shows Don Bradman advertising Peters Ice Cream. The Don knew his worth and was among the first cricketers to cash in on his popularity.

Of all the 80-plus books I have written, published, edited or ghosted, the one which shocked and surprised most and led me down so many unexpected avenues was my biography of the maverick Australian professional Cec Pepper. Only 500 were printed across two editions. Interest in his career was limited as he was from a bygone era, had never represented his country and only a few were still alive who had see him play Lancashire League cricket. But it was a rollicking yarn with an 'x' factor: Don Bradman. *Wisden* loved it:

> '"Those who dared cross Don Bradman had a habit of disappearing," is a splendid opening line, and* Pep: The Story of Cec Pepper, the Best Cricketer Never to Represent Australia *was one of the year's most unexpected treats. Cecil Pepper, Ken Piesse, reminds us, was a garrulous, profane, six-smashing, leg-spinning all-rounder, who collected more than 14,000 runs and 1800 wickets in the Lancashire Leagues. His greatest hours came in the Victory Tests of 1945, when-alongside Keith Miller-he starred for the Australian Services XI. On their tour of Britain, he averaged 42 with the bat and 27 with his leggies and flippers.*
>
> *'The defining moment in his career, such as it was, came soon after the Services XI returned home. At Adelaide in December 1945, they played South Australia. Pepper bowled to Bradman and, according to legend, had him plumb lbw twice in an over (both with the flipper) only to be denied on each occasion. "What do you have to do to get the little bastard out?" Pepper asked the umpire, before, perhaps ill-advisedly suggesting: "You're a fucking cheat." That was that, and Pepper, as the subtitle says, never did play for Australia. Piesse is protective of his subject, and fiercely partisan; the result is extremely entertaining.'* [114]

---

114   Alex Massie, *Wisden 2020.*

Pep was a larger-than-live character, big and brusque who flaunted convention and authority and treated women flippantly, loving and leaving them. For years Pepper lived in a menage-a-trois and had at least four boys with four different women, only one in wedlock. At the time of publication, in 2018, I knew of only three, but a fourth sibling, Londoner Robert Butlin, contacted me early in 2024:

'Dear Ken

'I've just read the fascinating book that you wrote about the life of Cec Pepper after tracking down a copy in a Sydney bookshop. I live in England but managed to get a copy sent over here as I couldn't find a copy in this country.

'The book (and his story) has particular significance to myself because Cec was also my father. I was born in December 1964, just a couple of months after Paul (another son). My mother had first met Cec as long ago as 1959 but had kept their affair secret over the subsequent years and I was also kept out of the spotlight as I grew up and sadly never made contact with my father after my mother died in the early 1970s.

'I don't know if you'd be interested in any further information, but I'd love to hear from you as I'm only now trying to discover more about my past and relatives. I've been doing some research into the cricket archives of the Lancashire League so got quite a few details from his time at Burnley but really feel I've only scratched the surface about his amazing life and career.

'I haven't made any attempt to contact any of my half-brothers as yet. I thought it might be best to write to you first as someone with an overview of my father's life.

Top: My 2018 biography of the maverick Australian Cec Pepper was rated one of the year's 'unexpected treats' by Wisden. Back then, I knew of only three Pepper sons, but in 2024, a fourth, Londoner Rob Butlin made contact. He'd met his Dad only once, when he was a toddler.

Above: My *Complete Guide to Australian Football* was launched at the MCG in 1993 and updated in 1995. Rex Hunt and Paul Salmon were among the guests of honour, Rex contributing the foreword. Later, Fish and I combined in writing his autobiography.

I appreciate this is a message completely out of the blue but if you are able to contact me I'd be absolutely delighted.

'Sincerely

'Robert Butlin'

Having children outside the sanctity of marriage was considered highly scandalous at the time. Like his wartime buddy Keith Miller, Pep lived in the moment, not knowing what was to come. I wrote to Robert and he enjoyed my recollections of meeting one of his half brothers, Paul Tetlow, in a café in the heart of Leeds. I was running late and wondered how I would recognise him. There must have been 200 in a huge room. The first face I sighted was Paul's. He was a deadringer for his Dad with the same wide face and toothy grin. I laughed, he smiled and we had a mighty hour together.

By chance, Pep's third son, Hugh Lake also contacted me, from Suffolk. He'd heard about my researches. He too was a love child. When he contacted Pepper, Cec thought Hugh was wanting money and hung up. 'I only wanted to know if he'd like to see his grandchildren,' Hugh told me.

It was an emotional, roller-coasting journey. Arthur Morris wrote the foreword but with the complications of our Tori's tragic illness, publication was delayed and Arthur didn't live long enough to see the finished product. 'I always wondered if he had his time again whether he would have been less opinionated on the field,' Morris said. 'It may have helped him to have the Test cricket career he wanted… and deserved.'[115]

Cec's brother Keith and sister Alma signed the sheets inserted into the original hardbacks. Keith, 97, said it was 'the best bloody book on cricket and a cricketer that I've ever read – but I am biased!' The mayor of Parkes

---

115   *Pep: The Story of Cec Pepper, the Best Cricketer Never to Represent Australia*, Ken Piesse (cricketbooks.com.au, Melbourne, 2018)

hosted a launch for the book in council chambers. The little wild west town known for its annual Elvis Festival was so proud of its most famous summer son. Effervescent Keith bowled up to me after the speeches and said: 'Fancy a beer… you've deserved it.'

IN MAY 2024, Rob Butlin, Pep's fourth son – and there may be more – wrote again:

'Dear Ken

'Thanks for getting back to me so promptly. Sorry about the slight delay in responding. My mother (Jean Butlin) worked in banking in the north of England which is where she met my father (in 1959) and continued to see him over the next few years. The impression I get is that he didn't want to really know my mother once I'd been born but, having read one of her diaries in more detail, I believe he may have met me briefly late in 1968, when I was four. I don't recollect the meeting, but I seem to have taken a liking to him – which my mother didn't approve of. My mother and Gran moved from the north of England to the Midlands in order to keep me "secret" but didn't like it there and yearned to return to the North. I've attached a few excerpts from my mother's diaries (from 1966 and 1969) which seem to suggest I had an unusual accent for where I was living. They actually encouraged me to say, "Damn Daddy Pepper" (October 7, 1966 entry) which certainly shows they unfortunately didn't harbour particularly good feelings about him.

'These were very different times to nowadays and the difficulties of being a single parent were obviously quite a

challenge. It's a shame I was kept out of the limelight and away from my father but I can only assume they thought it was for the best. They didn't want to create any sort of "scandal".

'Yours sincerely

'Robert Butlin'

HAVING SUCH ACCESS to little-known and fresh material is a lifeline for any writer.

I conducted 35 to 40 fresh interviews for the biography of Geelong's enigmatic, mesmerising superstar Gary Ablett snr. Allan Jeans had tired of his flippant attitude and wild behavior at Hawthorn. He had a season with Myrtleford, walking into the local pub with his footy kit over his shoulder. 'My uncle told me I might be able to get a game with you,' he said to Greg Nichols, Myrtleford's captain-coach. He was outstanding all year, playing as a goalkicking centreman. One day against Wangaratta Rovers at home, Ablett kicked five and took a soaring, sky-high mark on top of an opponent's shoulders, a little like the pride of Longwarry, Peter Knights. 'You just don't see marks of that quality, especially in the bush,' said Bill McMaster, Geelong's long-time recruiter. He hi-tailed it back to Geelong as fast as he could, telling Billy Goggin and Tommy Hafey he'd just seen the best country footballer in his lifetime. 'If he was available right now, next week, I'd place him straight in the centre,' he said.[116]

Ablett's best was extraordinary, eclipsing everyone. He was the AFL's Michael Jordan. But he was a troubled soul and struggled with life even in a big country town like Geelong. Malcolm Blight had just become coach and Ablett missed back-to-back early sessions. Blight heard he wasn't showing up again that night. Blight had a one-two-three-you're out

---

116   *Ablett, the Gary Ablett Story* (Information Australia, Melbourne, 1994)

theory. He was ready to sack him on the spot. They met at the Balyang Wildlife Sanctuary, just near the Barwon. Blight spoke about the need for Ablett to be a leader, set a better example and be a mentor for the young ones. 'We all know you can play Gary,' he said. Motioning to a small pine bridge stretching across a section of a lake, he said: 'Either you walk over that bridge with me, Gary – or I'm going to push you off.'

There was a pause, for four maybe five seconds, the two men eyeballing each other, neither dropping their gaze. 'Suppose I'd better go and get my gear then,' said Ablett, re-igniting his fabulous career which was to see him kick 100 goals or more in three consecutive seasons. My fresh interviews made for a bestseller. One Friday night, just before the book was due to print, Ablett rang. Susan answered. 'Ken,' she said. 'It's Gary Ablett.' Gary wanted 'in' on the book after-all and yes would sit down for an interview. But he wanted too much money. I'd deliberately written around many of his misdemeanors. I wanted it to be a hero book and it remains one of my very best.

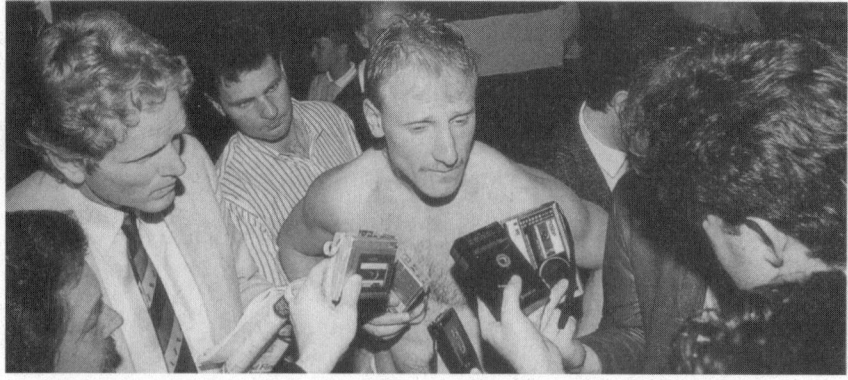

Gary Ablett snr was rarely at ease at interviews, but he was always in demand, so spectacular were his goalkicking feats. The *Herald Sun's* Tony de Bolfo (far right) and I are among his inquisitors in this press conference at Kardinia Park in the early '90s.

ANOTHER BEST-SELLING biography followed in 1995, *Warne Sultan of Spin*, the mid-career story of a mischievous, girl-crazy kid from the Melbourne bayside with the rare ability to spin the ball like no one before, or since. Many of Warnie's school buddies and teammates from Brighton to the Australian Test team contributed, ensuring a lively read. If there was fun to be had, Shane was always up front and centre. His buddies called him 'The Moth'. Anywhere a light was on, he'd appear. Some of his schoolboy escapades were hilarious. Legendary Melburnian Weg (Bill Green) did a series of classic cartoons. Cricket tragic and commentator Rex Hunt contributed a visionary foreword, saying Warnie could become the greatest bowler of all. 'Shane dared to be different,' Rex wrote. 'And that's why he has assumed such star status. We have never seen a spin bowler with the same flair, panache and sense of theatre. Thanks to Shane, it seems every second kid you meet now wants to bowl leggies.'[117]

Warnie signed a copy for one of my Dad's old hockey pals, Don Moyes. 'Nothing to do with me,' he said. Deep down, I know he enjoyed it, despite not appreciating the full-length picture on page 131 of his model wife Simone Callahan in white high heels and a matching G-string.

Warnie's biography and David Warner's The Bull, published almost 30 years later, virtually promoted themselves, Warner's story gaining some extra momentum after my 2023 springtime podcast appearance on *You Can't be Serious* with Sam Newman and for a few minutes, Don Scott. The two had been warring in the lead-up and I was the meat in their peculiar sandwich as Sam sounded off. Even a sailor would have blushed at some of the language. Neither took a backward step and when Sam said, 'Go on, piss off.' Don did… never to return. Sam and I continued on, Sam keen to know why Warner was so polarising. 'He didn't have your Grammar education Sam,' I said.

Sam smiled and continued: 'You've written a lot of books Ken. How many?' '88'. 'My godfather… where does this one rate?'

'It's in the Grand Final, among my very best.' And it was.

---

117 *Warne Sultan of Spin*, Ken Piesse (Celebrity Publishing, Melbourne, 1995)

29
THRILL OF THE HUNT

'That is why we Australia love beating you England in anything…'

Time stands still in Port Chalmers, gateway to the stunning Edwardian city of Dunedin in New Zealand's dreamy deep south. Misty clouds shroud a century-old church nestling in the foothills near our cruise ship. An albatross hovers majestically in the wind, its huge wingspan unmistakeable, before it soars effortlessly up through the clouds. Everything is serene and unspoilt. The evening sun illuminates the tree-lined, rocky coastline. It's postcard perfect.

We'd just trekked up Dunedin's Royal Terrace and visited Olveston, one of its grandest private homes, finished in 1906 and in impeccable order, with all its original furniture and artefacts, including a Steinway, a large library of classic books and in the glassed-off garage, a lovingly restored 1921 Fiat. I ask Vivienne, our hostess, if there is anything on cricket. 'No,' she says smiling. 'But there are some on trekking and many on travel. I've just dusted them.'

The library is dimly lit to help preserve the spines of the books. Its 100-year-old wallpaper, sourced from America, is still pristine.

The beautifully maintained cottage garden, with all its herbaceous borders, flows rhythmically, with multi textures and colours with bulbs, annuals, hydrangeas and roses. A woodland area includes a stunning copper beech, its canopy so formidable that it entirely blankets the two o'clock sun. The serenity is marked, yet we are only 10 minutes from town.

We had initially intended to spend our day at Carisbrook, Dunedin's original Test cricket venue, superseded now by the leafy Otago University cricket ground. A 20-year-old Dennis Lillee had opened the bowling there against the locals in 1970. Greg Chappell was first change and made 80-odd from No.5. It was often a green top and invariably a two-jumper job. 'Do you go past the old Test cricket ground?' I asked the bus driver. 'You know, Carisbrook?'

'We do,' he said. 'But there's nothing there now. It's an industrial estate – only some gates from the original ground have survived.' Everywhere we cruise, Cairns, Norfolk Island, Fiji, Vanuatu or NZ, we like to find the nearest cricket ground.

Thanking the driver, we instead headed uptown to our favourite group of second-hand bookshops, including the best, Dead Souls in Princes Street. In the window was a pristine copy of *Dance Bands of North Otago*, the author a Colin Dorsey. While the cricket stock was limited, there was a Noel Streatfeild first edition, complete with its original dustjacket and a Cecil Beaton I had not seen before – both gratefully procured for Jessie, our collecting daughter.

He recommended we also visit the 'esoteric little bookshop' in the main street back at Port Chalmers before re-embarking. On arrival, the gent was playing an early JJ Cale album, on vinyl. 'JJ' often recorded from his front verandah. On some tracks, he's so laidback, he's almost asleep. I particularly love his ever-so-soft introduction: 'One, Two, Three, Four' leading into *Crazy Mumma*. We were immediately at ease and spent almost an hour there, chatting and perusing. 'Sorry I didn't have more for you,' he said. 'We loved every moment,' I said. 'Especially your taste in music.'

We'd eagerly anticipated our mid-cruise visit to Christchurch and its spectacular jewel-in-the-crown rose garden on the fringes of the Avon. Despite two earthquakes during a horrific six-month period in 2010-11, the Botanical Gardens had been unaffected. It was the city's only large open space of safety.

Fifteen minutes south, a large library also beckoned: books, matchday brochures and small, ultra-rare fixture cards, including some from Australia's post-war Test tour in 1946. There was also an uninterrupted, immaculate run of the *NZ Cricketer* magazine from the mid-'60s, sourced for my collecting mate Bruce Hockings. I bought almost everything. The collection had been considered irrelevant by the NZ Cricket Council and discarded. *(Several years earlier Cricket Victoria had also disposed of hundreds of books once housed in an ornate bookcase immediately outside its magnificent teak lined delegate's room in Jolimont. It kept only its* Wisden *set for its move to the Junction Oval.)*

Inside the early editions of the NZ Cricketer were some rare images, old and new, from Australian Test legends Charlie Macartney and Alan Kippax pictured together at the Basin Reserve in the '20s through to NZ's first express bowler Gary Bartlett, 'The Marlborough Meteor' whose international career was to end ignominiously after the 1968 Indians, frightened out of their wits, labelled him a thrower. Clips of his action are damning. The magazine had been edited by Dick Brittenden, the most famous and enduring of all NZ sportswriters. In the sixth year of publication, he apologised that the cover price had to increase from 40 to 45 cents. As I perused the volumes, several KEN PIESSE requests for NZ books appeared. I was just 15 at the time and working two paper rounds to help satisfy my growing obsession. I'd forgotten I'd taken out the advertisements but was glad I had. A Mr Gregory in Christchurch wrote and offered his collection. He was downsizing. Would I like the lot? Dad advanced me the money and when seven big boxes arrived late one early spring afternoon, it was like Christmas had come early. There must have been almost 150 books, all originals, all hardbacks. Most of the NZ standards were there: Brittenden, Cameron, Carman, Reese, Reid and Sutcliffe. To help pay for them, I missed a season of under-age football and worked winter weekends selling flower seeds. When the arrears had reduced below $100, Dad told me not to worry about the rest.

I still have all of Mr Gregory's books, the jackets all protected by acid-free plastic ensuring their longevity. After all, I am only the current caretaker. Picturing all those boxes neatly stacked on the front doorstep at No.26 Deauville St. Beaumaris remains an indelible image from my childhood.

I'VE ALWAYS TREATED books as treasures. They have a special feel and smell. Like good friends and conversation, they are a constant to be enjoyed again and again. You immerse yourself in a story and can be found in your same easy chair hours later. The best writers have a flair for producing words so compelling you want to read and re-read them. Red Smith was a doyen and Jack Fingleton, Alan Ross and Paul Edwards in any Grand Final field among cricket writers. Fingleton's *Cricket Crisis* and *Brightly Fades The Don* are among my most dearest. Jack autographed both for me during the Centenary Test. He could be cantankerous, but he liked the fact that a 21-year-old so loved his signature books.

I am always keen to enhance my collection with a superior dustjacket or a signature. The provenance of an old book adds to the adventure, especially if a previous owner has been noteworthy, or notorious.

George Hele, the ex-Bodyline umpire, possessed a small library of classics which included several Fingleton's, a signed and inscribed *Australian Summer* by Neville Cardus (released in 1937) and all four of Percy Fender's wonderfully chunky tourbooks from the 1920s and early 1930s. As a former Test cricketer, his writings commanded an immediate respect, but in one, he did question whether a young Don Bradman was just a flash in the pan…

George's son, Ray, was one of our District cricket stringers at *The Age* and asked if I would like to see his father's books. George was 86 and his eyesight was failing. He wanted them to go to a good home. I ventured out to Thornbury and spent two hours with him. He'd written his name and address in each of the books, sometimes twice as he had moved from Adelaide to Melbourne. Having paid him by cheque, I filled two Benson & Hedges cricket bags to the brim and staggered back onto the tram to town. It was the summer of the Centenary Test, cricket's ultimate birthday party. Every living Ashes Test cricketer had been invited to Melbourne, including 84-year-old Fender, who had played his maiden Ashes Tests in Australia in 1920-21. Legally blind, he was accompanied by his 13-year-old grandson Nicholas Bensted-Smith. Nick's role was to describe the play. Mr Fender could tell purely from the sound of the bat hitting the ball how good a shot it was. We did an interview for *The Age* and afterwards, in the tiniest handwriting, Mr Fender autographed each of his four books.

Only months earlier, I'd submitted a story for the paper's finance pages about the collectability of *Wisden* and how they were a pleasurable hedge against inflation, fiscally fun and at the time the equivalent in worth of BHP shares. Our business editor Barrie Flint liked the story and said his elderly neighbour had recently been widowed. Her husband just happened to have *every* Wisden since 1890. Would I like them? Talk about being in the right place at the right time! I fitted yellow cardboard jackets to each and even carefully Letrasetted WISDEN and the year on the spines. They were all immaculate – the most thrilling of finds. And in this era of typewriters and contact books, a cornerstone for much of my early writings and research.

WHEN I WAS EIGHT OR nine, Dad's youngest brother, my uncle Dick helped fuel my passion for collecting when he presented me with a handful of cricket books he'd owned since his teens. Among them was Patsy Hendren's *My Book of Cricket and Cricketers* (1927) and Charlie Macartney's *My Cricketing Days* (1930). 'Charley Mac' was hero-worshipped by thousands, including a young Don Bradman, who was 12 when he saw Macartney power to a big Ashes century at the Sydney Cricket Ground in 1921. The young Don told his father he would not rest until he, too, had also played on the famous old arena. In time I was to add a dustjacket to my Macartney book. It shows him striking a straight drive with menacing ferocity. It's an original Herbert Fishwick, taken with a revolutionary telescopic lens during the 1920-21 summer which Macartney dominated. Known as the father of modern sports photography, Fishwick's action photographs are clear and dynamic taken even from long range, sitting with the crowd. The Macartney is still my all time favourite early dustjacket.

On school holidays from the age of 12, I'd go to town at first light with Dad and from 9am visit the many secondhand bookshops which were Melbourne institutions: Berry's in Flinders Lane, Fabian's near the RMIT, upstairs at the Hill of Content at the top of Bourke Street and, until 1980, HA Evans and Son in Swanston Street. At Gaston Renard's in Little Collins Street I purchased Arthur Mailey's *Googlies* and Frank Lee's *The Ashes*, two good condition between-the-wars cricket cartoon books for $6. I still have the receipt. Collins, downstairs in Elizabeth Street, had mint-condition copies of RS Whitington's *Simpson's Safari* at 25 cents each. I bought all six, wrapped them in brown paper and added them to a store of other remainders, thinking I might one day sell cricket books as a sideline…

I would also visit Robertson and Mullens, one of the earliest of all central city bookshops, which traded in both new and second-hand books. One time they had a rare Beldam and Fry, *Great Bowlers and Fielders, their methods at a glance* (1907), one of two in the set. I didn't have the $7 but didn't think to ask them to put it away for me. Twenty-four hours later it was gone. I since have acquired a nice copy to go with its companion volume *Great Batsmen*, but at about 30 times the cost!

Second-hand catalogues from Charles Steggell, Roland Cole, Ted Brown and Martin Wood in the UK arrived regularly and I still remember my disappointment when Wood advised he could no longer supply hard-to-get volumes as he wanted to keep them 'in circulation' in England so he'd have the opportunity re-sell them again. John McKenzie had no such set of rules and soon I'd added a set of *Cricket: A Weekly Record* to my library.

ALMOST ALL OUR TRAVELS, within Australia and beyond, become book crawls, the towns with pre-loved bookshops always favoured over those which don't.

One Friday, on the way to Bendigo for a speaking engagement, our Holden broke down on 'Transmission Hill', the slow climb out of

Sunbury, forcing us to hire a car for the weekend. Bendigo is a mecca for book collectors. The Bendigo Book Mark on the main drag had just acquired a very large library of rare between-the-wars autobiographies and tour books, all in excellent condition. Sitting on a small stool, eyeing all these gems, rarely had I been so mesmerised. I bought the lot: two very heavy boxes worth. The night went well and we duly returned our borrowed car, only to learn that our own car was still in the repair shop and likely to stay there into the following week. We staggered onto the railway platform with our finds weighing upwards of 30 kilograms – and somehow got them home.

Our UK Ashes trips invariably include time in Hay-on-Wye, the acclaimed International Booktown, just a morning's rail and bus trip from the city of song, Cardiff. In 2015, the Test ended a day early late on the Saturday and we were having a counter tea with some of our fellow tourists when four gents walked in with T-shirts proclaiming: I'VE BEEN TO HAY-ON-WYE. 'That's it,' said Susan. 'That's what we're doing tomorrow. Hay-on-Wye, here we come.'

Ignoring the torrential dawn rains – reminiscent of monsoonal Brisbane in its rainy season – we took a fast train and linking bus and had the best time. Never will I forget spying a leatherbound edition of Don Bradman's *Farewell to Cricket* behind the counter in one shop. Only 500 were produced. It was expensive but I wasn't going to leave the UK without it.

Over five or six trips, I've visited second-hand bookshops from Bath, Buxton and Eastbourne through to the Peak District and the Yorkshire Dales. The collecting bug and thrill of the hunt is irresistible. One year we were too early to visit Sir Winston Churchill's Chartwell, so went into nearby Oxted for morning tea. All 18 of us were settling in one of the charming little town's ye olde tea rooms eyeing the scones and jelly slices when I spied a man over the road placing an OLD BOOKS sign outside his shop. Immediately excusing myself, I emerged all triumphant 20 minutes later with a dozen or so books so precious that I even seat-belted the box into the front of our bus. Our friends were sure it had all been carefully pre-planned. But it was a sheer fluke. I never did have that cuppa, or slice…

Every four years, in-between the cricket, touring and having High Tea at the Ritz – one of our Ashes rituals – we post boxes of books back to Melbourne. One year there were 21. Susan was forever tripping over book stacks in our hotel room. Like Charlotte Collins in Jane Austen's *Pride and Prejudice*, she would dutifully follow her parcel-toting husband to the nearest post office. At Eastbourne one time I'd run out of tape and asked the shop assistant if he could please reinforce a corner of one. 'The tape's over there,' he said officiously. 'It's two pounds.' 'That is why we Australia love beating you England in anything,' I said. I had the two pounds, but back home, the girls automatically provided any extra tape. It was just part of the service. Fearing an international incident of Bodyline-like proportions, the gent relented and passed me the tape with a 'here you go, Sir'.

THE THRILL OF the hunt can be easier closer to home, like in New Zealand, one of our regular cruise destinations. Everyone is house proud and the cities clean and enticing. The North Island township of Napier is a particular favourite for its art deco rebuild[118] and its vibrant stand of pohutukawa trees and sunken gardens bordering its main street, Marine Parade. It also possesses a gem of a bookshop, the Little Bookshop, on the fringes of nearby McLean Park, which in 2024 hosted not only cricket

---

118   The town and the Hawke's Bay area had been devastated by an earthquake in 1931. Two hundred and fifty-six people died. The rebuild took years.

and rugby internationals but the iconic Tom Jones in his only NZ concert. From the classics to kid's books, there are tens of thousands of titles, all beautifully curated.

On our initial visit, my box of purchased books was so heavy that Anne, the owner, paid for a taxi to take us back to the ship. She insisted on cleaning some of the books before packing them for us. This time our bounty required a second box and a backpack. There was Andy Flanagan's whimsical *On Tour with Bradman* with a near perfect dustjacket, Alan Ross's *Australia 55* – among the most lyrical of all cricket books – and some 1950s NZ Cricket Almanacks, the Arthur Carman ones. A bigger and more expansive suitcase was duly purchased in Auckland to help cart them all home. Happily there are few weight limits on the Pacific Explorer…

Our fortnight away happened to coincide with the first of two mismatches between New Zealand and South Africa at Mount Manganui's new Blake Park. The integrity of Test cricket was on trial as the cream of South Africa's best players had been committed to a home-soil Twenty20 tournament. Six of South Africa's XI were new to Test cricket, including its captain. In only his seventh Test innings, NZ's Rachin Ravindra scored a century on the first day and another on the second. He also took two cheap wickets with his handy finger spinners. While cruise guests visited the nearby thermal springs, walked the Mount or frequented the coffee bars in town, we delighted in spending two sessions at the cricket watching a star of the future. Ian Smith, Jeremy Coney and John Bracewell, all old friends, were among the old Kiwi Test legends in the broadcasting box. Shaking their hands before play, I asked Bracewell: 'How are they coming out?' 'He had to stop,' broke in Coney, ever the jokester. 'Anger management reasons.'

NZ Test grounds are wide and airy with grassy mounds and little shade. Admission is $30 – or $20, if you happen to possess a Senior's card. Spectators bring their own easy chairs or lie on beach towels. On arrival you're told to slip, slop and slap. At lunch, a guitarist played a lovely acoustic set from Neil Young to Neil Finn. On match-eve, wild winds had threatened to derail the Test with the 11 hospitality tents on either side of the southern media box bending and bowing and large sections of the small perimeter fences being upended.

The pitch lacked the pace of some but the bounce was even and the contest initially keen, despite the disparity in experience and class.

Kane Williamson's 30th and 31st Test centuries contained few of Ravindra's wristy drives or pulls, but it was a miracle he was even playing after a succession of serious injuries including a full knee reconstruction. Few have been more sporting or as ambassadorial and at his sublime best, he rivals Bert Sutcliffe and Martin Crowe as NZ's premier batsman. His long-time mentor has been the noted Australian batting coach Trent Woodhill – also an advisor to David Warner. Woodhill marvels at the careers of both men. He particularly admires Williamson's pursuit of perfectionism. Williamson once complained to Woodhill how it had been weeks since he felt the sweet sensation of truly middling the ball, yet he'd just made back-to-back Test 100s!

South Africa was outclassed at the Mount, the game stretching into a fourth day only because NZ's captain Tim Southee preferred not to enforce the follow-on. By fielding a team of fledglings, South Africa compromised the very fibre of almost 150 years of Test cricket and triggered worldwide condemnation and censure. Its administration said it needed the monies from its own premium T20 tournament to help fund Test cricket into the future.

IN A LIFETIME OF collecting, my most expensive and rewarding purchase came in 2011, a multi-faceted library once belonging to Casino's 'Mr. Cricket' Gordon Vidler. There were 51 boxes on three large crates. Gordon lived in Spring Hill in the northern Rivers region of New South Wales and had been a cricket aficionado since he was knee-high. We had corresponded for years. Among the collection were dozens of large Walkers Studios original photographs from the Scarborough Festival, dating way back. There were also hundreds of books, brochures, magazines, Fleet St. photographs, a vast array of cuttings, cigarette and trade cards and many excellent condition cricket catalogues and rarely seen advertising dodgers.

Mr Vidler had died, aged 90, on the centenary of Don Bradman's birth, on August 27, 2008. His son Bob said every farm conversation would always include cricket and the Don. 'It didn't matter what we were discussing, tractors, feed, whatever,' he said. 'Dad would always find a way of talking about Bradman.' Mr Vidler's enthusiasm for cricket and collecting matched mine. Born in Kyogle in 1917, he attended Cowongla Public School and moved with his parents to the family's farm in Spring Grove in the early 1930s. There was no power or telephone until 1960. Cricket was his life. Unable to play in Sydney because of farm responsibilities, he was a long-time player in Casino and Lismore and competitive even into his late 50s when he aggregated 500 runs and averaged 71 at Lismore third grade level in the mid-'70s.

He loved anything to do with the game, keeping scrapbooks, collecting cards and researching and compiling stats. His photograph collection branched into several other sports including tennis, which post-war enjoyed a status and profile almost equivalent to cricket. Seeing an image he liked, Gordon would write away for it, to the newspapers in Sydney and Melbourne and to many in the UK. One of the rarer photos, of the

1959-60 Australian touring team to New Zealand, came direct from the secretary of the Auckland Cricket Association: 'thought you'd like to have this.' It's addressed to Gordon at Spring Grove Rd via Cusine (sic), country New South Wales… but it still found him. 'Dad loved it when the latest envelope or package would arrive with the mail,' said his son. 'He was collecting right up until the end. He just loved it.'

I've known only one other bigger collector, Pat Mullins, a solicitor from Indooroopilly in Brisbane. So vast was his library that his books were double stacked on wooden shelves, all bowing with the excessive weight. He bought everything on cricket, kept scrapbooks and helped me with several 1980s anthologies – one in which he uncovered a newspaper cutting where a gold digger traded a nugget for admission to one of Melbourne's big matches.

My biggest single book purchase was Don Neely's heavyweight *Men in White*, the boxed subscriber's edition, limited to 1200 copies, A1 in size and weighing more than 20 kilograms. No bigger, more spectacular cricket book has ever been issued. Don was in Melbourne on business and brought my copy with him. I took the underground into the city and met him at his hotel, the old Southern Cross. One coffee became two and then three and by the time I got back on the train it was peak hour and standing room only. Wedging myself and Don's special book into a corner, somehow I was able to protect it from being knocked by fellow passengers. One of the rare images in Don's magnum opus was a team photograph of the 1927-28 Australians to NZ, a side which included the Xavier College prodigy Karl Schneider, who at 154cm (5ft 1in) was known, even by his own family as 'The Little Squirt'. Tragically, he was to die young from leukaemia, aged 23, when he seemed set for stardom. A biography of his life was published in 2024.

30

TIM TAMS AT MONBULK

'She likens me to Mr Darcy from her favourite Jane Austen novel, Pride and Prejudice: *aloof, despotic and friendly only when it suits...'*

It's hard to surprise Susan, but I did this Saturday in early October. It had been raining cats and dogs all week. All turf cricket was off. 'Fancy a leisurely drive up to the Dandenongs?' I suggested. Susan was staggered. 'Normally you say it's out of the question,' she said. She likens me to Mr Darcy from our favourite Jane Austen novel, *Pride and Prejudice:* aloof, despotic and friendly only when it suits – or when I am with my gym, swimming or cricket buddies. She says she was so close to doing a runner during our first year of marriage.

Working freelance is liberating, but the hours are long. I was saying yes to everything. I had to. And deadlines had to be met. And that was tough on her. It's good that we work on the high seas now. She says she'll stay with me while we are cruising.

Anyway, back to that springtime Saturday: we set up a picnic at a barbeque area in Monbulk and were about to have a cuppa and a Tim Tam. Suddenly I heard the unmistakeable thwack of bat on ball and some clapping from nearby. It was one of those crisp, clear days in the hills. Noise travels. Sure enough, a cricket match beckoned – it was on a hard wicket. We upped stumps, followed the voices and found the ground, just at the end of a clearing and for 15 minutes or so, camped at the deep cover fence. The match had just started and the new ball bowler, while pacy, was spraying them everywhere. 'Top of off,' I called. 'Make him play... hit the stumps... full and straight... c'monnn.' Everyone looked around in amazement. Who was this strange bloke yelling from the sidelines? 'You just can't help yourself, can you!' said Susan.

Few cricket tragics can pass a cricket match without stopping. I certainly can't. There must be something in my DNA: I like to mentor. It's not being big-headed. There's a reason why only 500 have played for Australia in 150 years. They are the creme de la crème. I wasn't – but I mixed with the best and learnt their lessons.

At Kingston one of the very promising teenage lads, Brendan McCoy, could bat but kept flicking the ball in the air to mid-on. The legendary Barry Richards was visiting family in Beaumaris and I asked him for a remedy. 'Get him to rock the baby,' he said. 'Rock the baby?' 'Yeah. Try it.' So Barry had me cradling my two hands and rocking an imaginary baby from side to side. 'Now,' he said. 'Play an off drive.' I did. Suddenly everything was in rhythm. I shared the lesson with young Brendan. He hadn't heard of Barry, but suddenly took more notice when I said Sir Donald Bradman had selected him as his opener in his best ever XI.

Now 'rocking the baby' has a legendary status with the Mt. Eliza lads. And if one spies me hitting bottom-handed across the line, rather than playing impeccably straight, he'll say: 'Master, are you rocking the baby?'

One Tuesday in the nets at Mt Eliza, a young teenage kid was bowling leggies. He had good energy at the crease, overspin and bounce, but not the follow through he needed for maximum sidespin. 'This is how Shane Warne would do it,' I said, bowling from ten o'clock and completing an exaggerated follow through with my arm almost behind my back. The kid spun his very next ball sharply. 'Yeesss!' I said. 'Warnie would be so proud of you.' There were smiles all round. Soon afterwards, another of the juniors, young Sam approached: 'Master,' he said. 'That's so funny. That kid you were coaching... that's Sebi Warne, Warnie's nephew!'

At Frankston Heat, one of 'my' boys Steve Stubbings was playing first XI regularly. He'd had a season or two in Derbyshire. He'd learnt his lessons well from his days in the thirds. Towards the end of a net he started to play a series of fancy trick shots: ramps, switch-hits and reverse sweeps. 'Stubbo, what are you doing?' I yelled. 'Master, this is the way we play now, especially in the one-dayers.'

At Kingston we had a very promising left-arm wrist spinner Benny Burton. He was bowling to a left-hander who had just come in. His first ball, full length and spinning away, induced a top edge high into the air for an easy caught and bowled. I suggested to the batsman, Kieran, that he play straighter, especially early and maybe show the kid a little more respect. 'Get stuffed, Master!' he said.

In my first year with the Mounties, Housie and Juzz enlisted me as a coaching consultant and advisor to the first XI and after winning the semi, everyone went ballistic. Harey, our secretary, almost had to call for slab reinforcements. I kept telling the boys there was one more to go. The job was only half done. They were brave in the Grand Final but lost. The following year, having again won the semi, I fielded a phone call from Juzz about 10pm on the Sunday night. 'Masteerrr!' he yelled. 'We're in the Big One again.'

'You'd better not be partying...'

'No, we're not,' he said. 'There's one more to go...' And broke up laughing.

Once in the nets at Mountie, one of the young blokes, Sammy Webster, asked me how many wickets I'd taken. '746,' I said, 'and you're about to become No. 747.' And he was. I love it when the lefties run at you.

Cricket breeds the most amazing friendships. The stats and solo feats are often forgotten, but rarely a face... or a nickname. I get 'Master' most – thanks to Mike Sheahan – but over the journey have had many. At Beaumaris I was 'Mantis' (the preying mantis... I was long and thin), at Kingston 'KP', at Port Melbourne I'm 'Guru' and now at Mt Eliza, I get 'Jurassic' which is fair enough as I am in my 70th year.

I'm with the sixth XI, the Rock Stars, so named because our two team principals Andrew Cox and Phil Leonard by night front The Fauves, one of Melbourne's great underground rock bands. We won the 'C' division Mornington Peninsula flag in 2023, my first premiership in 37 years. Participation is by invitation only. The previous year, around exam time, the club was short in all the grades so Phil's lads all joined me in the thirds. We were defending only 100 and the other mob was 0-30 and cruising when Phil enlisted me from my favourite Tully's Orchard end with the breeze going from left to right. One of our lads, Bergs, had to leave early so we were down to 10. I got lucky, took a wicket in my second over – thanks to a nicely judged catch by our first-gamer Hollywood – another in my third and another in my fourth on the way to a career-best six-for[119] and we won by two or three runs. Francis Leach of Melbourne radio fame took two stumpings and a catch and Phil insisted I play full-time down the grades with him from then on.

We have so much fun. Our 'keeper Maxie likes to chat to the batsmen

---

119   My six for 19 from eight overs was judged the club's best individual performance for 2021-22. I have the Wally Wedgwood jnr. plaque on my library wall to prove it.

when I'm bowling. 'Mate,' he'll say. 'This old fella is easy. We whack him at training. Use your feet... get down to him... just smash 'im.' It has resulted in so many dismissals, stumped Maxwell, bowled Piesse. Two flattish leg breaks followed by a slightly slower, higher one, dropping six inches shorter... pure gold.

In one of our 2024 games, two of the boys, Rug and Joe, abused each other from long range, swearing and sounding off for almost a minute after a hasty throw landed in mid pitch. Joe had done well to quickly launch it back, creating doubt for the batsmen running between wickets – but wicketkeeper Rug was unimpressed. And said so, forcibly. 'They're losing it,' one of the opposition players called from the sidelines. We still won the match and afterwards the lads kissed and made up over multiple Coronas and chardies. We made it through to another Grand Final, looking to go back-to-back but our opposition was about 20 years younger than us... and in my case 35 years younger!

I'd joined the Mounties having done my achilles in my last game with the Kingston Saints, forcing me to miss an entire year. Kingston was about to enter Premier League ranks, thanks to the enterprise of the visionary Phil O'Meara and didn't need another oldie robbing a young kid of a place in the fourths. My ankle had been sore all year. It was a very hot day. Oakleigh had a thickset, very whippy fast bowler who specialised in fast yorkers. He clean-bowled two or three of our kids while I was at the non-striker's end. 'You're about to blow up,' I said to him. 'Never seen a redder face in my life.' Maybe it was Karma but in calling' yes' for a single to get down his end, the achilles just snapped. I had to retire hurt for the one and only time, across more than 800 games of cricket.

The front oval at St Bedes was our home ground and one day Juice Wintle, a star first XI player, was having a game in the threes alongside his Dad, Wally and hit an awesome straight 6 over the Brothers' second story accommodation quarters and into the Mentone RSL's carpark. Had it been at the MCG it would have landed in the back rows of the second level of the Shane Warne. It was huge.

I'd always favour the younger spinners, but this day was on early when one failed to show. A beefy left hander misread the wrong-un and it ballooned not too high straight to mid-on where our opening bowler Doughie fluffed it. Take two Master: a wrong-un again, this time a little wider and this time the fella picked it up like he was Babe Ruth and calmly smacked it over the cyclone fence and onto Beach Road. A bloke turning right towards the Mentone shops, stopped, picked up the near new ball and drove off with it, laughing hysterically. Lucky for us all, Fab had a spare.

Another time three or four fellas were having a bucks' night/afternoon. The groom, a very hairy fella, ran onto the ground in a Mankini and took up a fielding position at backward square next to me. It was not a pleasant sight. 'Play on boys,' he said. 'Mate,' I said. 'Unless you piss off you're going to get a stump rammed up your backside.' I stopped the game and he soon retreated, calling us all a pack of fairies.

Most of the teams had 'home' umpires in the thirds. My Mum liked to come to see me play. She knew I was opening this particular day and just as the fella was running in for his first ball, she moved from mid-off to directly behind the bowler's arm. It was impossible not to be distracted. Luckily for me the ball was wide. I called to Chopper our umpire: 'Chop, can you tell that good looking young lady behind the bowler's arm to move? It's my Mum.' Later she explained that I'd always taught her to get behind the bowler's arm so she could see if the new ball was swinging.

Box Hill had a very old and crusty home umpire who liked to finish matches early. He was hard of hearing but reckoned he could hear the nicks perfectly well, thank you. And he also liked to uphold most lbws, even the ones pitching outside leg stump. 'It would have hit,' he'd say. Box Hill's captain and I agreed pre-match that we both could have two Decision Reviews – and this day, used them all!

Kingston's practice captain Sheeza would allow six or seven bowlers in every net, bar the firsts. I called him the Rock-ape. 'Rocky,' I said one day. 'Can we possibly get an eighth bowler down here? We haven't got enough…' 'Geezus Master,' he said. 'You're lucky to be playing here. Just shut up and get on with it.'

Porno was captaining our thirds one day at Ormond. We were on the smaller oval close to the railway line, adjacent to the ones, who were on the main ground. I'd arrived early so warmed up with them. They were defending less than 100. Our fast bowler, Matty Walsh was known as the Bear. We needed him to strike early and often. Bear was big, energetic and genuinely fast. I was in the covers, for my speed, agility and powerful throwing arm… just a stone's throw from their game. 'C'mon Bear,' I yelled. 'Hit him in the stumps mate.' He took an early wicket. 'Yeesss!' I said, not realising that in our game, our fast bowler Jonty was almost in his delivery stride and forced to abort. 'Bloody hell Master,' said Porno. 'Any chance of you concentrating on our game?'

The pride of Port Melbourne, Peter Bedford, coached us for a couple of years. One day our fourth XI, captained by the Cougar (JR Noonan) was all out for 12. Wheels was beside himself. 'Geezus JR. Twelve… twelve… TWELVE. Surely someone could have got a partnership, somewhere. Twelve. I just can't believe it,' he said before walking away, shaking his head in disbelief. He was so angry. But that's the game. Eleven guys or girls walk onto the park every Saturday not knowing what is going to happen. It's one of the joys of the game. Long live cricket.

LAST WORD

It rarely rains at Canadian Bay when I walk and swim with the pups. Serendipity? Maybe. The skies tend to open only when we are safely back home. Unlike my Beaumaris buddy Drew, known to all as 'The Rainman' for good reason, I don't possess a raincoat. So, why did it rain in Cardiff during its historic first Ashes Test match in 2009? We'd come 13,000 miles to see the Aussies retain the Ashes. This was match 1 and our lads were way ahead in the game... before the rains forcing an early finish to Day 4. At 2-20 in its second innings, England was facing defeat, unless the deluge continued and the banks of the Taff broke. As our tour group headed towards the exit and the seven-minute stroll through stunning Sophia Gardens to the CBD and the front bar of the Holiday Inn, I said to Susan on the quiet: 'We're in trouble here. We haven't got tickets for tomorrow.'

'What!'

'It's true. They sold them only in four-day blocks. We haven't got tickets tomorrow. None of the groups have.'

'Okay... so who plays here? Who runs the ground?'

'Glamorgan... Glamorgan County Cricket Club.'

'Do they have an office here?'

By now it was really bucketing and we were soaked but made the 200-yard trek around to the offices of the GCCC and asked if we could please see someone important.

'Someone important?' said the girl. 'Yes, maybe your secretary or ticketing executive. My name is Ken Piesse. I'm a cricket writer… from Melbourne.'

'Please give me a moment sir.'

A lass came down to greet us and said she was the PA for Paul Russell, the club's chairman. He was upstairs entertaining guests. 'I'll give you two minutes,' she said. Mr Russell duly appeared, laughed at our general dishevelment and said when it rains in Cardiff, it really rains. How could he help?

'Mr Russell,' I said. 'We've come from the other side of the world. There's 20 of us. We've loved every moment we've been here. Everyone has been so kind. But we haven't got tickets for tomorrow. There's going to be 20 very disappointed Australians.'

'Do you have a credit card?' he asked.

'Yessir.' Within minutes he returned, holding 20 tickets to the member's reserve. There is a God. And it all started with Susan.

Cricket may be my obsession but Susan is the guiding light and love of my life – along, of course, with my pups, Belle and Leo. It's a standing joke that when I walk upstairs from the library I'll say to Susan, 'How is my all-time favourite person in the whole world?' 'Belle,' she'll call. 'Daddy wants you.'

In the early days at our first home in Seaford, I'd have cricket magazine lay-outs all over our loungeroom and down the corridor. Susan wasn't allowed to touch anything. I'd be typing relentlessly in the front bedroom while listening to the La De Das, Uriah Heap and Deep Purple. Journalism was all 'hard' copy back then. Susan so wanted to ditch that old Adler. She hated the clack-clack-clacking *and* my old Silver ghetto blaster – and was so relieved when our boy James requested it.

I've been away a lot, but Susan and the family still love me and have my back. Jessie realises when she marries, do it on a Saturday out of season, or at worst in early October as there's often a washout.

Susan is used to my maverick ways and crazy eccentricities, wearing odd socks and T-shirts inside out. She reckons I have so much face and care about appearances only when it counts, when we're cruising or at public speaking gigs at places like the Crown. She likens me to Homer Simpson. I couldn't care if I had a chicken drumstick stuck to my eyebrow. It's one of the joys of freelancing. Wear what you want. Singlets, shorts, thongs. Way to go. The girls at the post office barely recognise me if I happen to come in wearing a suit. But they, too, have my back. Jessie and Bec make mince pies and gingerbread for them every Christmas in appreciation and when the queues are long and the staff run off their feet, I always jolly any disgruntled customers in the queue, saying how the girls are doing their best and we'll all be served ASAP.

The kids were indoctrinated early into barracking for Hawthorn, all except for James, our eldest. Ron Barassi had returned to Melbourne and wrote to him saying the Demons loved that he was now a supporter. James collects sci-fi books and vinyl records, has eight synthesizers and an arsenal of beautifully crafted model cars – all with their original boxes. He also has a working, ever-expanding railway. His wife Alzina is very understanding. For fun, James self-publishes books for young adults. And, like me, insists on his beer being full-strength. One day when James was in his mid-teens, we sighted a mega skip, on the road, just a few doors up from our house in Bareena Drive, Mt Eliza. We'd just updated our Queen-sized bed and the old mattress was in the garage. It didn't fit even into our hatchback to take to the tip… so… under the cloak of darkness that night, James and I hauled it up to the skip. It was so tall we couldn't see into it. With a one-two-three-heave, we threw the mattress into it and there was huge BANNGGG! There was nothing in it. We bolted home. No doubt our neighbours knew the identity of the culprits.

Melinda, our first-born daughter, was the fastest runner on the beach at Somers and one year won the Victorian women's longbow championship. She and her husband Wayne dote over their son Orion, the littlest star of the family. The week he was born I nominated him for membership at the Melbourne Cricket Club, but being the son of a boatbuilder, he is more likely to be a sailor. Minnie and Wayne married on the first December Saturday one summer, forcing me to miss a game. That was tough. But walking my daughter down a grass aisle for the first time was really something. She wore an exquisite white dress with wonderful hand-embroidered braiding – all her own work. It was a memorable night with a set of brilliant speeches and a live band – but not to everyone's taste. Midway through their first bracket, Tori, our second-born daughter asked: 'When does the music start?'

Tori was always cheeky, exuberant and explosive. I blame her grandfather and his fun-loving brothers. Tori was a talented calligraphist and for years, in impeccable fountain pen, would painstakingly number the limited editions I published. She could play *Stairway to Heaven* blindfolded. Even Ritchie Blackmore would have been impressed. She had the best cover drive in the family, flew incredibly high on the swings and was my tennis partner on lazy Sunday afternoons at Somers, where we had a holiday house. One day she was in a semi-final against a girl far her superior. This lass had been playing since she was knee high. I told Tori it was a final and to play her hardest. Anything could happen. Run down every ball. Treat every point like it's match point. She lost, but she took a game or two off the other girl.

She'd always been one of the sharpest, most intelligent and happiest of all our kids. On Minny's first day of preps, Tori and I accompanied her to school. Tori even sat down with the older kids, on cue. She was three going on 13. When Nanna would come to mind the kids, Tori would know where everything was. She and Mike were engaged to be married. He still comes each year to our family Christmas.

Jessie, daughter No.3, helps index most of my books and is a whizz at Photoshop. She can outpace an Olympic walker and select the best tomatoes in town. We attend the big concerts together and have seen Prince, the Stones, the Eagles, Stevie Wonder, Carole King, Graham Nash and CSN. One very rainy night in Colac – Aaron Finch and Luke Hodge country – we saw the legendary Neil Young, star of *Live at Massey Hall*, maybe the best live album ever recorded. The backing band, *My Morning Jacket* played too long and I clapped them off the stage. We wanted the real thing. We were both soaked and Jessie changed into a pair of my waterproof golf trousers on the way home. Jessie collects PG Wodehouse and Cecil Beaton first editions, likes big dogs, loves Paris and dresses just so. We agree there are few greater albums than Steven Stills' Manassas. She came with me into the Hawthorn rooms after a game one day and recognising so many would be in a state of undress, I covered her face with my suitcoat. She was only seven. All was forgiven when Jason Dunstall signed her Hawthorn scarf.

Another night I took the three eldest girls to the footy at the MCG. St Kilda was playing Collingwood. It was a milestone game for another of my Beaumaris buddies Stewie Loewe, maybe his 300th. We were in the AFL members and were surrounded by the Magpie army. Collingwood ran out first to tumultuous, prolonged cheers. When St Kilda entered, there was widespread booing. To even the odds, I started clapping and yelled: 'Go Saints, go Stewie.' The dirty looks we got from the Collingwod fans would have stopped an army. Jessie and the little Champ (Tori) were amazed at the fanaticism.

Working freelance from home, the kids would always be upstairs at my feet, until the noise escalated beyond even my limits and I'd yell: 'Mummy. HELLPPP!' Susan would appear and there'd be a stampede down to the kitchen. Jessie must have been no more than three when she first crawled up the stairs, giggling. 'Who's that?' I said. I bought her a little green plastic desk and she worked beside me every day until she started school. She was developing a work ethic even then.

Our youngest Bec rowed in the junior Olympics for Canberra and played several years of AFL, without her mother knowing. I was in ANU's footy team picture one year and Susan was puzzled why I had this glossy print of a women's football team behind me in the library. 'Hey,' she said, 'that's you! What are you doing in the picture? And… there's Beckie! What's going on?' She hadn't wanted her to play, but Bec loved the game. Always had. On Friday nights we'd talk about the next day's match, where she was playing and what she needed to do. This day she was at centre-half back so I told her not to give her opponent any space. Be one step ahead. Impede. Harass. Block. Force her to the boundary – a little like Big Mike in *The Blind Side* – without the aggression. Her opponent started to pinch her, up and down her side. 'What are you doing?' said Bec. 'Give me some space!' said the girl. 'All day! All day!' said Bec. I so loved hearing that.

I'd try and match her best rowing times at Michelle's gym and rang her one day, all triumphant: 'I've just done a 3.45 for 1000 metres.' I was pretty chuffed. Mind you, I'd almost blown up doing it. 'Good job, Dadda,' she said. 'Funnily enough,' she said, 'I was going to ring you. I did a 3.40 this morning.'

Every night at bedtime I'd read the kids stories. My favourites were *The Elephant and the Bad Baby*, *Guess How Much I Love You* and *Duncan and Delores*. I'd always add 'commercials', how the bad baby liked to eat

Big Macs on the side and how Duncan, a cat, had a fetish for Coca-Cola. In the end I'd plead with Bec to allow me to read a bedtime story, but at 14, she finally said to me 'maybe not tonight Dadda'. She and Aaron also married on a Saturday – on the eve of our fifth XI finals. I had to miss another match, but at least the wedding was at Blackheath where Don Bradman once made a century in three overs…

With Jess (left) and Bec at Mt Eliza. Sundays were particularly pleasant when the girls agreed to accompany me to the nets.

ACKNOWLEDGEMENTS

We were on the fast train to Yass to spend some quality time with our youngest daughter before a wintertime P & O cruise to sunny Fiji. The gent sitting next to me had his head buried in a Ken Follett thriller for most of the trip. So weighty was it you could easily have used it as a door stop. 'The first sentence in, you're hooked,' he said.

I'm hoping you have found *Living The Dream* equally absorbing.

In a lifetime in cricket and football, I have been fortunate to get up close and personal with so many sporting icons. The lessons I learnt from Ernie Sigley and Bill Collins, among many, have been inspirational. And helped fuel a lifetime of interviews, fun and nostalgia, across multi media.

Good people are associated with sport. I've always been hungry to hear their stories and I have loved recounting some of my favourites to you in these pages.

So many of my pals, young and old have contributed to these memoirs from the toasts and roasts through to the stats detailing almost 1000 games of cricket and footy over 60 years – that's a lot of creams, cricket shirts, boots and jumpers.

My thanks, again, to publisher Michael Wilkinson and his team for their encouragement and artist Paul Marcolin for his expertise.

Three of my closest buddies Mark Browning, Geoff Poulter and my brother Jim read the draft and made valuable contributions. So did my wife of 46 fun-filled years Susan whose loyalty and support is unequivocal – for now!

GLOSSARY

AB	Allan Border	Davo	Alan Davidson
Al Pal	Alan Connolly	Denbeigh	Denis Swingler
Ando	Jon Anderson	Diggers	Simon Dignan
Arms	Graeme Anderson	DK	Dennis Lillee
		Duck	Wayne Carey
Barks	Trevor Barker	Dusch	Darren Duscher
Bazz	Nick Baron		
Bear	Matty Walsh/ David Warner	Eggie	Stevie Morris
		Evil	David Sincock/ Russell Sincock
Beefy	Ian Botham		
Beeks	Brian Keogh		
Bergs	David Bergin	Fab	Phil O'Meara
Beva	Robert Bevilacqua	Fish	Paul Salmon
Biff	Greg Dermott	Frankie	Francis Leach
Big Jake	Shane Jacobsen	Froggie	Alan Thomson
Billy	Peter Goggin	Funky	Colin Miller/ Jim Miller
Braddles	Sir Donald Bradman		
Brem	Ian Bremner		
Bung	Jason Dunstall	Joe	Andrew Cox
Bunk	Robert Tinsley	Jonty	John Noonan
		Juzz	Justin Grant
Cement-head	Shane Doyle		
Champ	Tori Piesse	Garth	Graham McKenzie
Chappelli	Ian Chappell	Gen	John Grant
Chuck	Leslie O'B Fleetwood-Smith	Griff	Matty Griffiths
		Gubby	Graeme Allan
Claggie	Kim Hughes	Groover	Darren Groves
Cocky	John McFarlane		
Coina	Marcus Lyon	Heada	Jason Mathers
Coo	Alan Cowen/ Andrew Cowen	Hitch	Alan Hitchcox
		Holidays	Simon McEvoy
Cooky	Ross Cook	Hollywood	Paul Goddard/ Shane Warne
Cougar	JR Noonan		
Couta	Mal Coutts	Housie	Lyle House
Crock	Paul Crocker	Huddo	Peter Hudson
Curly	Henry Bolte		
		JB	Darren Walker
Danger	Patrick Dangerfield	JL	Justin Langer

I 300

GLOSSARY

Johnny Normal	Johnny Keogh	Ronnie	Ron Nicholson
Juice	Luke Wintle	Rug	Russell Hobbs
Kanga	John Kennedy snr	Sam	John Newman
KD	Ken Davis/Ken Davis	Scotty	Luke Walker
Killa	Alan Killigrew	Sheff	Alan Shiell
		Simmo	Bob Simpson
La-La	Bob Bitmead	Slasher	Ken Mackay
Legs	Peter Leggett	Sobie	Garry Sobers
LJ	Laurie Nash	Spice	Ken Spicer
Luigi	Jimmy Earle	Stevie Mac	Stephen McMahon
		Stork	Hunter Hendry
Mac	Robert McKenzie	Stretch	Vic Aanensen
Magoo	Bryce McGain	Suds	Wayne Daley
Malcolm	Rodney Hogg	Super	Rob Elliot
Marty the Brain	Martin Lane	Swampy	Geoff Marsh
Mikey	Michael Holding	Swan	Bob Richards
Minnie	Melinda Piesse		
Mo	Leo O'Brien	Tang	Max Walker
Mocca	Mark Dunstan	Ted	Paul Wale
		The Bull	David Warner
Nin	Neil Harvey	The Kid	Dermott Brereton
Nuffy	Shane Davidson	The Little Fave	Johnny Martin
Nugget	Keith Miller	The Monster	Gerry Callahan
		The Rainman	Drew Payne
Ollie	Colin Powell	The Thorpedo	Ian Thorpe
Oysters	Ian Crawford	Thommo	Jeff Thomson
		Tiger	David Nankervis/
Pants	Darren Millane		Bill O'Reilly
Pep	Cec Pepper	Timmsy	Daryl Timms
Phanto	Bill Lawry	TJ	Terry Jenner
Piccolo	Peter Allan	Tubby	Mark Taylor
Plugger	Tony Lockett		
Porno	Shaun Graf/	Wal	Bob Cowper
	Chris Murphy	Wally	Peter Wintle
Prezz	Wayne Hicks	Wheels	Peter Bedford
Prockie	Mike Procter	Whitt	Peter Whitty
Pup	Michael Clarke	Willie	Jack Potter
		Wok	John Watkins
Red	Ian Redpath		
Rig	Bob Bryce	Yab	Allan Jeans
Rocky/Sheeza	Darren Sheehan		

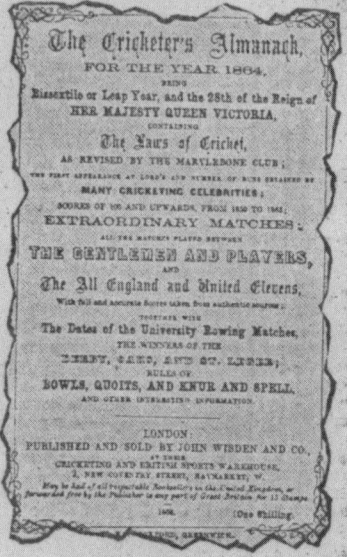

One of my first feature stories in the business pages of *The Age* in 1974. I was just 18 and already a *Wisden* devotee.

KEN PIESSE BIBLIOGRAPHY

Born 1955, Mordialloc, Melbourne; the youngest of four children

1973-78	Reporter, *The Age* (David Syme & Co)
1978-80	Chief cricket & football writer, *The Sporting Globe* (The Herald & Weekly Times)
1978-93	Editor *Cricketer* magazine (Newspress/Syme Magazines)
1980-87	Sports editor, *Sunday Observer* (Peter Isaacson Publications)
1984	Editor *Football Fan* magazine (Quadricolor Industries)
1984-2024	Cricket reporter 3MP, Sport 927, RSN
1990	Editor *Football Life* (Blake Publishing)
1994-98	Editor, *Australian Cricket* magazine (Mason Stewart)
1995	Editor, *Football Australia* (Champion Images)
2000-07	Editor, *Australian Cricket Tour Guide* (Emap)
2006-24	Editor, *Pavilion* magazine (Australian Cricket Society)
2007-24	Editor, *Universal's Cricket Summer Guide* (Umco)

HIS BOOKS & MAGAZINES

CRICKET

1978	*Great Triumphs in Test Cricket*
	Prahran Cricket Club's Centenary History
1979	*Cricket Digest annual 1978-79* (editor)
1980-83	*Cricket Year* (four editions: 1979-80, 1980-81, 1981-82, 1982-83, editor)
1981	*Calypso Summers* (with Jim Main)
1982	*Duel for Glory, England Tours to Australia 1861–1982* (with Jim Main)
	The Great Australian Book of Cricket Stories (editor)
	The Golden Age of Australian Cricket (editor)

1983	*Cartoonists at the Cricket* (editor)
	The A to Z of Cricket: Interviews with Australia's Leading Cricketers
	Donald Bradman (Famous Australians series)
1984	*Max Walker's Cricket in Australia* (1983-84 annual), editor
1986	*Bradman and the Bush: The Legend of Australian Bush Cricket* (with Ian Ferguson)
1988	*Match Drawn: A Cavalcade of Cricket Cartoons* (editor)
	Bradman & The Legends of Australian Cricket
1993	*Simply the Best: The Allan Border Story*
1994	*Cricket Skills & Secrets* (editor) – Updated seven times
1995	*Warne Sultan of Spin*
1996	*One-Day Magic*
	The Big Aussie Cricket Book
1998	*Wildmen of Cricket I* (with Brian Hansen)
1999	*The Taylor Years: Australian Cricket 1994–99*
	'Untapped' softback edition 2021
2000	*Cricket's Greatest Scandals* – Updated edition 2001
	The Complete Shane Warne
	Mark and Steve Waugh
2002	*The Waugh Zone, Australian cricket under the inspired captaincy of Steve Waugh*
	Bradmans of the Bush: The Legends and Larrikins of Australian Bush Cricket (with Alf Wilson)
	Magic Moments in Australian Cricket
2003	*Cricket's Colosseum: 125 Years of Test Cricket at the MCG*
	Glenn McGrath & Adam Gilchrist
2005	*Down at the Junction, There's A Cricket Ground: St Kilda Cricket Club – the First 150 Years*
	All Out for One and Other Cricket Anecdotes
2007	*The Ashes: An Illustrated History of Cricket's Greatest Rivalry*
	On Ya Warnie – Updated edition 2022
2008	*Our Don Bradman*

2009	*On Ya Richie*
	CC, the Colin McDonald Story (editor)
	Re-released as *Taking Strike*, 2015
	The Extraordinary Book of Australian Cricket
2010	*Great Australian Cricket Stories* – Reprinted 2011
	Brad Hodge, the Little Master
2012	*Dynamic Duos, Cricket's Finest Pairs & Partnerships*
	Encyclopaedia of Australian Cricket Players
	(with Charles Davis)
2013	*Great Ashes Moments*
2014	*Favourite Cricket Yarns* – Reprinted three times
2016	*A Pictorial History of Australian Test Cricket*
2018	*Australian Cricket Scandals, Ball tampering, bets, bribes, blow-ups!*
2022	*Ken Piesse's ABC of Australian Cricket*
	Fifteen Minutes of Fame, Australia's 70 One-Test Wonders
2023	*The Bull, David Warner, daring to be different*

'GHOSTED' AUTOBIOGRAPHIES

1988	*Hooked on Cricket, an Addict's A–Z Guide*
	(with Max Walker)
1999	*T.J. Over the Top* (with Terry Jenner)
2001	*Mahanama: Retired Hurt* (with Roshan Mahanama)
	Also published in Silanhese. Updated edition 2022.

FOOTBALL

1982-84	*The A to Z of Football* (with Jim Main)
	Three editions: 1982, 1983 and 1984 (the last two sponsored by Holden)
1983	*Football with the Stars* (with Daryl Timms)
1991	*Blues, Blinders & Ballbursters, stories, skills and secrets by Australia's football heroes*
1993	*The Complete Guide to Australian Football*
	Re-issued in 1995

1994	*Ablett, the Gary Ablett Story*
	Re-issued as *Ablett, Greatest Ever* in 1996
1993	*Just for Kicks* (editor)
1994	*Just for Kicks II* (editor)
2004	*Red, White & Black, Marching with the Saints*
2006	*The Greatest Game, Timeless Tales from the Greats of Aussie Rules*
2010	*The Bears Uncensored, Caulfield VFA, 1965-87*
2011	*Great Australian Football Stories* – Reprinted 2012
	Football Legends of the Bush
2014	*Stuey, my life with Stewart Spencer,* Fay Spencer (editor)
2015	*Favourite Football Yarns* – Reprinted three times

'GHOSTED' AUTOBIOGRAPHIES

1989	*Hooked on football,* with Dermott Brereton
1992	*Plugger, The Tony Lockett Story*
1993	*Dermott Brereton's 101 Favourite Football Stories*
1995	*The Goal King, Jason Dunstall's Own Story*
1996	*Dipper Tell the Kids I luv 'em,* with Robert DiPierdomenico
1997	*John Platten, The Rat, a football braveheart*
1998	*Libba, Living On The Edge,* with Tony Liberatore
2001	*The Big Fish, Paul Salmon's Own Story*

GENERAL INTEREST

1995	*Commando, from Tidal River to Tarakan, the story of No.4 Australian Independent Company AIF, 1941-45* (editor)
1999	*Dick Wicks the magnetic man*

KEN'S NOSTALGIA SERIES
(books published by cricketbooks.com.au)

2011	*It's Your Wally Grout,* a grandson's tale, Wally Wright
2012	*Cricket's Unsung Legend,* Jimmy Matthews' story, James Brear
	The Terror, Charlie Turner, Australia's greatest bowler, Ric Sissons
2014	*Miracle Match,* the day David downed Goliath, Brunswick St. Oval, July 6, 1963, Ken Piesse (VFL/AFL football)
2015	*The Silk Express,* the story of EA 'Ted' McDonald, Nick Richardson
	Lucky, The life of HL 'Bert' Collins, cricketer, soldier, gambler, Max Bonnell
	Reggie, Five Years of Fame, the story of Reginald Duff, Ric Sissons
2016	*Against All Odds,* how Victoria won the 1966-67 Sheffield Shield, Ken Piesse & Mark Browning
2018	*Pep, The story of Cec Pepper, the best cricketer never to represent Australia,* Ken Piesse – Reprinted 2019
2019	*Bob's Boys,* how Victoria won the 1969-70 Sheffield Shield, Ken Piesse & Mark Browning
	Dainty, the Bert Ironmonger Story, Max Bonnell
2020	*Invincible,* The life & Times of Sam Loxton, Martin Rogers
	Born to Play, the Barry Davis Story, Ken Davis
2021	*Born Lucky,* the story of Jack Potter, Australia's finest 12th man, Jack & Sarah Potter
2024	*Cricket's Lost Prodigy,* the Story of Karl Schneider, Michael Lefebvre

CLIPPINGS

BEAUMARIS FOOTBALL CLUB

Under 17s lightning premiership, St Kilda FC, Moorabbin:
'A wonderful performance. Every player is to be congratulated. They played magnificently. The first ever Beaumaris team to win a lightning premiership. Ballarat Districts (game 1) had a long ride for 26 minutes of football. St Kilda City thrashed us in a practice game, kicking 15 goals in one quarter. Things looked grim, yet we beat them in the semi and then won the big one too. Chris Powell set the pattern for the day, getting the ball at all costs. Kendrick Piesse dominated the rucks and didn't miss a knockout in three games. Shane Jacobsen kept popping up when wanted. Ken Robinson, Steve Kennedy and Mick Warr were a tough backline and Marty Lyons was the star of the series…' (1972)

Under 17s v Chadstone (away): 'The boys appeared as if they had been out all night. Very lethargic and disinterested. You know you are breaking your coach's heart. More endeavor. More effort. Everyone must do their share…' (1972)

Under 17s v Chadstone (home): 'When we win the ball from the centre we look like a football team. Kendrick Piesse and Peter Cornford are now consistently winning the hit-outs… a special mention and congratulations to Kendrick Piesse, a great game, but more especially for "keeping his cool". Don't punch or elbow. Play the game hard and fair.' (1972)

(Match summaries by Ted King)

THE AGE

Australia v England Press Test, Sydney: '(Paul) Fitzpatrick of England was unfortunate to be dismissed by a miraculous catch in the gully by man-of-the-match Ken Piesse (Sporting Globe/Sunday Press/Cricketer magazine, formerly of The Age). Piesse received a couple of bottles of something which will surely keep him happy when next he composes,' – John Edwards, Australia's team manager (January 1980)

(I was making G & Ts for the next six months thanks to Mr Gilbey)

CRUSADERS

Crusaders v Combined High Schools, Punt Road Oval, Richmond: 'Tangles (Max Walker) took a nice diving catch at backward square leg much to the relief of leg spinner Ken Piesse who had seen four of his previous seven deliveries to young Geoff Parker disappear to the square boundaries. Sixteen-year-old Parker top-scored with 34 and later in the summer won selection on the Australian Under 19 tour to India and Sri Lanka.' (November 21, 1984)

Crusaders v MCC XXIXers, Albert Ground: 'Bowling at first change, Piesse was unimpressed when MCC skipper (David) Shepherd danced down the wicket and said: "That's your wrong-un Piessey" and called "one" as he drove to mid-on. Shepherd was soon out, well stumped by Mark Foster from Piesse's bowling, a dismissal which caused the normally poker-faced Swan (Richards) to chortle with delight.' (December 12, 1984)

Crusaders v Brighton Grammar: 'Mark Foster (3 not out) and Ken Piesse (8 not out) say they were just starting to feel good when the innings was closed.' (January 23, 1985)

Crusaders v Carey Grammar: The Englishman (Paul) Smith made 64 (retired) with some excellent long-off hitting and dominated a third wicket stand of almost 80 with Piesse (24 retired).' (February 20, 1985)

Crusaders v Ansett Invitational XI, Punt Road, Richmond: 'Piesse was grateful to see an over-pitched leg-break land straight back in his hands, compliments of Keith Stackpole. Stacky (2) had played a maiden over from Piesse, before telling 'keeper Mark Foster: "It's him or me". He was out very next ball.' (March 1, 1985)

(Englishman Colin Cowdrey, aged 52, also played in that game, taking a catch at first slip from my bowling. Later he became Sir Colin for his services to cricket).

Crusaders v Politicians, Manuka Oval, Canberra: 'Ken Piesse and Giles Bush were quite the best of a modest attack. Piesse took the valuable wicket of Graham Evans (the PM's chief of staff), but should have had many more, given just a modicum of help from the field.' (March 15, 1985)

1985, Politicians v Crusaders, Manuka Oval. Trevor Chappell is the non-striker. I took one wicket but could have had more. I'd earlier made 18 before Trevor dismissed me with his slower ball.

Crusaders v Ivanhoe Grammar: 'David Emerson bowled 11 overs for 0-56 and Piesse 19 overs, 6-88, a brilliant catch by (Michael) Ephraims at mid-on to catch Peal (35) a highlight. He had to sprint back 20 metres and throwing himself in the air caught the ball one-handed before catapulting to the ground. It was a remarkable effort. Many consider him Victoria's No.1 fieldsman.' (November 20, 1985)

Crusaders v Ansett Invitational XI, Brighton Grammar: 'Piesse took three wickets in four balls after Swan (Richards) had taken the important wickets of (Graeme) Anderson (41) and (Ron) Steiner (22). (January 16, 1986)

Crusaders v Cricket Club of India, Keysborough Playing Fields: 'Nigel Murch, the blond bombshell only a little slower than in his heyday, was unimpressed to see team spinner Piesse disappear back to work. "We won't need you anyway," called Murch in earshot of everybody.' He was right, the Indian lads making just 63, Murch taking five wickets and Shaun Graf four. (January 23, 1986)

Crusaders v Politicians, Melbourne Cricket Ground: 'The Politicians started like there was no tomorrow. David Hookes made 26 from seven scoring shots, taking 13 runs in an over from Swan and helping himself to two 6s in five balls from Piesse. He was finally caught by David Richards, who had to run around from long leg to complete the skied catch.' (February 25, 1986)

Crusaders v Combined Technical Schools, Junction Oval, St Kilda: 'Piesse conceded 10 runs from his first over but was more accurate later and in 24 balls in mid-innings took 3-9.' (February 28, 1986)

Crusaders v Old Victoria, Junction Oval, St Kilda: 'Ephraims led a revival after Victoria was 3-12 and then 4-22 on a spongy wicket. He added 104 runs for the fifth wicket with Russell Sincock, the pair taking particular toll of Piesse's wrist spin. He had 61 runs hit off seven overs.' (March 4, 1986)

Crusaders v Essendon Grammar: 'Essendon's batting held out the strong opening trio of Reiffel, Balcam and O'Donnell and looked headed for an excellent first innings total. However, the middle-order batsmen were unable to match the spin of Piesse (4-18) and Johnstone (2-4).' (October 15, 1986)

Crusaders v Trinity Grammar: 'The game was a good one ending in a draw, with the last two boys in defending grimly against the wily spin of (Jim) Higgs and Piesse.' (November 11, 1986)

Crusaders v Ivanhoe Grammar: 'Ivanhoe were determined to make amends for the defeat of last year and opened most confidently. Our early bowling could not break through and it was left to K. Piesse to retard the scoring. He took 4-28, continuing his good form.' (November 19, 1986)

Crusaders v Singapore Cricket Club, Junction Oval, St Kilda: 'Crusaders faint hopes of victory rested squarely with Piesse's leg-spinning prowess. Given the ball in the eighth over with Singapore 0-10, he bowled 10 well-controlled overs, surviving a torrid onslaught from Stiller (38) and crucially dismissing Singapore's star in the last over,' the Crusaders winning by just one run.' (November 8, 1988)

PORT MELBOURNE

'Fine support also came from spinner Ken Piesse, who captured 17 wickets and medium pacer Steve Dunn 10. Both these players were in their first seasons with the club and their dedication and desire to do well and win will be an asset in the coming seasons.' (PMCC annual report 1985-86)

'The "Master" Ken Piesse proved on various occasions that he was a very worthwhile member of the team. His innings in the final was superb. His leggies provided the variety that was needed. Not always consistent with the ball, however, it personally gave me great pleasure seeing him play in the sub-district premiership, when two years ago, he told me he didn't think he was good enough for our standard. A very good trainer and a lesson to all young players. All of Port Melbourne loved his Sunday (TV) reports.' – Phil O'Meara (coach) (PMCC annual report 1986-87, Championship year)

'Ken Piesse, a dedicated worker in the nets and on the ground, bowled his tantalising leggies to capture 24 wickets at an average of 17.45 to have his personal-best season with the Burra. An extremely fascinating cricketer, his ability with either bat or ball and his agility in the field make him a pleasure to watch in action. His commitment to his teammates and our club is first class.' (PMCC annual report 1987-88)

'Ken Piesse with his leg spin bowling had his best season with the Burra to capture 28 wickets at 15.60 to win the A. Bogdanoff bowling award, indeed a fitting reward to this player as he is a fine example to any young player that if you're prepared to work at your particular skills at training then the rewards will come in the matches.' (PMCC annual report 1988-89)

'With the inclusion of Tony (Wright), the return of Brendan Doyle and Steve Nicholson and the players from the previous years with the exception of the person whose presence was missed the most, Ken Piesse to Frankston, it was expected the team would go well...' (PMCC annual report 1989-90)

(We missed the finals).

TOASTS & ROASTS

Ando (Sunday Press/3AW): 'I made the mistake of giving Master a taxi chit after one very, very long luncheon with Timmsy at the Golden Gate. He duly bought up the day's takings close to home, prompting a stern please explain from my editor.

'Once at Waverley, Brad Hardie had a huge blew with Mick Malthouse and waved his jumper up to the coach's box before storming out of the rooms immediately afterwards. Master was working for the Sunday Observer and I was his opposition at the Press. As Hardie stormed past us, he said, 'I reckon we should follow him,' and we did, right out to the carpark, despite Shane O'Sullivan from Footscray telling Master that he'd never speak to him again if we kept after Hardie. We duly spoke to Brad. It was clear he had no love for Malthouse but couldn't go on the record. We both wrote our stories. Hardie had won the Brownlow 12 months earlier. He was a big name in the game, just like the Daicos boys are today. Master saved me from being scooped that day.'

Bazz (Mt Eliza CC): 'After years of neglect, our old rundown nets at Mt Eliza were finally getting a touch up from the Council, but you Master had to stop them extending the roof due to your famous flighted deliveries, which were on show when knocking over Housie with a cracker of a ball during final's week, '24. Loved the celebration.'

Beva (Port Melbourne CC): 'You Guru fitted in brilliantly with us and had a thick skin. We lost count of the times at training when the Big Bird, 'Stretch' (Aanensen) gave it to you, calling you a Liberal bastard among many expletives and telling you to go back to where you came from.'

Mark Browning (Australian Cricket Society): 'Bath 2009: you were coming to town and wanted a game between your ACS tour group and Bath CC on their wonderful North Parade Ground. I organised the fixture. Tick. Then you asked if I could find an extra player, or two. Tick. Then you needed another and another. Tick. Tick. Five of us from the Prior Park School's staff team ended up representing ACS that day. The Bath boys belted us, but at least you and I got to bat together for nearly an hour against a bright pink Kookaburra six-stitcher on a gorgeous English summer's day on one of the best club grounds in the world.'

Wayne Carey (North Melbourne great): 'Ken and I have been mates ever since 1988 when I first walked into Arden Street. He has a unique knowledge of how the very best tick.'

(From Wayne's foreword in The Greatest Game, *2006)*

Couta (Frankston Heat CC): 'It was a high scoring game at Collingwood and they were coming at us, needing under 30. The ninth wicket fell and their No. 11 was taking guard. Master came up and said, "No matter what I say, hit this bloke in the stumps. Full and straight. First ball." He walked off and started to yell, "Couta, Couta bounce him. Chin music. Straight at him mate. Straight at him." We added a second backward square and Master put himself at square leg just in front. "C'mon Couta. Let him have it. Bounce 'im. Chin Chin. First nut." I bowled it at his stumps and it went straight through him, hitting his middle and leg. How sweet it is.'

KD, Ken Davis (co-author and former opponent): 'I witnessed Ken's 'wordsmithing' first-hand when he edited and published a book I wrote on my brother Barry Davis, entitled *Born to Play*. He was so positive and encouraging. The time he put in and the connections he made to convert the narrative from that of a novice writer to producing a book of which I'm very proud, was commendable and greatly appreciated by this old purveyor of leg-spin.'

Diggers (Frankston Heat): 'One Melbourne Cup day, I took Jaclyn, my new girlfriend and mother of my two boys to the cricket. We were playing North Melbourne at Ross Straw. It was a warm day and she had the shortest summer frock on, basking on a towel just to the side of the wicket. You asked: 'Who's taking fine (leg) today, lads?' Without hesitation, six all raced down so they could get a better look at Jac.

'I was trying really hard to get in the ones and one night broke Shaun Graf's ribs. Once he had recovered, he got me one-out in the nets facing himself, Wally (Cam Wallace), Steph Cottrell and Adrian Mack, all with new rocks, all steaming in. I was peppered. Afterwards you said to me: "Told you it would be best if you'd stayed in the thirds with the Master".'

Mocca (Australian Cricket Society): 'Early in my Over 60s career with the ACS I was keen to make an impression. We were at Elsternwick, my stamping ground. The tailenders were in and I was given the nod to loosen up for the next over. I needn't have bothered. The Master took a hat-trick – nine, ten, jack and we were into the beers early.'

Dusch (Port Melbourne): 'Don't forget our matchwinning partnership against Sunshine in the Grannie…'

Brendon Gardner (Frankston subbies CC): 'That back cover picture of you with Barass from 1980… there is a striking resemblance to a young D. Brereton, pre-mullet and pre-rinse.'

Adam Gilchrist (Australian Test legend): 'I haven't met many who rival Ken's passion and enthusiasm for the game.'

(From Gilly's foreword in Bradmans of the Bush, *2002)*

Peter Glenton (Australian Cricket Society): 'No-one surpasses your encyclopaedic knowledge of cricket at all levels. Others are better placed to recount your exploits – and misdemeanours – but playing cricket with you over the last few years has been a pleasure. Cricket became fun again. First time I kept to you: "Hmmm, this is interesting, that's a lot of flight, I haven't seen this much flight for a long time, definitely above the eyeline, stay down, stay down…" After a few balls, sure enough, the batsman charges down the track, eyes alight, head up, misses by a mile. "Be patient, it'll get here, it'll get here – we've got him!" My apologies for the ones I've missed, but let's hope we can snag a few more.'

Robert Harvey (dual Brownlow Medallist): 'Ken is passionate, expert, loyal and caring. He's at the top of the tree – among the best and most knowledgeable sportswriters. Years ago he got me out first ball at Port Melbourne but my old man got runs against him that day, so I always say we're square.'

Bob Hawke (Prime Minister): 'First time I have been caught out by a journalist in 25 years.'

Rug (Mt Eliza): 'Never met anyone who is keener or works harder on their game than you Master and the slips catches you are still taking at your age have been a joy to watch. The fly trap! Your love of the game is infectious, and it's great to be able to call you a premiership teammate.'

Housie (Mt Eliza): 'It was spring 2016 and the start of a new season and we were at centre wicket training. Just our firsts and seconds. Not much was being said at all. All of a sudden, this old bloke, in full gear, strides onto the field and without hesitation, positions himself at cover. Within one or two balls, he's chirping to the batsman on strike: "He's still on zero here lads. Still hasn't scored. Keep it tight. Top of off. Doesn't he know it's a one-dayer?" None of us had seen him before. As coach I wander over and introduce myself. "I'm Ken Piesse," he says. "Call me Master."'

Bob Hopkins (Australian Cricket Society): 'Have never forgotten the match against the Supreme Court at St Bedes when you took one of your one-handers to give an old bloke his fifth wicket. We all went home early that day.' (Bouncin' Bobby, then 70, took five for 6).

Hayden Jackson (Frankston Heat): 'After a rare away win against Geelong, Master, ever-perceptive, stopped our mini-bus at the North Geelong bottle-shop for some celebratory 'travellers'. The long drive home was extended by Master's new world record of 11 laps around the Mordialloc roundabout, each lap being accompanied by a raucous "YEAH". 'One more lads?' he asked. "YEAH". We sung the song so many times most of us were hoarse on arrival back at Jubilee Park.'

Legs Leggett (Australian Cricket Society): 'Having taken your hat-trick catch and being engulfed in a bear-hug which would have done Killer Kowalski proud, my ribs are still only just recovering.'

Darren Lehmann (Australian Test player & coach): 'Few match Ken's knowledge or have his rapport with the players. He showed me the player-by-player stats he keeps each summer – and has done for nigh on 40 years. It shows a great passion and enthusiasm for the game. He has been writing longer than I have been playing.'

(From Darren's foreword in All Out for One, *2005)*

Heada (Frankston Heat): 'Big Griff was about to bowl the first ball of the match one day at Moorooduc. It didn't matter who we had in the side. Griff would always take the new cherry downwind. I was at first slip and Master said: "Heada, take leg slip." The fella played a genuine leg glance, straight into the mitts. We'd got him very first nut.'

Tony McCallum (Beaumaris High School): 'Glad I could help with your maths back then mate – not that it mattered. You had much more important stuff on your mind, like cricket and footy.'

Holidays (Frankston Heat): 'It's a bleak June winter's day in Mt Eliza village in 2022. I'm walking along the street and there in the distance appears this burst of radiance. It's Master, decked out in full cricket creams, from bowling boots to vest — and even zinc cream on the nose.

"G'day Master," I said. "Have you been playing cricket?" Master shoots back: "No, mate, I'm just running a few errands and then heading down to the nets to work on my wrong'un.'"

William McInnes (leading Australian actor): 'Few can spin a yarn like Ken.'

Stevie Mac (Kingston Saints CC): 'In the lead-up to a third XI game at Bayswater, I'd impressed the Master in the nets, bowling my gentle mediums reasonably tightly. "You might be our weapon come Saturday, Mac," he said. Sure enough, in mid-innings I was called up. And second ball I got a wicket, courtesy of a gully catch by the great man himself.

'Might be my day,' I thought. A dot to the new batsman, then a swipe across the line to cow corner. Four. No harm. Looking to sneak an innie between bat and pad, I'm again smashed to cow, this time over the fence. Hmm. Ten off two balls. "Well bowled, Mac… unlucky," shouts Master.

'I thought that might be my day done but with Ted Lasso positivity, Master calls me up again for a second over, this time placing an outrider, Andy Heinrichs, at mid-wicket. The hitter is on strike. "Let's see if he's got any other shots," says Master. The first sails over Andy's head. As does the second and third. Andy suggests he stays on Mountain Highway. I'm bowling wider and wider, a little like Johnny Watkins years ago in Sydney.

"He's only got one shot Macca," the ever-optimistic Master calls, before another disappears, squarer this time; the fella's fifth maximum. Thankfully he miscues one and is off strike, but with one for 35 off my two, I was hardly Master's secret weapon. I didn't get another bowl all year. Or the next. 'The punchline? Master came on for me and bowled the cowboy first ball.'

Porno (Kingston Saints): 'Training was always fun with you Master. You only hit the top of the nets every second ball! You were the plank king. Only tough blokes like me could match you.'

Fab (Port Melbourne/Kingston Saints): 'Couldn't understand at Melton one day when you went off once and then again, exactly an hour later. Turns out you were doing golf updates from the Masters for 3MP "live" from Huntingdale…

'And what about the season at St Bedes when you tossed the coin eight times and lost eight straight? You got me to toss in our last home match and finally we won one.'

Ricky Ponting (Test legend/ACS patron): 'Like me, Ken reckons cricket is the best game ever invented. His writings bring us all closer to the action and gives everyone the best seat in the house.'

Mick Shaw (Beaumaris FC): 'I loved the day you hit Eddie Melai's fist with your chin.'

Bob Shield (Sydney club umpire & lover of cricket books): 'You have been a big part of many lives over such a long period, Ken. Thankyou.'

Craig Tansley (Mt Eliza): 'Kenny's most memorable innings with us came for our "B" grade warriors at Carrum Downs a few years back. It reminded me of Dean Jones and his double century in Madras. Never before or since had we played in such stifling humidity and having got to 10 or so, Kenny, our many-seasoned pro, was already gasping. Not wanting to run any more he just smashed 4s and a couple even disappeared over the fence at cow corner. By tea he was 70-odd, but we reckoned he needed an ICU unit. He lay on his back with his shirt off gasping for breath and was all but incoherent. It wasn't a pretty sight. We suggested he should consider retiring and applied ice packs, liberal sprays of cold water and even got an old fan to work, directing it in the direction of his overheated carcass. But no, defying the odds, out he stumbled again and got a dozen or so more before fatigue and their opposing skip knocked him over. But it was still an unforgettable knock: 86 of the best… almost matching his age!'

Joel Wylie (Frankston Heat): 'Does your famous nude lap at Jubilee Park get a mention, Master? Or the nude tee-off on the 12th at Flinders?'

Shaun Young (Frankston): 'After a washed-out game at Brighton, you and George (Voyage) went toe-to-toe with cricket trivia questions; each one crazier than the last. The Frankston boys were at one end and the Brighton boys at the other. The roars were deafening each time either yourself or George answered correctly.'

Trying to spin one big at Frankston's No.1 oval at Jubilee Park in 2022.
David Long

MASTER STATS

FOOTBALL

118 games, Beaumaris, 1967-78 (including 7 finals)
2 games, Mordialloc, 1975 (practice matches)
Long kick champion, Beaumaris state school 1965-66
Under 17s St Kilda Football Club lightning premiership 1972 (first ruck)
Under 17s South-East Suburban FL premiership 1972 (first ruck)
VFA Major Media Award, best story 1975
Senior best and fairest 1975
First XVIII SESFL Div II premiership 1977 (first ruck)
Runner-up best and fairest 1977
Best Player in finals 1977
VFL Major Media award, Best Feature Story, Sterling Cup (night competition), 1984
Australian Football Media Association Life Membership 2012

GOLF

Jim Power Cup, The Age Golf Day, Victoria GC, 1975
Portsea Pro-Am (C grade), 1990 (With 83 off the beater)

CRICKET

Beaumaris	1964-85, Federal District Cricket Association
Prahran	1971-76, Victorian Cricket Association (2nds, 3rds & 4ths only)
Crusaders	1984-91
Port Melbourne	1985-89, Victorian Sub-District Cricket Association (1sts only, bar one game in 2nds)

Frankston   1989-93, Victorian Sub-District Cricket Association
Frankston Peninsula   1993-2006, Victorian Cricket Association
                        (3rds & 4ths only)
Kingston Saints   2007-15, Victorian Sub-District Cricket Association
Mt. Eliza   2016-24, Mornington Peninsula Cricket Association
                        (3rds, 4ths & 6ths)

TOURS:
United Kingdom   1987, 2001, 2005, 2009, 2013, 2015, 2019
West Indies   1999
South Africa   1999, 2018
New Zealand   2016

BATTING STATISTICS

	Mts	Inns	No	HS	Runs	Ave	100s	50s
Beaumaris	173	193	19	106	2866	16.47	1	11
Prahran	12	12	1	20	78	7.14	-	-
Crusaders	66	44	20	31*	475	19.79	-	-
Port Melbourne	52	41	11	46*	444	14.80	-	-
Frankston	51	41	13	40	291	11.10	-	-
Frankston Peninsula	164	144	40	108	2131	20.49	1	7
Kingston Saints	93	101	11	96	1911	21.23	-	9
Mount Eliza	88	68	6	86	1338	19.18	-	5

BATTING AVERAGES

1967-68	Beaumaris Under 14s, 229 runs at 36.17
1970-71	Beaumaris Under 16s, 200 runs at 23.38
1994-95	Frankston Peninsula thirds, 196 runs at 27.67
1996-97	Frankston Peninsula thirds, 263 runs at 52.60
2018-19	Mt. Eliza fourths, 196 runs at 39.20
2020-21	Mt. Eliza fourths, 239 runs at 33.71

CENTURIES

108   Frankston Peninsula thirds v Prahran, 1993-94, Como Park, South Yarra

106   Beaumaris first matting (the Red Bluff XI), v Aspendale, 1975-76, Balcombe Park, Beaumaris

CENTURY PARTNERSHIPS

138*   Third wicket, with Matt McCoy, Kingston Saints thirds v Croydon, 2012-13

135   Sixth wicket, with Harrison Scott, Mt Eliza fourths v Dromana, 2020-21 (Harrison 80, me 46)

133   Third wicket, with Tim Dickens, Mt Eliza fourths v Carrum, 2019-20

126*   Seventh wicket, with Craig Bennett, Frankston Peninsula thirds v Camberwell Magpies, 1996-97

120*   Third wicket, with Phil O'Meara, Kingston Saints thirds v Noble Park, 2007-08 (Phil 83, me 32)

113   Fifth wicket, with Craig Wills, Frankston Peninsula thirds v Prahran, 1993-94

112   Ninth wicket, with Darren Groves, Frankston Peninsula thirds v Geelong, 1997-98

BOWLING STATISTICS

	Overs	Mds	Wkts	Runs	Ave	BB	5wI	10wM
Beaumaris	391.5	35	77	1301	16.90	5-59	1	-
Prahran	8	1	3	37	12.33	3-9	-	-
Crusaders	595.2	102	130	2095	16.12	6-88	4	-
Port Melbourne	613	128	90	1683	18.06	5-33	3	-
Frankston subbies	603.5	164	63	1348	21.38	5-51	2	-
Frankston Peninsula	797	167	130	2324	17.80	5-22	4	1
Kingston Saints	411.3		72	1713	23.79	4-28	-	-
Mount Eliza	515.1	56	108	1824	16.89	6-19	1	-

BOWLING AVERAGES

1970-71	Beaumaris Under 16s, 21 wickets at an average of 5.71 (best 4-2)
1988-89	Port Melbourne firsts, 28 wickets at 15.60
1995-96	Frankston Peninsula thirds, 17 wickets at 17.47
1996-97	Frankston Peninsula thirds, 31 wickets at 10.55
1997-98	Frankston Peninsula thirds, 17 wickets at 19.15
2013-14	Kingston Saints thirds, 16 wickets at 15.06
2017-18	Mt Eliza fourths, 9 wickets at 27.11
2020-21	Mt Eliza fourths, 20 wickets at 10.75
2021-22	Mt Eliza thirds, 14 wickets at 21.64
2023-24	Mt Eliza sixths, 26 wickets at 12.45

FIVE WICKETS IN AN INNINGS

1983-84	5-59, Beaumaris seconds
1987-88	5-33, Port Melbourne firsts v Moorabbin
	5-100, Port Melbourne firsts v Ormond
1988-89	5-33, Port Melbourne firsts v Elsternwick
1990-91	5-60, Frankston firsts v Noble Park
1992-93	5-52, Frankston seconds, v Brighton (from 26 overs)
1996-97	5-34, Frankston Peninsula thirds v Footscray (1st inns)
	5-34, Frankston Peninsula thirds v Footscray (2nd inns)
	5-22, Frankston Peninsula thirds v South Melbourne
	(the three five-fors were in consecutive innings)
2003-04	5-34, Frankston Peninsula thirds v Fitzroy-Doncaster
2021-22	6-19, Mt Eliza thirds v Baden Powell (from 8 overs)

DISTINCTIONS

1964-65	Best Junior Clubman, Beaumaris
1968-69	Beaumaris Under 14s premiership. Carried bat for 65 not out in the Grand Final, v Mentone, Shipstone Reserve, Cheltenham
1969-70	Five dismissals in a game (1 catch & 4 stumpings), Beaumaris Under 16 v Freighter-Heatherton, 1969-70

1970-71	Captain Beaumaris Under 16s
1971 & 1972	Victorian All High Schools representative XI
1972-73	Beaumaris first XI Second Turf premiership team, aged 17
1974 & 1975	Victorian Junior Cricket Union Under 21 team
1976-77	Captain Beaumaris first XI, aged 21
1983-84	Beaumaris second XI, best player in finals
1985-86	First ever 'six-for', Crusaders v Ivanhoe Grammar
1986-87	Port Melbourne first XI Championship team
1988-89	Port Melbourne first XI Twenty20 champions (Caulfield Cricket Ground)
1990-91	Runner-up Frankston club championship
1996-97	Jack Ryder Medal, Cricket Victoria best player award, third XI
2008-09	Kingston Saints inaugural Team of the Year (also honoured in 2009-10, 2010-11 & 2013-14)
2015	Australian Sports Medal for 50 years involvement in cricket
2017-18	Victorian Over 60s third XI, national champions, Canberra. Defeated New Zealand in final.
2018-19	3-3 including first-ever hat-trick, Australian Cricket Society v Richmond Union, McDonald Oval, Beaumaris
2020-21	A then-career best 6-36, Australian Cricket Society Over 60s v Essendon Over 60s, Elsternwick No. 2
2020-21	Hat-trick, Australian Cricket Society v Gippsland Goannas, Elsternwick No.2
2021-22	Wally Wedgwood Jnr award, best individual performance of the season, 6-19, Mt Eliza third XI v Baden Powell, Mt Eliza Football Ground
2022-23	Mt Eliza fourth XI premiership, Mornington Peninsula Cricket Association
2023-24	Australian Cricket Society Over 60s, Echuca Division 1 Championship team

AUSTRALIAN CRICKET SOCIETY

150-plus games, 1971-2024

Richard Elvins Over 60s Best Player Award 2017-18, 2018-19, 2019-20, 2020-21

Christopher Box Grainger ACS Cricketer of the Year Award 2018-19

Doug Manning Lifetime Achievement award 2022-23

SWAN RICHARDS' CRUSADERS

Best bowling 6-88 v Ivanhoe Grammar, 1985-86. Also took 5-37 v Haileybury College (UK), 1987-88, Keysborough Playing Fields and 5-54 v Singapore CC at the Junction Oval, St Kilda, 1988-89.

LIFE MEMBERSHIPS

Melbourne Cricket Ground Media Hall of Fame 1999

Frankston Peninsula CC 2003

Australian Cricket Society 2015

VCA/CRICKET VICTORIA MEDIA AWARDS

1975-76 District cricket writer of the year (The Age)

Cricket Victoria Major Media Award:

Sunday Herald Sun 2003-04

Inside Cricket/Fox Sports 2001-02, 2004-05, 2005-06

Pavilion magazine (Australian Cricket Society) 2011-12 & 2014-15

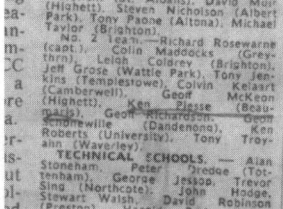 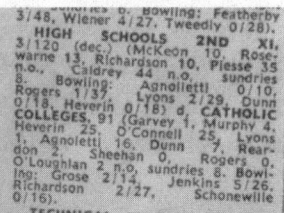 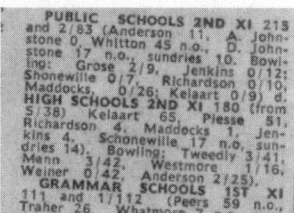

Scrapbook cuttings from the 1972-73 Melbourne secondary schools tournament in Melbourne. Future Test pair Dav Whatmore and Julien Wiener were among those to also play that December.

PREMIERSHIP PICS

1968-69, cricket: Our Beaumaris Under 14s premiership XI which defeated Mentone in the Federal District final at Shipston Reserve, Cheltenham. Back row, left to right: Phil Graves, Mitch Turner, Ken Ansell, Col Gooch, Steve Smith, Peter Cornford, Peter Davey, my best mate Coo Cowen, Steve Kennedy. Seating: Kevin Graves (co-coach), Russell Riddell (captain), Cheryl Riddell (scorer), me (vice-captain), Stan Anderson (co-coach).

1972, football: Our Beaumaris team which knocked over undefeated Ormond in the South-East Suburban Under 17s Grand Final at Spring Street, Black Rock. Standing, left to right: Ted King (mentor and coach), Andrew Warr, Charlie Scott, Michael Poynter, me, Peter Craven, Peter Cornford, Peter Cuming, Mick McNicholas, Steve Heath, Marty Lyons, Mark Ellwood, Shane Jacobsen, Steve Healey, Mick Warr, Ross Ellwood, Jim Spotswood snr (manager), Jack Lyons (assistant-manager). Kneeling: Peter McLeod, Dave Connell, Ian Letcher, Steve Kennedy, Ken Ansell (captain), Steve Coutelas, Ricky Collister, Trevor Albury, Chris Powell. Absent: Ken Robinson.

PREMIERSHIP PICS

1972-73, cricket: Our Beaumaris first XI which won the Federal District Turf 2 premiership at Moorabbin Park. Back row, left to right: Gary Rasmussen, Jimmy Macmillan, Shane Gooch, Jock Stewart, Dave Yeates, me. Front: Noel Newson, Dave Moran, Kevin Graves (captain), Ross Ellwood, Ron Cooper.

1977, football: The greatest thrill of all. Our 1977 senior Beaumaris team defeated hot favourites Chadstone in the SESFL Division 2 Grand Final at Jack Barker Reserve in Cheltenham. We'd trailed by three goals at half-time. I rucked virtually all day after Peter Cornford was injured in the lead-up to the finals. Back row, left to right: Jack Cornford (trainer), Steve Ellingworth, Reggie, Whitey, Fordy, Scan, Tony La Sala, Peter Linton, Corny, Ivan Wilde (trainer), Ronnie Nicho, Larry Warren, Mick Kirkby. Seated: Peter Marsh, Frank Reade (chairman of selectors), Chopper, me (vice-captain), Gerry Callahan (coach), Mick Shaw (captain), Rockstar, Rod Pasquill. Front: Pissy, Chuck, Whitt, Peter Mac, Steve Coutelas, Chris Batchelor, Snowy, Mal Smith.

2022-23, cricket: Our Mounties fifth XI were thrilled to knock off undefeated Pearcedale in the grannie on their dung-hill. The party went on and on and on. Back row, left to right: Bergs, Hollywood, Bernie Cooper, Mac, Joey, Maxy. Standing: Matty Green, Jason Ross, Foxy, Rug, Coina, Fabulous Phil and me. It was my first premiership in 37 years! Without Mac we were cactus.

A close up with Phil and Joey of Fauves fame.

INDEX

Aanensen, Vic 'Stretch' 138-145
Ablett, Gary snr 179, 197, 218, 270
   'The AFL's Michael Jordan' 269
Agar, Ashton 258
Agassi, Andre 180
Alcott, Errol 245
Alderman, Terry 119, 134
   19 lbws in one series 217
Allan, Graeme 'Gubby' 125
Allan, Peter 'Piccolo' 7
Allardice, Lachie 153
Allen, David 29
Ambrose, Curtly 201, 215, 229, 244
   'I don't care if I have no career left' 228
Amiss, Dennis 70
Anderson, Graeme 'Arms' 138-145
Anderson, Jon 167
Angelo, Jeff 75
Animals, The 21
Anne the Napier bookseller 280
Archer, Dave 155
Archer, Jofra 256
Armstrong, Norm 36
Arnall, Don 54
Arnold, Geoff 69
Arthur, Graham 116
Atherton, Mike 234
Atkins, Cam 151

Austen, Jane 280, 285
Austin, Dave 87-88
Australian Cricket Society 51, 53, 200, 252-261
   Miracle at Cooma 261
Aylett, Dr Allen 95

Bacher, Ali 144, 256
Bailey, Chris 90
Bailey, Trevor 80
Baillee, Ernie 91
Baldock, Darrel 'Doc' 116, 146, 147
Bancroft, Cameron 248
Barassi, Ron 'Barass' 66, 97, 108, 111, 253, 254, 294
Barber, Bob 28, 29
Barker, Geoff 84
Barker, Jack 96
Barker, Trevor 'Barks' 96, 167, 174
Barlow, Eddie 'Bunter' 8-12
Barnes, Alan 64
Barrie, JM 18
Bartlett, Gary 275
Bartlett, Kevin 'KB' 239
Beames, David 256
Beames, Percy 28, 79, 80, 92
Beasley, Simon 125
Beatles, The xi, 158
Beaton, Cecil 273

Becker, Gordon 7
Bedi, Bishen 104
Bedford, Peter 'Wheels' 54, 291
Bedser, Alec xviii
Beecher, Eric 88, 106
Beitzel, Harry xv
Bell, Graeme xvii
Belle the chesapeake 107, 293
Benaud, Daphne 159
Benaud, Richie 7, 11, 15-17, 23-25, 45, 48, 65, 222
   75th birthday interview 159
   Bradman regret 15
   Tied Test 16
Benjamin, Kenny & Winston 229
Bennett, Gordon 208
Bennett, Rex 156
Benstead-Smith, Nicholas 276
Bergin, David 'Bergs' 288
Bernard, Steve 'Brute' 238, 243
Berry, Darren 155, 238
Berry, Scyld 110
Bevilacqua, Robert 141
Bichel, Andy 238, 246
Bigelow, Doug 'Bigs' xv
Bingley, John 116
Binns, Peter 156
Bird, Vere 213
Bishop, Ian 214
Bishop, Pam 254
Bitmead, Bob 'La-La' 40
Black, Charlie 74
Blackmore, Ritchie 295
Bland, Colin 8, 213
Bleeser, Joe 38
Blewett, Bob & Greg 206, 238
Bligh, The Hon. Ivo 194
Blight, Malcolm 108, 269
   Ultimatum to Gary Ablett 270
Blues Brothers, The 124
Bogdanoff, Tony 144
Boland, Scott 259
Bolte, Sir Henry 199
Bonecrusher 209
Bonney, John 116
Boon, David 211
Booth, Brian 9, 15, 19, 25
   Apology from Bradman 41-42
Border, Allan 'AB/Captain Grumpy' 127-135, 185, 203, 206, 207-208, 226, 229, 231, 232
   Famous stand with Thommo 131
   'Unsociable and unpleasant' 217
   Sporting royalty 217
Borenstein, Mrs 75
Botham, Ian 'Beefy' 65, 90, 103, 104, 120, 130-132
Boyce, Pat 89
Boycott, Geoff 29, 185, 197
Brabham, Gary 224
Bracewell, John 281
Bradman, John 189, 197, 199, 260
Bradman, Sir Donald 10, 11, 15, 16, 20, 22, 23, 31, 47, 51, 57, 64, 67, 102, 105, 119, 147, 148, 160, 162, 182, 185, 187, 189, 197, 160, 162, 196-198, 215, 222, 225, 231, 232, 254, 264, 276, 277, 279, 283, 286, 298

INDEX

Apology to Brian Booth 41-42
Brokers peace deal with Packer 150
Cashing in on his popularity 263
Drops Garth McKenzie 45
Favourite all-time song 260
Purge on throwers 8
Sacking of Bill Lawry 63
Sacking of Bobby Simpson 15
Brassel, Steve 168
Brayshaw, Ian 'Braysh' 6, 7
Brearley, Mike 101
Bremner, Ian 6
Brereton, Dermott snr 192
Brereton, Dermott 'The Kid' 94, 124, 146, 171-175, 191-194, 205, 253
Dermie's dog KD 193
Brereton, Jean 192
Brewster, Gill 262
Bright, Ray 208
Brittenden, Dick 274
Brittin, Jan 204-205
Broad, Stuart 258
Brown, Bill & Barbara 200
Brown, David 30
Brown, EK 'Ted' 278
Brown, Mal 253
Browning, Mark 54
Buchanan, John 224, 259-260
Bull, Chris 155
Bunton, Haydn 92
Burge, Peter 21, 24, 30, 41
Burns, Creighton 74, 77
Burton, Benny 287
Butlin, Robert 265-267

Byrds, The 46
Byrne, Colonel Denis 140
Byrne, Jennifer 78

Cale, JJ 273, 274
Callahan, Gerry 'The Monster' 86
Cameron, Don 275
Campbell, Blair 55
Campbell, Todge 6
Candy, John 84
Cannon, William 161
Capper, Warwick 126
Cardus, Neville 276
Carew, MC 'Joey' 50
Carey, Wayne 'Duck' 146, 172, 176-180, 197
Carlstein, Peter 8, 10
Carlyon, Les 77, 84
Carlyon, Norm 4
Carman, Arthur 275, 281
Carroll, 'Turkey Tom' 116
Carter, Ron 79, 80
Carter, Sergeant 38
Casey, Ron 209
Casson, Beau 248
Chakrapani, VM 'Chuck' 46
Chamberlin, Dean 253
Chambers, John 27
Champion, Greg 192
Chappell, Greg 51, 70, 128-129, 132-133, 200, 232, 247, 273
Champions David Warner 195
Conversing with the Don 197
Five ducks in 22 days 232

Tour of a lifetime 196
Chappell, Ian   20-25, 39, 42-46, 49, 57,
            58, 66-69, 133, 135, 196, 206
   'An over ahead of the game'   24
   Inspiring speech at Port-of-Spain   66
   Merv Hughes rebuke   211
   Remarkable 1968-69 season   51
Chappell, Trevor   196
Charles, Peter   223
Cheatley, Barry 'Cheetah'   97
Cheesewright, Antony   119, 123
Chevell, Kevin   231
'Chickie'   244
Chipp, Don   150
Chisholm, Andrew   261
Chisholm, Wayne   243, 244
Christian, Michael   159, 258
Chuah, Aaron (son-in-law)   298
Churchill, Sir Winston   239
Clapton, Eric   46
Clarke, John   30
Clarke, Michael 'Pup'   258
Clarke, Wayne   100
Clayton, Scott   123, 125
Cole, Roland   278
Colebatch, Tim   78
Coleman, Bob   77
Coleman, John   98
Coleman, Lesley   76
Collier, Albert 'Leeta'   117
Collier, Harry   98
Collins, Bill   209, 210
Collymore, Corey   245
Compton, Denis   81

Coney, Jeremy   281
Conlan, Gerard   263
Connolly, Alan   9, 10, 31, 34, 40, 49, 56
Connors, Chuck   177
Coodabeen Champions, The   35
Cook, Ron   113
Cook, Ross   256
Coon, Dennis   255
Corbett, Ronnie   110
Corling, Grahame   18
Cosier, Gary 'Jaf'   144, 150, 205
Cosgrove, Bryan   39
Cosgrove, Ernie   104
Cosgrove, Mark   260
Coventry, Syd   117
Cowans, Norman   131
Coward, Mike   103, 110
Cowdrey, Colin   28, 232
Cowen, Alan 'Coo'   34, 35, 55
Cowen, Andrew 'Coo'   151
Cowen, Dorrie   34
Cowper, Bob 'Wal'   1, 3, 6, 19, 25,
            42, 52, 53, 55
   Assessment of Graeme Pollock   14
   Dropped for not being
   fit enough   30-31
Cowper, Dale   53
Cox, Andrew 'Joe'   288, 289
Cox, Peter   143, 144
Coyle, Lew   141
Cozier, Tony   240
Cozzo, Franco   93
Crawford, Ian 'Oysters'   157
Cream   46

INDEX

Creed, Colin	181	Deitz, Shane	260
Creedence Clearwater Revival	158, 210	Dekker, Desmond	244
Crimmins, Peter	35	Dell, Tony	58-62
Cripps, Patrick	179	Dempsey, Gary	108
Crocker, Paul	142	Dench, David	108
Croft, Colin	206, 214	Dennis, Chris 'Bones'	85
Crompton, Neil 'Froggie'	205	Dermott, Greg 'Biff'	138
Cronje, Hansie	197	Desira, Peter	112
Crowe, Jeff	185	Devlin, Bruce	127
Crowe, Martin	196, 282	Dexter, Ted	16, 28
Cullen, Tom	109	Dew, Stuart	165, 166
Curran, Kevin	116	Dharmesena, Kumar	258
Czeck, Mike	296	Di Pierdomenico, Robert 'Dipper'	173
		Dimattina, Michael	204
Dale, Adam	242	Ditterich, Carl 'Big Carl'	95-96
Daley, Wayne 'Suds'	140	Donovan, Jason	239
Dangerfield, Patrick	179	*Doobie Brothers, The*	79
Daniel, Wayne	134, 214	Dooland, Bruce	222
Davidson, Alan 'Davo'	15, 16	Dooley, Bill	100
Davidson, Shane 'Nuffy'	139	Dorsey, Colin	273
Davies, Geoff	42, 51	Douglas the labrador	254
Davies, Ray	21	Doull, Buce	177
Davis, Bobby	98, 99, 209	Doyle, Shane 'Cement Head'	140
Signing Polly Farmer	113-115	Drake, Ian	116
Davis, Ken 'KD'	63, 64, 111	Du Plessis, Faf	250, 257
Davis, Simon	149	'Aussies unlocked the fighter in me'	249
de Bruyn, Theunis	250	Dujon, Jeff	214
De Kock, Quinton 'Quinny'	250	Duncan, Ross	56, 57
De Lacy, Hec	92	Dunn, Jack	83
De Silva, Alzina (daughter-in-law)	294	Dunne, Steve	221
De Silva, Aravinda	138	Dunstall, Jason	171, 173, 176-177, 296
De Villiers, AB	250, 257	Duscher, Darren	143
Deep Purple	293	Dusty, Slim	xviii
DeFreitas, Phil 'Daffy'	234		

Dyer, Jack 'Captain Blood'	100, 117, 209, 210	Fitzgerald, Ella	xviii
		Fitzmaurice, Jim	6
		Flanagan, Andy	280
Eagles, The	296	Fleetwood-Smith, L. O'B 'Chuck'	105
Earle, Jimmy 'Luigi'	144	Fletcher, Keith	69
Eastwood, Ken	6, 57, 65	Flint, Barrie	277
Edrich, Bill	189	Flintoff, Tess	261
Edrich, John	69	Flynn, Errol	185
Edwards, Brendan	116	Fogarty, John	158
Edwards, John 'Darkie'	110	Foley, Bill	155, 156
Edwards, Paul	275	Foote, Les	116
Eicke, Wells	99-100	Forbes, Prue	50
Elliot, 'Uncle' Doug	209	Forster, Gary	62
Elliot, Rob	248	Fortune, Charles	11
Elliott, Matthew	246, 260	Foschini, Silvio	126, 167
Elphinstone, Robert	121	Foster, Mak	205
Elton John	85	Fothergill, Des	118-119, 148
Elvins, Richard	252	Francis, Bruce	64
Entwistle, Craig 'Wiss'	151	Fraser, Dawn	79
Erickson, Rick	74, 142	Fredericks, Roy	68
Evans, Godfrey	81	Freeman, Eric	45
Fankhäuser, Des	73	Gainey, RJ	197
Fanning, Fred	100	Gains, Grant	153
Farmer, Graham 'Polly'	114-115	Garner, Joel	134, 196, 214
Fauves, The	288	Gatting, Mike	222
Favell, Les	42, 150	Gee, Margaret	78
Fearnley, Duncan	132	Geddes, Allan	117
Fender, Percy	80, 81, 276	George the intern	122
Finch, Aaron	141, 296	Getty, John-Paul	186
Fingleton, Jack	46, 161, 275, 276	Gibbs, Barry	197
Finn, Neil	282	Gibbs, Lance	26, 49, 214
Fisher, John	99	Giddings, Al	83
Fishwick, Herbert	277	Gilbert, Dave	204

INDEX

Gilchrist, Adam	40, 238, 240, 242	Griffiths, Daryl	116-117
Gilligan, Arthur	46	Griffiths, Matt 'Griff'	151
Gillon, Cr Alec	85	Grimmett, Clarrie	197, 222
Gleeson, John	48, 68	Grout, Wally	22
Goddard, Trevor	7-13	Chainsmoking gambler	21
Goggin, Billy	269	Groves, Darren	51
Goggin, Peter 'Billy'	154	Gulle, Sam	89
Golden, Dave	37		
Goldsmith, Brett	90	Hadlee, Sir Richard	206
Gooch, Graham	217	Hafey, Tom	93, 253, 269
Goodes, Adam	125	Hall, Barry	168
Goodman, Tom	16	Hall, Wes	25, 26, 50
Gordon, Harry & Michael	78	Hamilton, Jack	94
Goss, Kevin	85	Hammond, Happy	99
Goss, Normie	176	Hammond, Jeff	67, 142
Gould, Shane	127	Hammond, Walter	12, 68
Gower, David	101, 217	Handley, Johnny	120
Graf, Shaun	154, 220	Hanif Mohammad	23
Grant, Chris	175	Hansen, Brian	189, 190
Grant, John 'General'	32, 40	Happell, Charlie	179, 180
Grant, Justin 'Juzza'	287	Happy Gilmore	103
Grant, Sandy	263	Harbourd, Noel	230
Graveney, Tom	54	Hare, Anthony 'Harey'	287
'Gravy'	245	Harmison, Steve	244
Greaves, Judge	180	Harris, Dickie	99, 100
Gregory, Mr	275	Harris Mr. P	xiv
Green, Bill, 'Weg'	271	Harrop, Brett & Dean	151
Greenidge, Geoffrey	68	Hart, John	161
Greenidge, Gordon	105, 106, 214	Harvey, Neil 'Nin'	57, 102, 121, 159, 196, 200, 254, 260
Greig, Keith	108		
Greig, Tony	70, 128	Harvey, Robert	142
Griffith, Adrian	239, 245	Hassett, Lindsay	47, 104
Griffith, Charlie	25, 26, 49	Hawke, Bob	49
Griffiths, Alec	116	Hawke, Neil	103

Haynes, Dessie 105
Healy, Gerard 126, 146, 185,
Healy, Ian 216, 222, 228, 229, 232, 240, 242
Heard, James 163
Heath, Kevin 35
Heinrichs, Paul 78
Hele, George & Ray 276
Heller, Bill 22
Hendren, Patsy 277
Hendrix, Jimi 21
Hendry, HSTL 'Stork' 121
Hendy, Peter 137
Henriques, Moises 245
Hernandez, Patrick 100
Hession, Robert 173
Heywood, Doug xv
Higgs, Jim 223
Hill, Benny 51
Hill, Freddie 85
Hills, Ben 78
Hitchcox, Alan 24
Hoare, Des 7
Hobbs, Greg 'Hobbsy' 91-92, 95-97, 108, 178
Hobbs, Jack 2011
Hobbs, Russell 'Rug' 289
Hobson, David 260
Hocking, Bruce 274
Hodge, Brad 110, 173
Hodge, Luke 296
Hoffman, Dustin 142
Hogg, Fred & Dulcie 210

Hogg, Rodney 'Hoggie/Malcolm' 102-104, 205, 210, 212-214
Hohns, Trevor 218
Holder, Noddy 82
Holding, Michael 'Mikey' 123, 172, 196, 214
Holt, Darrel 222
Holten, Val 38-39
Hookes, David 106, 128, 201, 205, 219, 258
House, Lyle 'Housie' 287
Howard, Bob 38
Howard, John 253
Howell, Verdun 116
Hudson, Andrew 227, 228
Hudson, Peter 'Huddo' 35, 36, 112, 113, 174, 253
Hughes, Frank 'Checker' 117
Hughes, Howard 97
Hughes, Kim 'Claggie' 124, 132, 133, 135, 185
Hughes, Merv 211, 215, 227
Hughes, Phil 248
Humphries, Gerry 142
Hunt, Geoff 81
Hunt, Rex 175, 271
Hurley, His Excellency General, the Honorable David 58
Hussey, Dave 154
Hussey, Mike 260

Iles, Geoff 'Chopper' 94
Illingworth, Eddie 54
Illingworth, Ray 55, 57, 60, 64

INDEX

Inverarity, John	48, 150	Jones, Dean	31, 110, 133, 149, 216-217, 229
Ironmonger, Bert 'Dainty'	148, 149		
Isaacson, Peter	112, 120	Famous double-100 in Madras	207-208
Jackson, Mark 'Jacko'	166-167	Jones, Jack & Sarah	98
Jackson, Paul	201, 204	Jones, Jeff	30
Jacobs, Bill	53	Jones, Simon	255
Jacobs, The Rev Garry	27, 28	Jones, Tom	281
Jaggard, Ed	45	Jordan, Michael	269
Jagger, Mick	43	Jordon, Ray	40
James, Darren	150	Joseph, David	245
James, Glenn	167	Joshua, Geoff	150
Jamieson, Ray	96	Joslin, Les	48
Jansz, Keith	151, 254	Judd, Chris	116
Jarman, Barry	22		
Jeans, Allan	156, 176-177, 191, 193, 210, 269	Kallicharran, Alvin	68
		Kallis, Jacques	249
Jenkins, Katherine	xviii	Kamahl	260
Jenner, Terry 'TJ'	34, 68, 173, 180-183, 221, 236-240	Kanhai, Rohan	68
		Kasprowicz, Michael	255
Jesaulenko, Alex 'Jezza'	43, 198, 214	Keddie, Bob	35
Jewell, Tony	167	Keenan, Peter 'Crackers'	116
Jim Power Cup	82	Kennedy, Dulcie	36
Jimmy the greyhound	174	Kennedy, John F	14, 43, 223
Johnson, Alan	111	Kennedy, John 'Kanga'	35, 36, 171, 173
Johnson, Bob	84, 85	Keogh, Brian 'Beeks'	157
Johnson, Ian	47, 190	Keogh, Johnny	141
Johnson, Len	199, 2009	Kerley, Neil	114
Johnston, 'Big Bill'	197, 198	Kernahan, Stephen	175
Jolly, Darren	167-169	Khawaja, Usman	21
Jolly, Deanne & Scarlet	168-169	Killigrew, Alan 'Killa'	141
Jones, Andrew	220	King Kong Bundy	124
Jones, Clem	8	King, Andrew	243
		King, Carole	296

King, Edmund' 'Eddie' 87
King, Ted 87, 243
Kingston Town 126
Kink, Rene 120
Kinks, The 46
Kippax, Alan 274
Kirby, Keith 32
Kirby, William 126
Kline, Lindsay 48
Knights, Peter 171, 269
Knox, Ken 79-80
Knox, Malcolm 201, 230
Kohli, Virat 7, 213
Krishnan, Raj 205
Kuuse, Andew 255

La De Das, The 293
Lahiff, Tommy 143
Laird, Bruce 66
Lake, Hugh 267
Laker, Jim 47
Lalor, Peter 249
Lamb, Allan 131
Lamb, John 77
Lane, Colin 75
Lane, Marty 'The Brain' 140
Langdon, Wally 6
Langer, Justin 'JL' 211, 223, 235, 244
Lara, Brian 183, 213, 228, 232, 237, 239
    Mayhem at St Johns 245
Larwood, Harold 40
Lawrence, Barry 116
Lawrence, Bridget 213

Lawry, Bill 'Phanto' 6-10, 15, 19, 29, 40, 45, 47, 48, 49, 50, 52, 56, 57, 67, 68, 207, 263
    Club match of the century 31-33
    Dead man walking 20
    His sacking 20, 63-65
    Nickname 19
    Stonewalling in Sydney 16-17
    'Wouldn't walk my dog on the MCG' 20
Lawson, Geoff 103, 108
Ledward, Jack 39
Lee, Brett 255
Lee, Frank 278
Leech, Francis 288
Lehmann, Darren 'Boof' 256, 260
Leigh, Howard 84, 111
Lemmon, Jack 120
Lennon, John 223
Leo the groodle 293
Leonard, Phil 288
Lewis, Mick 150
Liberatore, Tom 175
Liberatore, Tony 173, 175
Lillee, Dennis 55, 57, 60, 69-72, 105, 109-110, 121, 129, 132, 149, 214, 221, 233, 239, 273
    'A lawbreaking maverick' 133
Lindsay, Denis 13-14, 40
Lindwall, Ray 198
Livitsanis, Mr 74
Lloyd, Clive 68, 214, 240
Lloyd, David 'Bumble' 257
Lloyd-Webber, Andrew 182

INDEX

Linton, Peter 86, 87
Lockett, Tony 'Plugger' 125, 146-147, 173-175, 179
Lockett, Vicki 146
Loewe, Stewart 100, 256
Long, Michael 163
Lord twins 99
Lord, Normie 36
Lowry, Leigh 151
Loxton, Annie 103
Loxton, Sam jnr 50, 56-57, 132, 159-160, 187-188, 196, 199
Loxton, Sam snr 198
Luckhurst, Brian 72
Lyon, Garry 175
Lyon, Nathan 257
    Drops ball on AB De Villiers 256
Lyons, Marty 87

Macartney, Charlie 274, 277
Macdonald, Duncan 14
MacGeorge, Peter 87
MacGill, Stuart 223, 236, 242, 246
Mackay, Ken 'Slasher' 48, 50, 79
Madden, Simon 171
Mailey, Arthur 278
Mallett, Ashley 48, 68
Malone, Mick 106
Mann, Hassa 35
Mann, Neil 100
Markram, Aiden 250
Marley, Bob 244
Marriott, Stevie 34
Marsh, Geoff 'Swampy' 211, 238, 240-243

Marsh, Rod 69, 70, 110, 121, 132-133, 200, 204
Marshall, Malcolm 134, 214
Martin, Chris 220
Martin, Johnnie 'The Little Fave' 7, 18, 22
Martyn, Damian 223, 248
Massie, Bob 67
Masterton, Billy 138
Mathers, Jason 'Heada' 151, 153
Matthau, Walter 120
Matthews, Greg 202
Matthews, Leigh 95, 165, 171, 179, 253
Maxwell, Shane 'Maxie' 288-289
McBurney, Glenn 'The Fireman' 140
McCabe, Stan 133, 234
McClean, Dave 141
McCormack, Basil 117
McCoy, Brendan 286
McCullum, Tony 37
McDermott, Craig 133
McDonald, Ian 92, 94, 190
McDonald, Colin 47, 195
McDonald, Trevor 39
McEnroe, John 120
McFadyen, Brian 'Freddie' 204
McFarlane, Glenn 169
McFarlane, John 'Cocky' 140
McFarline, Peter 79, 84, 102, 128-129
McFeeters, Ian 157
McGain, Bryce 154, 254, 261
McGilvray, Alan 11, 47, 104
McGorrie, Ian 75

McGrath, Glenn   15, 221, 228, 233, 234, 239, 240, 244, 245, 254-255
   Career-making dismissal   228
   Fitness fast-tracking   231
McGuane, Micky   159
McGuire, Eddie   147
McKenna, Peter   xi, 210, 253
McKenzie, Nick   78, 225
McKenzie, Graham 'Garth'   7-11, 21, 23, 26, 44, 45
   Rates the best   12
McKenzie, John   278
McKenzie, Robert 'Mac'   142
McKernan, Corey   146, 172, 173
McLeod, Jack   36
McLeod, Keiran   287
McMahon, Sally   178, 179
McMaster, Bill   269
   Rediscovers Gary Ablett   269
McNamara, Brad   204
Meckiff, Ian   8
Melai, Eddie   86
Meldrum, Ian 'Molly''   85
Menzies, Sir Robert   16, 32, 194, 195
Merrett, Thorold   xv
Merriman, Bob   135, 207
Michael, George   164
Michelle's gymnasium   297
Millane, Darren   165
Miller, Colin 'Funky'   238, 239, 242-246
Miller, Geoff   132
Miller, Greg   177-180
Miller, Jimmy   151, 154
Miller, Justin   150

Miller, Keith 'Nugget'   xiii, 13, 16, 47, 93, 181, 184-190, 195, 220, 267
   Bridgetown blow-up with Ian Johnson   190
   'Don Bradman ruined my life'   187
   Shock axing from touring team   188
Miller, Peg   190
Milne, Margaret   239, 243
Milne, Rick   243
Minogue, Kylie   239
Mitchell, Neil   78
Mohr, Bill   92, 195
Mooney, Mr   74
Moore, Darcy   121
Moore, Jarred   151
Moore, Kelvin   193
Moore, Peter   121, 124, 125
Morello, Joe   21
Moriarity, Jack   117
Morris, Arthur   47, 260, 267
Morrissey, Greg   114
Mortensen, Ole   138

Moss, Jon   154
Mott, Matthew   151
Moule, WH 'Bill'   194
Moyes, Don   271
Mueller, Jack   117
Mullins, Pat   284
Murch, Nigel   54, 150
Murch, Suzie   54
Murdoch, Lindsay   89
Murphy, Chris 'Porno'   291
Murphy, Johnny   108

INDEX

Murray, John 30
Murray, Will 225
My Morning Jacket 296

Nankervis, Brian 153
Nankervis, David 'Tiger' 151, 153
Nash, Graham 296
Nash, Laurie 'LJ' 92, 93
Neely, Don 284
Neitz, David 125
Nettlefold, Michael 85
Newman, John 'Sam' 92, 209
   'You can't be serious' 271
Newton, Bert 115
Newton, Bill 115
Ngini, Lungi 250
Nichols, Greg 269
Nicholls, Eddie 240
Nicholls, John 'Big Nick' 79
Nicholson, David 'Chuck' 86
Nicholson, Rod 102
Nicholson, Ronnie 73-74
Nicklaus, Jack & Jack jnr 127
Nolan, Mick 108, 116
Nolte, Nick 83
Noonan, John 'Jonty' 291
Noonan, John 'JR' 291
Norman, Greg 173

Oakley, Ross 97
Obuya, Kennedy Otieno 155
O'Brien, Leo (football) 113-115
O'Brien, Leo (cricket) 146, 159, 160, 162, 223
O'Donnell, Gary & Lisa 164
O'Donnell, Simon 202
O'Keeffe, Kerry 'Skull' 67-68
Ollington, Lionel 'Nappy' 89
O'Meara, Phil 'Fab' 138-145, 289, 299
O'Neill, Norm 8-10, 19, 21, 40-42, 104
   Denounces Chuckin' Charlie 26
   Remarkable throwing arm 41
O'Reilly, Bill 'Tiger' 12, 47, 102-105, 135, 158, 195, 213
O'Rourke, Jeff 'Chopper' 290
Osborne, Richard 125
O'Toole, Jack 210
Our Waverley Star 209

Packer, Kerry 42, 65, 79, 106, 128-130, 199
Pagan, Denis 178, 179
Page, Percy 117
Paine, Tim 250, 254
Palm, David 121
Palmer, Scott 136, 146, 164, 165, 169
Parish, Bob snr 129, 196
Parker, Geoff 126
Parkinson, Sir Michael 158, 186, 196, 220
Parks, Jim 29, 30
Parr, Orion 295
Parr, Wayne (son-in-law) 295
Partridge, Joe 9
Pascoe, Len 66
Pataudi, Nawab of 44-46
Patterson, Patrick 214, 216
Pattinson, Darren 247

Pawson, Tony 70
Payne, Andrew 'Drew' 37, 254, 292
Payne, Garth 38
Pepper, Alma 267
Pepper, Cec 'Pep' 14, 222, 257, 264-269
    4 sons with 4 different women 267
    'Cec was also my father' 265
    'The year's most unexpected treat' 264
Pepper, Keith 267-268
Perkin, Graham 45, 46, 72, 77-78, 195
Perry the chihuahua 34
Pert, Gary 175
Perry, Neramiah 239
Perussich, Lee 141
Peter the hairdresser 146
Peters, Noel xv
Phelan, Terry 108
Philpott, Peter 41
Piesse, Anne (my sister) 21
Piesse, Dick (my uncle) 277
Piesse family xi-xvii, 72-76, 86
Piesse, James (son) 89, 126, 293-294
Piesse, Jessica 'Jess' (daughter) 127, 176, 192-193, 273, 294, 296, 297
Piesse, Jim (my brother) xv, 21
Piesse, Jim (my uncle) xvii, 115
Piesse, Ken/Kendrick xi-298
    1977 Grand Final boilover 86-88
    1980 Press Test 110
    'Being' Keith Miller for a day 184-185
    Best 72 hours of all 256
    Biggest ever football story 167-170
    Lucky escape at Plugger's farm 174
    Nude lap 195
    Nude rock 'n roll 90
    Playing Michael Slater into form 239
    Public Enemy No.1 153
    'Stumped Whitla bowled Warne' 205
    Thirty Grand Finals 165-167
    Thrill of the hunt 272-284
    Training under Barass 108
Piesse, Kenneth Charles (my Dad) xv-xvii, 9, 33, 37, 44, 46, 72, 77, 110, 252, 275, 277
    Second World War 73
Piesse, Melinda 'Min' (daughter) 101, 110, 295
Piesse, Patricia, nee Thomas (my Mum) xv-xvii, 19, 37, 39, 44, 72, 80, 95, 110, 256, 290
Piesse, Rebecca 'Bec' (daughter) 169, 277, 294, 296
Piesse, Richard (first cousin) 37
Piesse, Susan (my wife) 72, 82, 89, 101, 107, 111, 124, 139, 157, 166-167, 169, 179, 192, 203, 236-238, 243, 253-255, 270, 273, 270-280, 285, 286, 292-294, 297
Piesse, Victoria 'Tori' (daughter) 127, 253, 267, 295-296
Pippos, Angela 258
Pithey, Tony 10
Platten, John 'The Rat' 150, 173, 176
Player, Gary 83
Pollock, Graeme 'Little dog' 8-14, 23, 49, 210, 213
    209 against Richie Benaud's International Cavaliers 7

INDEX

Pollock, Peter 'Pooch'   7-14, 40
Pollock, Shaun   235
Ponsford, Bill snr   30, 35, 160-161, 195
    'No-one could chase Bradman'   162
Ponsford, Billy jnr   162
Ponsford, Geoff   160-161
Ponsford, Megan   162
Ponting Foundation, The   253
Ponting, Ricky   24, 201, 221, 229, 238-239, 248, 259
    Australian Cricket Society patron   200
    Signed by Kookaburra at 13   248
Popescu, Alex   115
Postle, Bruce 'Poss'   77-78
Potter, Jack 'Pottsy'   6-9, 18, 19, 22, 40, 221
    'You've just ruined the match'   10
Poulter, Geoff 'Poult'   88, 95
Powell, Colin 'Ollie'   260
Pratt, Bob   92, 113
Prendergast, Denis   155
Presley, Elvis   158
Prince   296
Prince Charles, His Royal Highness   203
Princess Margaret, Her Royal Highness   186
Prior, Tom   102, 103
Procter, Mike   40
Pyle, Gomer   38

Quantok, Rod   xviii

Rabada, Kagiso   250
Radley, Clive   102
Rainsbury, Ken   178
Ramadhin, Sonny   214
Randall, Derek   213
Ranjitsinhji, KS   38
Ravindra, Rachin   281-282
Redpath, Ian 'Red'   6, 9, 10, 19, 64
Reed, Lou   79
Reed, Ron   90
Reese, TW 'Tom'   275
Reeves, George *Superman*   xi
Reid, Bruce   211
Reid, John (older)   275
Reid, John (younger)   206
Reiffel, Paul   204, 233
Rendell, Matty   123-125
Renneberg, Dave   18
Richards, Barry   12, 49, 106, 213, 234
    'Rocking the baby'   286
Richards, Bob 'Swan'   138, 206
Richards, David   201
Richards, Lou   209, 210
Richards, Viv 'Smokin' Joe'   105, 106, 134, 211-12
    The best No.3 since Bradman   213
    'Nasty racist Australians'   215-216
Richardson, Jeff   39
Richardson, Richie   222, 228
Richardson, Vic   11, 46
Riches, Bruce 'The Frog'   83, 84
Richmond, Graeme   112, 113
Riddle, Clay   151
Ring, Doug   159, 208
Rioli, Cyril   166

Ritchie, Greg 207
Rixon, Steve 233
Robb, Jimmy 90
Roberts, Sir Andy 133, 196, 214
Roberts, Brian 'Whale' 93-94
Roberts, Michael 85
Roberts, Neil 'Coconut' 85, 92
Roberts, Sandy 208, 209
Robinson, Austin jnr 129
Robinson, Austin snr 71
Robinson, Peter 261
Robinson, Smokey 79
Rolfe, Doug 109
Rollingstones, The 43, 296
Roos, Paul 'Roosy' 151, 168, 169
Root, Joe 251
Rosemary the tourist 244, 246
Ross, Alan 275, 280
Ross, Graham 143, 144
Rothwell, Barry 19
Roughead, Jean & Jarryd xv
Rowan, Lou 49, 57
Rowe, Lawrence 105
Rumph, Peter 'Hughie' 94
Runyan, Damon 244
Russell, Paul 293
Ryan, Tom 32
Ryder, Jack 'The King' 198

Saints, The 90
Salmon, Lachie 172
Salmon, Paul 'The Big Fish' 163, 164, 171-175
    Paul's family 164

Schimmelbusch, Wayne 106
Schneider, Karl 284
Schwab, Alan 97
Scott, Don 35, 83, 95, 113, 146, 171, 271
Selby, Des 24
Sellers, Basil 204
Sellers, Rex 22
Sessions, Bob 171
Sharland, WS 'Jumbo' 91
Sharpe, Duncan 157, 199
Sharrock, John 'Shadda' 98, 113
Shaw, Tony 146, 165
Sheahan, Mike 80, 84, 288
Sheahan, Paul 19, 48-49, 68, 71
Sheedy, Kevin 84, 163, 165, 175
Sheehan, Darren 'Rocky' 291
Sheldrake, Bill 37
Shepherd, Barry 14
Shepherd, David 159
Shiell, Alan 'Sheff' 102, 129
Shoaib Akhtar 233
Siddle, Peter 247
Sidebottom, Garry 112
Sidhu, Navjot 241
Sigley, Ernie 158-159, 193, 210
Simpson, Bobby xiii, 9, 10, 19-22, 26, 30, 31, 39, 42, 45, 48-49, 54, 110, 133
    Australian coach 207-208
    Bradman sacking 15
Simpson, Homer 294
Sinatra, Frank 78
Sincock, David 'Evil dick' 7, 23
Skilton, Bob 179
Skinner, Geoff xi, 27, 62

INDEX

Slater, Michael 230, 239
Smallhorn, Wilfred 'Chicken' xv
Smith, Graeme 257
Smith, Ian 281
Smith, Mal & Nick 85
Smith, MJK 'Mike' 27, 28, 30
Smith, Neil 'Doughie' 290
Smith, Norm 54, 163
Smith, Patrick 157
Smith, Red 275
Smith, Robin 229, 234
Smith, Steve (football) 87
Smith, Steve (cricket) 196, 247-249, 257
   'Lyon can do what he likes' 257
   Sports scandal of the century 248
Snead, Sam xv
Snow, John 3, 30, 57, 64
Sobers, Sir Garfield/Garry 'Sobie' 12, 13, 23, 26-27, 41, 50, 54, 213
Solomons, Harry 132
Southee, Tim 282
Spicer, Ken 'Spice' 206
Springfield, Dusty 54
Stackpole, Keith 'Stacky' 6, 19, 56, 57, 64, 65, 175
Starc, Mitchell 250
Steele, Ray 129
Steggell, Charles 278
Stevens, Anthony & Kelli 178
Stewart, Gary 209
Stewart, Ian 116
Stewart, Jimmy 127
Stokes, Ben 8, 256
Stone, George 173, 191

Strachan, Graeme 'Shirley' 95, 146
Streatfeild, Noel 233
Street, Tony 149
Stubbings, Steve 151, 287
Stynes, Jim 168
Sutcliffe, Bert 275, 282
Sutherland, James 257
Sutherland, Jane 76
Sweeney, Mr 107
Swingler, Denis 'Denbeigh' 140
Symonds, Andrew 151, 213
Symmonds, Donna 239

Taber, Brian 'Tabbsy' 195
Tamblyn, Mike 222
Tanner, Les 77
Tavare, Chris 132
Taylor, Greg 77, 84, 89
Taylor, Mark 'Tubby' 24, 78, 211, 217, 226-228, 231-232
   Australian of the year 230
   Not as Tubby 231
Taylor, Peter 'Peter Who' 182, 210-211, 227
Tendulkar, Sachin 213
Tetlow, Paul 267
Thomas, Amanda & Wilfred (my grandparents) xviii
Thomas, Grahame 19
Thomas, Helen 79
Thomas, Jean xv
Thoms, George 195

Thomson, Alan 'Froggie' 1-5, 54, 55, 57, 70, 84
   Refuses to bounce John Snow 3
Thomson, Jeff 'Thommo' 67, 69-71, 100, 130, 214
   'Blood on the pitch' 71
   Famous stand with AB 131-132
Thorpe, Ian 'The Thorpedo' 126
Thurmer, Linda 124
Timms, Daryl 'Timmsy' 85, 111, 120, 122, 184-185, 193
Tinsley, Robert 'Bunker' 138, 142
Titmus, Freddie 29, 34
Todd, Ron 100
Tony the greengrocer xiii
Tossol, Peter 94
Trainor, Francis 98
Trengove, Alan 175
Tretheway, Peter 24
Tribe, George 138
Trueman, Fred 103, 109
Trumper, Victor 45
Tryon, Lady Dale 'Kanga' 203
Tuck, Michael 171
Turner, Alan 71
Turner, Glenn 65
Turner, Neville 260
Twain, Mark xviii
Tyson, Frank 3

Uriah Heep 293

Valentine, Alf 214
Van Vugt, Geoff 142
Van Zanen, Jan 143
Verity, Hedley & Ray 74
Vidler, Bob 283, 284
Vidler, Gordon 270, 271, 283-284
Viljeon, Ken 'Boss' 13
Villiers, Fred 112
Vivienne the Dunedin guide 272
Voss, Michael 125

Wade, Doug 'The Fatman' 82, 113, 114
Wadekar, Ajit 44, 48
Walker, Luke 'Scotty' 151
Walker, Max 'Tang' 67, 69, 173, 176, 205
Wallis, Jim 116
Walsh, Courtney 201, 214, 229
Walsh, Matty 'Bear' 291
Walsh, Mike 243
Walters, Doug 18, 19, 21, 25, 39, 49, 50, 56, 67, 68, 80, 109, 233
   A star is born 29-30
   In 'Queer street' 56
   Sleeping-in in the Caribbean 66
Ward, John 27-28, 53
Warne, Jackson 224
Warne, Sebi 287
Warne, Shane 'Warnie' 15, 19, 21, 104, 145-146, 178, 182, 187, 197, 205, 219-225, 227, 231, 233, 236-242
   Addictive personality 220
   Axed in Antigua 242
   Chick magnet 237-238
   'I was extra driven' 225
   Fifteen years of bullying 222
   His flipper 221

INDEX

Sulking at St Johns   246
Warne, Simone   224, 225
Warne, Summer   224
Warner, Candice   250
Warner, David 'The Bull'   195, 256-257, 271, 282
    Flare-up with de Kock   250
    Sports scandal of the century   248
    The most divisive of all   249
Warner, PF 'Plum'   160
Wasim Akram   221, 233
Waters, Roy   37
Watkins, John 'Wok'   68
Watson, Graeme 'Beatle'   53-54
Watson, Tim   143, 164, 177
    Tim's family   164
Waugh, Mark   229, 234
    Three classic 100s   235
Waugh, Steve   150, 157, 195, 201, 204, 217, 229, 234, 23i9, 241-242, 246
    Bowls 3 bouncers in a row at King Viv   211
    Drops Shane Warne   242
    Incites Curtly Ambrose   228
Wearmouth, Ronnie   100
Webster, Sammy   288
Weekes, Sir Everton   213, 239
Whatmore, Dav   109, 149, 157, 199
Whitington, RS 'Dick'   13, 56, 188, 278
Whitla, Alan & Jimmy   205
Whitten, EJ 'Ted'   77, 112, 179
Whitty, Peter 'Whitt'   88
Wiener, Julien   108
Wilder, Billy   120

Wilkins, Phil 'Redcap'   71, 102
Williams, Greg   125
Williams, Marita & Sam   251
Williamson, Kane   282
Willingham, Graham   78
Willis, Bob   120, 131, 132
Wintle, Luke 'Juice'   289
Wintle, Peter 'Wally'   290
Winneke, Sir Henry   81
Wodak, Judge Tom   156
Wodehouse, PG   296
Wonder, Stevie   296
Wood, Graeme   216
Wood, Martin   278
Woodfull, Bill 'Woody'   73
    Famous rebuke of Plum Warner   160
Woodhill, Trent   282
Woodward, Jimmy   103
Wooldridge, Ian   33
Worner, Mike   111
Worrell, Frank   16, 17, 49
Wynd, Scotty   175
Wynette, Tammy   124

Yallop, Graham   103-104
Young, Neil   282, 296

Zimbalist, Efrem jnr   37
Zimmer, Ian   157

Ken Piesse proves that Ken Piesse gets by (lines) in the Sunday Observer

Observer sport

BY KEN PIESSE

MOORE BACK FOR 'PIES

By Ken Piesse
By Ken Piesse
By Ken Piesse
By Ken Piesse
Sports Editor

KEN PIESSE

PETER Moore has just returned from a month in Singapore looking forward to the challenges of leading Collingwood successfully in 1982.

Moore resumes training with his teammates in the New Year and although the Collingwood captain is not named usually until March, the blond ruckman is expected to have a second term as skipper.

"It gets a bit difficult sometimes," Moore said.

"It puts more pressure on you. You got to be a bit more concerned about others than your own form sometimes."

EXCLUSIVE!

"The first year was difficult. You've got to establish yourself with the players, supporters, media and everybody.

"I'm hoping in '82 that I'll be a bit different."

It's unlikely Moore will be challenged for the captaincy of Australia's most famous and parochial football club.

This time last year Moore was overseas enjoying a seven-week skiing holiday in France and Australia.

But he's concentrating on his football this time and while he was in Singapore visiting his wife's parents, trained regularly.

He is looking forward to playing alongside Graeme Teasdale.

"He'll be a great boost, Moore said.

— KEN PIESSE

EXCLUSIVE
by Ken Piesse

COLLINGWOOD and Hawthorn are likely to me

— KEN PIESSE

WAR AND PIESSE

TV RECORDERS
Rental — Purchase — Lease
With General & Adult Movie Packages

recorder including movie packages from

$8.56 WKLY.

Slightly more wkly

- 1 YEAR'S SUPPLY OF MOVIES
- 2 FULL LENGTH MOVIES TO KEEP
- 4 MOVIE PACKAGES AVAIL INCL. PERMANENT LIBRARY MEMBERSHIP GENERAL & ADULT

View movies not seen on TV in the intimacy of your own home

HOME DEMONSTRATION TONIGHT ALL SUBURBS
Ring now **211 5666**
9am to 9pm incl. weekends
PAL TV RENTALS P/L trading as
VIDEO MOVIE SALES & RENTALS

Ken Piesse at VFL Park

By Sports Editor Ken Piesse

IT'S piracy! Alarmed VFL clubs are planning concerted action to stop sweet-talking interstate bounty hunters from enticing some of the League's future champions away from Melbourne.

Interstate clubs are copying the dawn raids which highlighted interstate recruiting to Melbourne in the 1960s and 1970s — and the VFL clubs don't like it.

"The alarm bells are ringing," Richmond's vice-president and one of the original recruiting kings, Graham Richmond, says.

"There are a lot of clubs having uneasy nights at the moment."

Richmond is losing three uncontracted youngsters to Western Australia — Colin Waterson, 22, Peter Lane, 21, and Daryl Freame, 23. A fourth Tiger, Ian Scrimshaw, 26, is also heading west.

"Waterson is off his head going," Richmond says.

"He showed tremendous improvement last year and was coming along nicely.

"League rules don't permit us to enter into contracts with these blokes and interstate clubs present us with a fait accompli before we know anything about it.

"They're hitting the promising young players, the 21 and 22-year-olds. It's a very serious situation. All we can do is smile and wish them the best of luck."

Most WA clubs have sent recruiting officers to Melbourne, and more raids

...MORE KEN PIESSE PAGES 1-48

CRICKET YEAR 1981

EDITED BY KEN PIESSE

Send $7.95 to 'Cricket Year 1981'
Peter Isaacson Publications, 46 Porter Street, Prahran 3181.
I would like to order ..... copy/copies of 'Cricket Year 1981' @ $7.95 each, postage included. I enclose $..... in cheque □, money order □, Bankcard □, American Express □, Diners Club □
Card No. ☐☐☐ ☐☐ ☐☐☐ ☐☐☐☐☐☐
Signature
Name
Address
Post Code

Ken Piesse proves that football never dies in the Observer